English Situational
Conversations on Construction Techniques & Management

建筑技术与管理
英语情景会话

盛根有 著

中国建筑工业出版社

图书在版编目（CIP）数据

建筑技术与管理英语情景会话/盛根有著. —北京：中国建筑工业出版社，2008
ISBN 978-7-112-10466-6

Ⅰ. 建… Ⅱ. 盛… Ⅲ. 建筑-英语-口语-高等学校：技术学校-教材 Ⅳ. H319.9

中国版本图书馆 CIP 数据核字（2008）第 173049 号

《建筑技术与管理英语情景会话》是迄今为止在建筑业中尚未有的建筑科技实用英语会话专著。全书分五部共 45 个情景对话单元，包括建筑企业管理人员英语情景会话、建筑工程技术人员英语情景会话、建筑经济管理人员英语情景会话、建筑试验与测量人员英语情景会话，以及建筑公司后勤供应人员英语情景会话。这些会话涉及到建筑工程技术与管理诸多学科和施工的方方面面，从工程投标——施工——竣工——验收等符合当今国际工程承包与施工惯例的整套会话内容。全书具有四大特点：英汉对照、音标注音、短文翻译、专业词语替换与参考。

本书是针对建筑院校的学生，也可作为涉外建筑企业工程技术人员和管理干部学习和培训专用教材；同样适用于从事建筑出国劳务、工程承包的各类人员学习和提高其建筑英语水平，必选、必备、必读、必用之书。

* * *

责任编辑：程素荣　　责任设计：郑秋菊　　责任校对：张　虹　兰曼利

English Situational
Conversations on Construction Techniques & Management

建筑技术与管理英语情景会话

盛根有　著

*

中国建筑工业出版社出版、发行（北京西郊百万庄）
各地新华书店、建筑书店经销
北京嘉泰利德公司制版
廊坊市海涛印刷有限公司印刷

*

开本：880×1230 毫米　1/32　印张：11¾　字数：376 千字
2009 年 9 月第一版　2016 年 12 月第六次印刷
定价：28.00 元
ISBN 978-7-112-10466-6
（17390）

版权所有　翻印必究
如有印装质量问题，可寄本社退换
（邮政编码100037）

前　　言

《建筑技术与管理英语情景会话》是在中国改革开放中孕育，在为解决施工实际、促进生产力快速发展的知识创新尝试中诞生，又在与时俱进中逐步完善、反复锤炼、不断升华。《建筑技术与管理英语情景会话》是为振兴中国建筑工业，使其更好更快地融入全球一体化之中，并拓宽在国际建筑市场中的占有率；为满足建筑院校学生想学习和提高本专业英语会话水平而又苦于无书的迫切要求；为弥补建筑业广大工程技术人员、管理人员英语水平薄弱，特别是专业英语会话又缺失，给涉外施工带来了无法克服而一时又无法解决的头等难题——语言障碍，人人是聋子、个个是哑巴，有口不会说，有耳又听不懂的被动，尴尬而又十分无奈的实际困难而精心撰写的。

只因建筑工程技术人员和管理人员其工作性质决定了他们肩负着领导和指挥的角色，所以他们的英语水平，特别是口语怎样，直接关系到施工企业的形象、效益，甚至全局。本书唯一的目的是落实国际建筑施工合同规定的工作用语——英语，乙方人员与甲方代表、施工监理以及配合施工的相关人员，用英语进行工作交谈，改写中国工程技术和管理人员与外国专家面对面地直接交谈工作，无须二传手——译员的新篇章。该书的指导思想是从涉外建筑企业施工特点出发，着眼于施工实际，又服务于施工，促进企业健康、持续、科学发展。全书囊括了各类工程技术和管理人员在各自工作实际会话用语。如建筑工程技术人员英语情景会话这部设有十四个情景对话单元：主要涉及建材询价、报价与订购、施工计划实施与工程进度统计、工程质量监督与施工安全检查、图纸研究与工程索赔、工地参观，以及国外建筑考察等整套国际通用的施工会话内容。这些会话涉及施工的不同工序所使用的不同材料，不同材料所要求的不同施工工艺，不同施工工艺所采用的不同的施工方法以及不同工程所遵循的不同的质量标准和施工规范等内容。如果你有施工经历或亲临施工现场目睹建设者是怎样施工的，你一定会感到《建筑技术与管理英语情景会话》是一部真实的工作写照，也是作者首次把施工及其相关联的工作以最全面、最逼真的情景展示给你；这也是作者融实用性与科学性，集知识性与创造性于一体，形成了独树一帜的创作新思维、新理念；更是作者四十多年潜心研究向社会递交的答卷。是理论联系实际的产物，是基本教育理念运用于教学实践的尝试，是普通英语融入专业英语的创新。本书做到了简明、直观、地道、上口，符合英美英语口语表达习惯和特点。读者可立刻将书中的内容用到工作中，也可就某一具体问题现学现用，会收到事半功倍、立竿见影的效果。可以说"一书在手万事不求，译员不在无须发愁"。

该书具有下列四大特点：

1. 英汉对照：全书情景对话单元——学说英语均采用英汉对照的模式给读者展示出英汉两种语言的不同表达方式。通过对照和比较会一目了然地看到这两种语言并非 1 + 1 就完全等于 2，实际上各自有着各自表达特点、方式和习惯。通过全书的学习一定会使读者懂得在哪种语言情景中说哪些话，用哪些词语更得体、更恰当、更准确，并采用哪种语体、语气、语态和外国人进行交谈更合适、更习惯，收到的效果更理想。

2. 音标注音：全书口语练习中的专业词语均注有国际音标，每个词语都是根据《新英汉词典》和《现代高级英汉双解辞典》注音，以满足不同程度读者能按照国际音标规范其发音的需要，使其不仅能规范发音而且能保障发音准确，为今后轻松上口，确保口语水平既循序渐进又能扎扎实实地稳步提高铺平了道路。

3. 短文翻译：该书口语练习中均设有短文翻译（英汉互译）。设立这些短文翻译练习的目的不仅训练了学生对翻译技巧的运用，以培养其翻译能力，更重要的是通过翻译获取相关的专业词语，拓宽视野，为未来专业的发展奠定了基础。

4. 专业词语替换与参考：全书口语练习中均附有更专业化的词语供替换与参考，这些词语是根据每个情景对话实际需要而精挑细选，特意补充的。兼有两种作用，其一是替换口语练习中黑体词语，目的是打破传统教学模式，把一种死的语言变成活的语言；其二是满足读者实际工作的需要，而提供的参考和备查的词语。为学子终生奠基，为读者起航插翅。

书后还附有口语练习答案——汉语参考译文。

本书所有的插图均由盛莉绘制。

承蒙卞显敏、董延才、窦道义、David 和 S. Mcculloch 等专家型领导给予的关心和支持，在此特表示感谢！

本书不仅是生土地培育的禾苗，也是工作实践的再现。1993 年动笔，披阅十五载，九易其稿，仍有不尽人意之处，疏漏和不妥在所难免，诚望广大读者、同行赐教。

作者　盛根有

2008 年 8 月 8 日于西安

CONTENTS

Part One 1

English Situational Conversations with Managerial Personnel in the Construction Enterprise

Situational Dialogic Unit 1 2
    Talking about Introducing Construction Enterprise
    S. W. E: 1. Construction Enterprises
             2. Structure of Huaxia Construction Engineering Corporation

Situational Dialogic Unit 2 11
    Talking about Inviting Cooperative Partners
    S. W. E: Enterprise Managerial Personnel

Situational Dialogic Unit 3 17
    Talking about Meeting Cooperative Partners
    S. W. E: 1. Labour and Wages Management
             2. Organization Scheme

Situational Dialogic Unit 4 23
    Talking about Chairing a Production Meeting
    S. W. E: Terms about Management of Enterprises

Situational Dialogic Unit 5 29
    Talking about Making a Policy-decision
    S. W. E: Deciding Items

Situational Dialogic Unit 6 35
    Talking about Consulting Tenderings
    S. W. E: Terms about Submit Tender and Invite tender

Situational Dialogic Unit 7 41
    Talking about Engineering Contract Negotiated
    S. W. E: Contract Management

Situational Dialogic Unit 8 49
    Talking about Signing a Contract of Works
    S. W. E: 1. Terms about Contract Clauses
             2. Contract Party

目　　录

第一部 ·· 1
建筑企业管理人员英语情景会话

第一情景对话单元 ······································· 2
　　谈论建筑施工企业介绍
　　　替换词语：1. 建筑施工企业
　　　　　　　　2. 华夏建筑工程总公司机构设置
第二情景对话单元 ······································ 11
　　谈论邀请合作方
　　　替换词语：企业管理人员
第三情景对话单元 ······································ 17
　　谈论会见合作当事人
　　　替换词语：1. 劳动工资管理
　　　　　　　　2. 组织关系
第四情景对话单元 ······································ 23
　　谈论主持生产会议
　　　替换词语：企业管理相关术语
第五情景对话单元 ······································ 29
　　谈论作决策
　　　替换词语：决定事项
第六情景对话单元 ······································ 35
　　谈论咨询投标事宜
　　　替换词语：投标与招标相关术语
第七情景对话单元 ······································ 41
　　谈论工程承包合同洽谈
　　　替换词语：合同管理
第八情景对话单元 ······································ 49
　　谈论签订工程合同
　　　替换词语：1. 合同条款相关术语
　　　　　　　　2. 合同当事人

Situational Dialogic Unit 9 ·· 55
    Talking about Prolonging the Construction Contract Term
    S. W. E: Kinds of Contract
Situational Dialogic Unit 10 ··· 61
    Talking about Completion Certificates Issued
    S. W. E: Building Appraisement
Situational Dialogic Unit 11 ··· 69
    Talking about Congratulations and Giving a Banquet
    A. Congratulations on Completion Ceremony
    B. Giving a Banquet to Cooperative Partners
    S. W. E: 1. Congratulation on Something
           2. Banquet, Wines and Drink
           3. Chinese Food
           4. Parts of Staple Food

Part Two ·· 79
English Situational Conversations with Building Engineering and Technical Personnel
Situational Dialogic Unit 12 ··· 80
    Talking about Introduction of Building Engineering and Technical Personnel
    S. W. E: Building Engineering and Technical Personnel
Situational Dialogic Unit 13 ··· 87
    Talking about Building Investigation Abroad
    S. W. E: Terms about Ancient Architecture
Situational Dialogic Unit 14 ··· 95
    Talking about Studying Building Working Drawings
    S. W. E: 1. Kinds of Drawing
           2. Verify Drawing
           3. Drawing Instruments
Situational Dialogic Unit 15 ··· 103
    Talking about Inquiring Price of the Building Materials
    S. W. E: 1. Kinds of Building Materials
           2. Exchange Tables of Weights and Measures (一)

第九情景对话单元 ··· 56
　　谈论延长施工合同有效期
　　替换词语：合同的种类
第十情景对话单元 ··· 61
　　谈论完工证书的颁发
　　替换词语：工程评价
第十一情景对话单元 ··· 69
　　谈论祝贺与宴请
　　A. 祝贺工程落成庆典
　　B. 宴请合作方
　　替换词语：1. 祝贺某事
　　　　　　　2. 宴会及其酒、饮料
　　　　　　　3. 中餐
　　　　　　　4. 部分主食

第二部 ·· 79
建筑工程技术人员英语情景会话

第十二情景对话单元 ··· 80
　　谈论建筑工程技术人员介绍
　　替换词语：建筑工程技术人员
第十三情景对话单元 ··· 87
　　谈论国外建筑考察
　　替换词语：古代建筑相关术语
第十四情景对话单元 ··· 95
　　谈论研究建筑施工图
　　替换词语：1. 图纸的种类
　　　　　　　2. 审阅图纸
　　　　　　　3. 绘图仪器
第十五情景对话单元 ··· 103
　　谈论询问建筑材料价格
　　替换词语：1. 建筑材料种类
　　　　　　　2. 度量衡换算表（一）

Situational Dialogic Unit 16 ·· 109
　　Talking about Quoting Building Materials
　　S. W. E：1. Exchange Tables of Weights and Measures （二）
　　　　　　 2. Management of Materials
Situational Dialogic Unit 17 ·· 115
　　Talking about Purchasing Building Materials
　　S. W. E：1. Exchange Tables of Weights and Measures （三）
　　　　　　 2. Building Materials Enterprises
Situational Dialogic Unit 18 ·· 121
　　Talking about Construction Plan
　　S. W. E：1. Execution Program(me) of Works
　　　　　　 2. Schedule of Works
Situational Dialogic Unit 19 ·· 130
　　Talking about Kind of Buildings
　　S. W. E：1. Terms about Modern Architecture
　　　　　　 2. Some Parts of Building
Situational Dialogic Unit 20 ·· 140
　　Talking about Inspecting Construction Progress
　　S. W. E：1. Building Elements
　　　　　　 2. Building Codes and Standards
Situational Dialogic Unit 21 ·· 149
　　Talking about Inspecting Quality of works
　　S. W. E：1. Management of Quality
　　　　　　 2. Instruments and Tools for Quality
Situational Dialogic Unit 22 ·· 157
　　Talking about Inspecting Construction Safety
　　S. W. E：1. Safety in Production Management
　　　　　　 2. Labour Protection Appliances
Situational Dialogic Unit 23 ·· 166
　　Talking about Visiting a Worksite
　　S. W. E：1. Building Construction
　　　　　　 2. Construction Organization and Management

第十六情景对话单元 …………………………………………… 109
　　谈论建筑材料报价
　　　替换词语：1. 度量衡换算表（二）
　　　　　　　　2. 材料管理
第十七情景对话单元 …………………………………………… 115
　　谈论订购建筑材料
　　　替换词语：1. 度量衡换算表（三）
　　　　　　　　2. 建材企业
第十八情景对话单元 …………………………………………… 121
　　谈论建筑施工计划
　　　替换词语：1. 施工程序
　　　　　　　　2. 工程计划/进度表
第十九情景对话单元 …………………………………………… 130
　　谈论建筑物种类
　　　替换词语：1. 现代建筑相关术语
　　　　　　　　2. 建筑物一些部位
第二十情景对话单元 …………………………………………… 140
　　谈论检查施工进度
　　　替换词语：1. 房屋构件
　　　　　　　　2. 建筑规范与标准
第二十一情景对话单元 ………………………………………… 149
　　谈论检验工程质量
　　　替换词语：1. 质量管理
　　　　　　　　2. 质量检测器具
第二十二情景对话单元 ………………………………………… 157
　　谈论检查施工安全
　　　替换词语：1. 安全生产管理
　　　　　　　　2. 劳动保护用品
第二十三情景对话单元 ………………………………………… 166
　　谈论参观一家工地
　　　替换词语：1. 建筑施工
　　　　　　　　2. 施工组织与管理

Situational Dialogic Unit 24 ·· 175
    Talking about Claims of Works
    S. W. E: Claim Terms

Part Three ·· 183
English Situational Conversations with Building Economic Managerial Personnel

Situational Dialogic Unit 25 ·· 184
    Talking about Accounting
    S. W. E: Economic Managerial Personnel
Situational Dialogic Unit 26 ·· 190
    Talking about Opening a Bank Account
    S. W. E: 1. Kinds of Bank
            2. Kinds of Opening an Account
Situational Dialogic Unit 27 ·· 196
    Talking about Money Exchange
    S. W. E: 1. Terms about Currency
            2. Main Moneys of the World
Situational Dialogic Unit 28 ·· 202
    Talking about Applying for and Using Credit Card
    S. W. E: 1. Banking Facilities
            2. Cardinal Numeral
Situational Dialogic Unit 29 ·· 211
    Talking about Telegraphic Remittance
    S. W. E: 1. Remittance and Other
            2. Percent, Fraction and Decimal
Situational Dialogic Unit 30 ·· 217
    Talking about Accounts
    S. W. E: Classifications of Accounting
Situational Dialogic Unit 31 ·· 222
    Talking about Financial Budget Preparation
    S. W. E: Terms about Budget

第二十四情景对话单元 ·············· 175
　　谈论工程索赔
　　替换词语：索赔术语

第三部 ·············· 183
建筑经济管理人员英语情景会话

第二十五情景对话单元 ·············· 184
　　谈论会计工作
　　替换词语：经济管理人员
第二十六情景对话单元 ·············· 190
　　谈论开立银行账户
　　替换词语：1. 银行种类
　　　　　　　2. 开立账户种类
第二十七情景对话单元 ·············· 196
　　谈论货币兑换
　　替换词语：1. 货币术语
　　　　　　　2. 世界主要货币
第二十八情景对话单元 ·············· 202
　　谈论申请与使用信用卡
　　替换词语：1. 银行业务相关术语
　　　　　　　2. 基数词
第二十九情景对话单元 ·············· 211
　　谈论电汇
　　替换词语：1. 汇款与其他
　　　　　　　2. 百分数，分数和小数
第三十情景对话单元 ·············· 217
　　谈论会计科目
　　替换词语：会计分类
第三十一情景对话单元 ·············· 222
　　谈论财务预算编制
　　替换词语：预算术语

Situational Dialogic Unit 32 ·· 228
    Talking about Computing the Unit Cost
    S. W. E: Ordinal Numeral
Situational Dialogic Unit 33 ·· 236
    Talking about Fixed Assets and Current Assets
    S. W. E: Accounts and Others
Part Four ·· 241
    English Situational Conversations with Construction Testing and Surveying Personnel
Situational Dialogic Unit 34 ·· 242
    Talking about Concrete Test
    S. W. E: 1. Concrete Design and Test 2. Defects of Concrete
Situational Dialogic Unit 35 ·· 248
    Talking about Steel Reinforcement Test
    S. W. E: 1. Steel Bar Strength 2. Types of Steel Bars
Situational Dialogic Unit 36 ·· 256
    Talking about Welding Test
    S. W. E: 1. Welding Defects 2. Terms about Welding Test
Situational Dialogic Unit 37 ·· 264
    Talking about Piling Test
    S. W. E: Terms about Piling Test
Situational Dialogic Unit 38 ·· 270
    Talking about Surveying
    S. W. E: 1. Types of Surveying 2. Geometry
Situational Dialogic Unit 39 ·· 278
    Talking about Construction Surveys
    S. W. E: 1. Surveying Lines 2. Surveying Instruments and Others
Part Five ·· 287
    English Situational Conversations with Administrative Personnel in Construction Company
Situational Dialogic Unit 40 ·· 288
    Talking about Booking Airline Tickets

第三十二情景对话单元 ·················· 228
  谈论计算单位成本
  替换词语：序数词
第三十三情景对话单元 ·················· 236
  谈论固定资产和流动资产
  替换词语：账目和其他

第四部 ·················· 241
建筑试验和测量人员英语情景会话

第三十四情景对话单元 ·················· 242
  谈论混凝土试验
  替换词语：1. 混凝土设计与检验　2. 混凝土缺陷
第三十五情景对话单元 ·················· 248
  谈论钢筋试验
  替换词语：1. 钢筋强度　2. 钢筋式样
第三十六情景对话单元 ·················· 256
  谈论焊接试验
  替换词语：1. 焊接缺陷　2. 焊接检验相关术语
第三十七情景对话单元 ·················· 264
  谈论打桩试验
  替换词语：打桩试验相关术语
第三十八情景对话单元 ·················· 270
  谈论测量
  替换词语：1. 测量的种类　2. 几何图形
第三十九情景对话单元 ·················· 278
  谈论施工测量
  替换词语：1. 测量线　2. 测量仪器与其他

第五部 ·················· 287
建筑公司后勤人员英语情景会话

第四十情景对话单元 ·················· 288
  谈论订购机票

　　　　S. W. E: 1. Air Routes and Others
　　　　　　　　2. Main Air Corporations throughout the World
Situational Dialogic Unit 41 ·· 294
　　　Talking about Telephoning an International Call or Sending a Telegram
　　　S. W. E: 1. Terms about Telegram
　　　　　　　　2. Telephone and Its Idioms
Situational Dialogic Unit 42 ·· 301
　　　Talking about Posting Letters and Parcels
　　　S. W. E: 1. Terms about Letter
　　　　　　　　2. Stamps　3. Kinds of Parcel
Situational Dialogic Unit 43 ·· 308
　　　Talking about Shopping
　　　S. W. E: 1. Stores and Others
　　　　　　　　2. Some Terms of Articles
Situational Dialogic Unit 44 ·· 315
　　　Talking about Seeing a Doctor
　　　（A）Seeing a Surgeon
　　　（B）Seeing a Physician
　　　S. W. E: 1. Medical Staff and Departments of Hospital
　　　　　　　　2. Surgical Disease, Treatment and Medicine/Drug
　　　　　　　　3. Diagnosis, Symptoms and Medicine/Drug
Situational Dialogic Unit 45 ·· 324
　　　Talking about Purchasing Some Food for Site Canteen
　　　A. Buying Some Grain and Oil
　　　B. Buying Vegetables, Fruits and Condiments
　　　C. Buying Some Meat and Sea Food
　　　S. W. E: 1. Kinds of Grain　2. Sorts of Edible oil
　　　　　　　　3. Kinds of Vegetable
　　　　　　　　4. Dried Vegetables and Condiments　5. Fresh Fruits
　　　　　　　　6. Meats, Eggs and Fowl　7. Fish and Sea Food

Key to Spoken Practice——Chinese Reference Translation ············ 336

替换词语：1. 航线和其他用语
2. 世界主要航空公司

第四十一情景对话单元 ··· 294
谈论打国际电话还是拍电报
替换词语：1. 电报相关术语
2. 电话以及相关习语

第四十二情景对话单元 ··· 301
谈论邮寄信件和包裹
替换词语：1. 信件术语
2. 邮票 3. 包裹的种类

第四十三情景对话单元 ··· 308
谈论购物
替换词语：1. 商店及其他
2. 部分商品术语

第四十四情景对话单元 ··· 315
谈论看病
（A）看外科医生
（B）看内科医生
替换词语：1. 医务人员和医院的科室
2. 外科疾病，治疗和药物
3. 诊断/检查，症状和药物

第四十五情景对话单元 ··· 324
谈论给工地食堂采购食物
A. 买粮油
B. 购买蔬菜、水果和调味品
C. 购买肉和海味
替换词语：1. 粮食种类 2. 食油种类
3. 蔬菜种类
4. 干菜和调味品 5. 鲜果
6. 肉类，蛋和禽类 7. 鱼类和海味

口语练习答案——汉语参考译文 ·· 336

Part One
English Situational Conversations with Managerial Personnel in the Construction Enterprise
(Situational Dialogic Unit 1-11)

第一部
建筑企业管理人员英语情景会话
(第一至十一情景对话单元)

Situational Dialogic Unit 1
第一情景对话单元

Learn to Speak English

Talking about Introducing Construction Enterprise

Bolton: Could you please give us a brief introduction to your corporation, sir?

Guojia: All right. But what are you eager to know?

Bolton: Many things. Who is your manager?

Guoja: I'm in charge of CCEC (China Civil Engineering Corporation). My surname is Guo, given name Jia.

Bolton: Mr. Guo. I'm glad to meet you here.

Guoja: Thank you. Me too.

Bolton: Is your corporation a state-owned enterprise or a private one?

Guojia: A state-owned one, has established more than 20 years, which mainly contracts various kinds of overseas industrial and civil construction works and provides labor service.

Bolton: Your corporation is a big enterprise, which is well known both at home and abroad. But how much registered funds does it have?

Guojia: 500 million Yuan (R. M. B.) for overseas business.

Bolton: Oh, Too much it is! It's an abundant capital funds.

Guojia: That's indubitable, sir.

Bolton: How many staff and workers are there in yours, I'd like to know?

Guojia: The total number of staff and workers are 600,000.

Bolton: What about their composed structure?

Guojia: Quite well. Of them are over 1,000 senior engineers, senior economists and experts, 5,000 engineers, economists and other related administrative talents.

Bolton: They're all your engineering and technical personnel and managerial personnel. And your skilled workers?

Guojia: Quite good. We've all kinds of skilled workers in civil construction and installation works, machinery and decoration works, testing, surveying and maintenance works.

Bolton: Oh, really and truly nice! Do they all have higher construction abilities?

学说英语

谈论建筑施工企业介绍

波尔顿：先生，请把贵公司简单介绍给我们，好吗？

郭　佳：好吧。但不知你们热衷于想了解些什么情况？

波尔顿：许多情况。谁是贵公司的经理？

郭　佳：我全面负责中土公司（中国土木工程公司）的工作。我姓郭，名佳。

波尔顿：郭先生，我很高兴在此见到您。

郭　佳：谢谢！我也一样。

波尔顿：贵公司是一家国有企业还是一家私营企业？

郭　佳：是一家国有企业，已创建了二十多年，主要承包海外各种工业与民用建筑工程施工并提供劳务。

波尔顿：贵公司是名扬海内外的大企业。那贵公司拥有多少注册资金？

郭　佳：海外经营注册资金5亿元人民币。

波尔顿：啊，可真多呀！贵公司可谓资金雄厚。

郭　佳：那是无可置疑的，先生。

波尔顿：我想知道贵公司有多少名职工？

郭　佳：总共有60万名职工。

波尔顿：职工的配置结构怎样？

郭　佳：相当不错。其中拥有1,000多名高级工程师、高级经济师和各类专家，5,000名工程师、经济师以及相关的专业管理人才。

波尔顿：他们都是你们的工程技术人员和管理人员。那你们的技术工人怎样？

郭　佳：很好。我们拥有从事于土建与安装工程、机械与装饰工程、试验、测量与维修工程的各种技术工人。

波尔顿：啊，确实不错！他们都具有较高施工技能吗？

Guojia: Naturally. They're good at studying and have not only a good grasp of Chinese traditional construction techniques but also advanced world construction technology.

Bolton: There are so many dab hands in our corporation, Your talents are galaxy, technical capacity is very strong, and your corporation has a competitive one in the world.

Guojia: Right. That's not arguing fact.

Bolton: How many construction companies and technical service units are there in yours?

Guojia: 40 construction companies and 16 technical service units. They're ready to take part in international tendering and contract completed projects.

Bolton: Wonderful! Your completed machinery and equipment, technical capacity disposal, and managing experience is rich. It must undertake a variety of construction works in many parts of the world, is that right?

Guojia: Yes, of course. Please look at all sorts of the buildings in the picture books which were built by us in recent years.

Bolton: OK. Let me have a look.

Guojia: What do you think about them? Are they beautifull?

Bolton: Oh, wonderful! Beautiful!

郭　佳：自然是。工人们乐于学习，不仅较好地掌握了中国传统施工技术而且还掌握了世界先进的施工技术。

波尔顿：贵公司有这么多能工巧匠，真是人才济济、技术实力雄厚，在世界上很有竞争实力。

郭　佳：对。这是不争的事实。

波尔顿：那贵公司有多少个施工公司和技术服务单位？

郭　佳：拥有40个施工公司和16个技术服务单位。他们都乐于参加国际投标与承包成套工程项目。

波尔顿：好极啦！贵公司设备齐全，技术力量配套，管理经验丰富，一定承建了世界上许多国家的各种建筑工程，对吗？

郭　佳：那当然啦！请看这些画册上的各式各样的建筑物，全都是我们公司近年来承建的。

波尔顿：好。我来看看吧。

郭　佳：你觉得怎么样？漂亮吗？

波尔顿：啊，好极了！漂亮！

Spoken Practice 口语练习

1. **Pair Work:**

   A acts as a manager of a Construction Corporation, B acts as a welcome guest who wants to know something about the Corporation. Use the following expressions:

   A: Can I help you, sir?
   B: Yes, I'd like to...
   A: But what information do you...?
   B: It's...

2. **Answer the following questions in accordance with the actual situation:**

   1) Who is in charge of your company now?
   2) When did your corporation establish?
   3) How many staff and workers are there in your corporation?
   4) What construction projects does your company mainly undertake?
   5) How many registered funds for oversea are there in your corporation?

3. **Read & interprete the Following Passage:**

   ### Corporation

   A corporation is legal entity, having an existence separate and distinct from that of its owners. The assets of corporation belong to the corporation itself, not to the stockholders. The owners of a corporation are called stockholders and their ownership is evidenced by transferable shares of capital stock. The corporation is responsible for its own debts, and must pay income taxes on its earnings. As a "separate legal entity," a corporation may enter into contracts and sue and be sued as if it were a person in court.

4. **Change the Following Direct Speech (直接引语) into Indirect Speech (间接引语):**

   1) Tom said to his friend, "I'm studying specialized English about architecture now."

2) Teacher said, "Don't open your books first, try to think and explain the differences between direct speech and indirect speech."
3) An expert said, "Failure is the mother of success."
4) "What's your job?" asked a foreigner.
5) "You studied in An Architectural Engineering College before, didn't you?" asked a manager.

5. **Substitute the Following Words & Expressions:**

1) Use the following **Construction Enterprises** (建筑施工企业) to replace the black words in the following sentence:

Bolton: How many **construction companies** and **technical service units** are there in yours?

波尔顿：那贵公司有多少个施工公司和技术服务单位？

Construction Enterprises [kənˈstrʌkʃən ˈentəpraiziz] 建筑施工企业
China State Construction Engineering Corporation 中国建筑工程总公司
[ˈtʃainə steit kənˈstrʌkʃən ˌendʒiˈniəriŋ ˌkɔːpəˈreiʃən] /CSCEC
Civil Construction Engineering Corporation 土木建筑工程总公司
[ˈsiːvl kənˈstrʌkʃən ˌendʒiˈniəriŋ ˌkɔːpəˈreiʃən] /CCEC
Construction Installation Engineering Corporation 建筑安装工程总公司
[kənˈstrʌkʃən ˌinstəˈleiʃən ˌendʒiˈniəriŋ ˌkɔːpəˈreiʃən] /CIEC
Road & Bridge Engineering Corporation of China 中国路桥工程总公司
[roud ənd bridʒ ˌendʒiˈniəriŋ ˌkɔːpəˈreiʃənəv ˈtʃainə] /RBECC
No.1 Construction Engineering Company 第一建筑工程公司
[ˈnʌmbə wʌn kənˈstrʌkʃən ˌendʒiˈniəriŋ ˈkʌmpəni]
Construction Decoration Company 建筑装饰公司
[kənˈstrʌkʃən ˌdekəˈreiʃən ˈkʌmpəni]
Construction Materials Supplying Company 建筑材料供应公司
[kənˈstrʌkʃən məˈtiəriəlz səˈplaiŋ ˈkʌmpəni]
Construction Transportation Company 建筑运输公司
[kənˈstrʌkʃən ˌtrænspɔːˈteiʃən ˈkʌmpəni]
Construction Engineering Branch 建筑工程分公司
[kənˈstrʌkʃən ˌendʒiˈniəriŋ brɑːntʃ]

Construction Engineering Brigade 建筑工程施工队
[kən'strʌkʃən ˌendʒi'niəriŋ bri'geid]
Construction Engineering stock company 建筑工程股份公司
[kən'strʌkʃən ˌendʒi'niəriŋ stɔk 'kʌmpəni]
Construction Engineering limited company 建筑工程有限公司
[kən'strʌkʃən ˌendʒi'niəriŋ 'limitid 'kʌmpəni]

2) Use the following **Structure of ... Construction Engineering Corporation** (华夏建筑工程总公司机构设置) to replace the black words in the following sentence:

Bolton: What about their **composed structure**?
波尔顿：职工的配置结构怎样？

Structure of Huaxia Construction Engineering Corporation
华夏建筑工程总公司机构设置

董事会 Board of Directors

总经理办公室 President Office

经营管理部 Management & Administration Dept.	劳动人事部 Labour & Personnel Dept.
综合计划处 Planning Division	财 务 处 Financial Affairs Division
业务一部 1st Business Dept.	科 技 处 Science & Technology Division
业务二部 2nd Business Dept.	质量监督处 Quality Supervision Division
海外公司 Overseas Company	设计咨询公司 Design & Consulting Company
亚 洲 处 Asia Division	物资供应处 Material Supply Division
欧美太处 Europe-America-Pacific Regional Division	动力设备处 Equipment Division

建筑技术与管理英语情景会话

驻巴黎代表处 Representative in Paris	施工管理处 Construction Administration Division
驻香港办事处 Hong Kong Office	工厂管理处 Factory Administration Division
非洲处 Africa Division	建筑科研所 Building Science Research Institute
分公司 Branch	建筑职工医院 Construction Staff & Workers Hospital

Situational Dialogic Unit 2
第二情景对话单元

Learn to Speak English

Talking about Inviting Cooperative Partners

Kuaile: On behalf of Chairman of the board, Mr. Bian, general manager, Mr. Dong. I'd like to invite you to dinner. Thank you for your cooperation with us many years. I hope you can join us, Mr. Tweed.

Tweed: I'm very grateful for your invitation. I'd be very happy to do so, but what's the latest news, please tell me?

Kuaile: CSCIC has accomplished the installation task of eighty-thousand meter gas and water supply mains.

Tweed: Is that true, young man?

Kuaile: Yes. That's the first piece of good news.

Tweed: Another one, please say it quickly?

Kuaile: We've won the tender for Queen Hotel.

Tweed: OK. Chinese builders are great! I should go to congratulate. But unfortunately, I have to attend a conference tomorrow. I'm afraid I couldn't.

Kuaile: Not tomorrow, this evening, sir.

Tweed: That's fine, but where will you hold it?

Kuaile: In Hilton Hotel. Here's your invitation card. Would you honor us with a visit? Do come with your wife, please.

Tweed: Yes, I'm delighted to accept your invitation. Come on time. Thanks a lot.

Kuaile: See you evening, sir.

Tweed: See you evening.

学说英语

谈论邀请合作方

邹　乐：我代表董事长卞先生，总经理董先生请您赴宴，以感谢您多年的合作。希望您能光临，特威德先生。

特威德：非常感谢你们的邀请。我很高兴应邀，但不知有什么最新消息，请告诉我好吗？

邹　乐：中建安装总公司已完成了8000米煤气管道和给水干管的安装任务。

特威德：当真，小伙子？

邹　乐：真的。这只是第一条好消息。

特威德：另一条是什么，请快点说？

邹　乐：我们中了皇后大酒店标。

特威德：好啊！中国建筑工人真伟大！我应该去庆贺。但不凑巧，我明天得参加个会议，恐怕不能前去。

邹　乐：先生，不是明天宴请，而是今晚。

特威德：那好。在哪儿举行？

邹　乐：在希尔顿饭店。这是给您的请柬。如蒙光临，不胜荣幸！请务必带上贵夫人。

特威德：是的，我很高兴接受您的邀请。准时光临。多谢！

邹　乐：晚上见，先生。

特威德：晚上见。

Spoken Practice 口语练习

1. **Pair Work:**

   A clerk on behalf of her general manager invites some inspectors to have a dinner party because they work together more than two years and finally completed the building project. Inspectors are too busy to attend it, and the clerk tries to persuade them to attend it.

2. **Answer the following questions in accordance with Learn to Speak English:**

   1) Whom would you like to invite to dinner on behalf of Chairman of the board, Mr. Bian, general manager, Mr. Dong?

   2) Why is Mr. Tweed very happy to accept the invitation?

   3) Will they hold the dinner in Baiyui Hotel or Hilton Hotel?

   4) Would they like to invite other welcome guest to the dinner beside Mr. Tweed?

   5) What time are they going to hold their dinner?

3. **Read & Interpret the Following Passage:**

   ### Welcoming Speech

   Ladies and gentlemen,

   Following the increasing rapidity of our communications with foreign countries, we're having a large number of learners and experts from different countries. Today, we feel very much honoured to have Mr. Henry Smith with us. Prof. Smith is well known to the world for his achievements in the field of architecture.

   First of all, let me, on behalf of all present here, extend our warm welcome and cordial greetings to our distinguished guest.

   Now let us invite Mr. Henry Smith to give us a lecture on management of construction enterprises.

4. **Try to Put the Following into English**：

> 请　柬
>
> 兹定于 2005 年 10 月 16 日（星期五）晚 7 点至 8 点，在白云宾馆举行宴会，敬请贵公司史密斯先生和夫人光临。

Explanatory Notes 注释：

1. 请柬也称请帖，分正式和非正式的两种。非正式的请柬就是平时所说的邀请信和邀请条，一般用于亲朋好友之间。正式请柬则用于招待会，庆祝大会等正式的社交场合。
2. 正式请柬措词精练，标准。行文不使用第一人称而用第三人称。如"I would like you to come to dinner."应改为"Mr. and Mrs. Smith cordially invite you to dinner"
3. 正式请柬应包括邀请人的姓名，活动内容，时间，地点等相关信息。正式的请柬一般都邀请夫妻双方。

4. **Substitute the Following Words & Expressions**：

Use the following **Enterprise Managerial Personnel**（企业管理人员）to replace the black words in the following sentence：

Kuaile: On behalf of **Chairman of the board**, Mr. Bian, **general manager**, Mr. Dong. I'd like to invite you to dinner. Thank you for your cooperation with us many years. I hope you can join us, Mr. Tweed.

邻乐：我代表董事长卞先生，总经理董先生请您赴宴，以感谢您多年的合作。希望您能光临，特威德先生。

Enterprise Managerial Personnel 企业管理人员
['entəpraiz ˌmænə'dʒiəriəl ˌpəː'nel]
Chairman of the Board ['tʃɛəmən əv ðə bɔːd] 董事长
Director of the board [di'rektə əv ðə bɔːd] 董事
president; general manager ['prezidənt 'dʒenərəl 'mænidʒə] 总经理
vice-president [vais 'prezidənt] 副总经理
manager ['mænidʒə] 经理

manageress ['mænidʒəres] 女经理
deputy manager ['depjuti 'mænidʒə] 副经理
business manager ['biznis 'mænidʒə] 经营经理
sale's manager [seilz 'mænidʒə] 销售经理
project manager ['prɔdʒekt 'mænidʒə] 项目经理
production manager [prə'dʌkʃən 'mænidʒə] 生产经理
engineering manager [ˌendʒi'niəriŋ 'mænidʒə] 工程经理
site director [sait di'rektə] 工地主任
chief of division [tʃi'f əv di'viʒən] 处长
factory director ['fæktəri di'rektə] 厂长
chief of section [tʃi:ʃ əv 'sekʃən] 科长
workshop manager ['wə:kʃɔp 'mænidʒə] 车间主任
section chief ['sekʃən tʃi:f] 工段（股）长
clerk [klɑ:k klə:k] 办事员，职员
materials checker [mə'tiəriəlz 'tʃekə] 材料员
secretary ['sekrətri] 秘书
storekeeper [stɔ:'ki:per] 库管员

Situational Dialogic Unit 3
第三情景对话单元

建筑技术与管理英语情景会话

Learn to Speak English

Talking about Meeting Cooperative Partners

Lihua: Excuse me. You're Mr. Henry. Smith from Canada, right?

Henry: Yes. You're...

Lihua: Oh, I'm Mr. Luo's secretary, Miss Lihua. OK, please come in.

Henry: OK. Thank you.

Lihua: (after a while) Allow me introduce you to Mr. Luo, Main contractor, general manager of CCEC. This is Mr. Smith, building owner of CHC. (They both shake hands and say...)

Henry: How do you do, Mr. Luo? I've often heard about you. Nice to meet you here today.

Luojie: How do you do, Mr. Smith? I've often wanted to meet you and have my wish fulfilled nowadays. Welcome!

Henry: Thank you. It's a great pleasure to have the opportunity of meeting you, Mr. Luo.

Luojie: The pleasure's all ours. Please sit down, Mr. Smith. Would you like a cigarette?

Henry: No. Thank you, Mr. Luo.

Luojie: What would you like to drink, wine or coffee?

Henry: Wine, please. It's very thoughtful of you to have arranged all this for me. Thank you for all you've done for me.

Luojie: Oh, it's what I should do. If it's convenient, now let's begin our discussion about Labour and Wages Management first.

Henry: All right, sir.

Luojie: Please, Mr. Smith.

学说英语

谈论会见合作当事人

李　华：对不起，请问您是从加拿大来的史密斯·亨利先生吗？

亨　利：对呀！您是……

李　华：啊，我是罗先生的秘书，李华小姐。好吧，请进。

亨　利：好吧，谢谢！

李　华：（过了一会儿）请允许我把您介绍给中国土木建筑工程总公司，总承包人，总经理罗先生。这位是加拿大住房公司的建筑业主，史密斯先生。（双方握手并说……）

亨　利：罗先生，您好，常听人谈起您。很高兴今天在此见到您。

罗　杰：史密斯先生，您好，我一直想结识您，今天终于如愿以偿。欢迎光临！

亨　利：谢谢！我能有机会见到罗先生深感荣兴。

罗　杰：我们都感到非常荣兴！请坐，史密斯先生。抽支烟吧？

亨　利：谢谢！罗先生，我不会抽烟。

罗　杰：您想喝点什么，酒还是咖啡？

亨　利：请来杯酒吧。您为我安排得很周到，感谢您为我所做的一切。

罗　杰：啊，这是我该做的。如果方便的话，咱们现在就先开始讨论劳动工资管理吧。

亨　利：好吧，先生。

罗　杰：请吧，史密斯先生！

Spoken Practice 口语练习

1. Pair Work:

Suppose you're visiting a Construction Engineering Company, a manager meets you in his office. Try to say what you both talk.

2. Answer the following questions in accordance with Learn to Speak English:

1) Whom does Mr. Luo meet in his office?

2) Does Mr. Henry. Smith come from Canada or U. K. ?

3) Who is general manager of CCEC?

4) Mr. Henry Smith is a building employer, isn't he?

3. Reading & interpretation:

Functions of the Board of Directors

The primary functions of the board of directors are to work out corporate policies and to protect the interests of the stockholders. Specific duties of the directors include hiring high-ranking officers for the corporation and setting these officers' salaries, declaring dividends, and reviewing the findings of both internal auditors and independent auditors.

4. Put the Following into English:

名 片

CSCEC 文华 经理
海外公司
中国建筑工程总公司
地 址：中国北京百万庄
邮政编码：100037　　　传 真：010-8548986
电 话：010-87654321（宅）　　010-81234567（办公室）
E-mail：Wenhua@ yahoo. com www. China com.

5. Substitute the Following Words & Expressions:

1) Use the following **Labour and Wages Management**（劳动工资管理）to replace the black words in the following sentence:

Luojie: Oh, it's what I should do. If it is convenient, now let's begin our discussion about **Labour and Wages Management** first.

罗杰：啊，这是我该做的。如果方便的话，咱们现在就开始讨论劳动工资管理吧。

Labour and Wages Management 劳动工资管理
['leibə ənd 'weidʒiz 'mænidʒmənt]
labour discipline management 劳动纪律管理
['leibə 'disiplin 'mænidʒmənt]
adjustment of working hours 调整工作时间
[ə'dʒʌstmənt əv 'wə:kiŋ 'auəz]
wages grading system ['weidʒiz 'greidiŋ 'sistəm] 工资等级制度
wages/ salary ['weidʒiz 'sæləri] 工资，薪水
wages level ['weidʒiz 'levl] 工资水平
working year ['wə:kiŋ jiə] 工龄
money award, bonus ['mʌni ə'cw:d 'bounəs] 奖金
prize [praiz] 奖品
certificate of merit [sə'tifikit əv 'merit] 奖状
quota of enterprise-staff ['kwoutə əv 'entəpraiz sta:f] 企业定员
level of labour quota ['levl əv 'leibə 'kwoutə] 劳动定额水平
labour-assignment ['leibə ə'sainmənt] 劳动力分配
recruitment of labour [ri'kru:tmənt əv 'leibə] 劳动力招收
three-shift workday system [θri:ʃift 'wə:kdei 'sistəm] 三班制
eight-hour workday [eit 'auə 'wə:kdei] 八小时工作日
day shift [dei ʃift] 白（日）班
night shift [nait ʃift] 夜班
swing shift [swiŋ ʃift] 中班
treatment of staff and workers 职工待遇
['tri:tmənt əv sta:f ənd 'wə:kəz]
wage plan [weidʒ plæn] 工资计划
numbers of staff and workers ['nʌmbəz əv sta:f ənd 'wə:kəz] 职工人数
labour and wages ['leibə ənd 'weidʒiz] 劳动工资双方

2) Use the following **Organization Scheme** (组织关系) to replace the black words in the following sentence:

Lihua: (after a while) Allow me introduce you to Mr. Luo, **Main contractor**, general manager of CCEC. This is Mr. Smith, **building owner** of CHC. (They both shake hands and say...)

李华:（过了一会儿）请允许我把您介绍给中国土木建筑工程总公司，总承包人，总经理罗先生。这位是加拿大住房公司的建筑业主，史密斯先生。（双方握手并说……）

Organization Scheme 组织关系

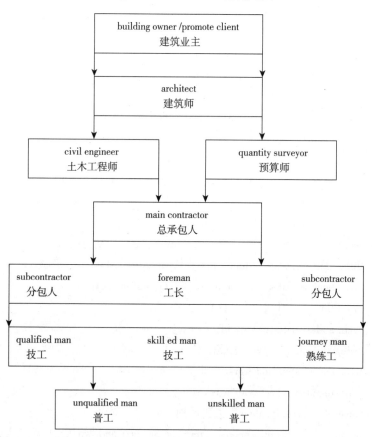

Situational Dialogic Unit 4

第四情景对话单元

Learn to Speak English

Talking about Chairing a Production Meeting

Charles: Is everybody present, Mr. Lan?

Lantian: Yes, all present and correct, Manager.

Charles: Ladies and Gentlemen, the meeting begins (Everyone claps). This meeting is to discuss and work out the economic target figures and production plan. Mr. Lan, please report last year's economic target figures and production plan.

Lantian: All right, Manager.

Charles: Mr. Wan, please read and talk over this year's economic target figures and production plan.

Wanhai: OK, sir.

Charles: Let Mr. Jian give us his views about the plan.

Jiandan: Thank you. Let's begin by looking at the general plan of this project.

Charles: Now let's start discussing the program. Who would like to say?

Lantian: Let me say a few words, manager.

Charles: OK. Please.

Lantian: I think the plan is more practical plan than last one. Undoubtedly, we must fufill it.

Charles: OK. Anyone else?

Jiandan: It saves both time and money. It's a good plan, so I have no more to say, sir.

Wanhai: Yes. That's just what I'm going to say. I agree to this plan.

Charles: Now let's vote by a show of hands.

W. L. J.: OK. Please.

Charles: Those against. Show your hands, Please. —OK. No. Those in favour. Show your hands, please. We all agree to this plan. And then that's all for the meeting.

学说英语

谈论主持生产会议

查尔斯：大家都到会了吗，蓝先生？
蓝　天：是的。如数到齐，经理。
查尔斯：女士们，先生们：会议开始（全体鼓掌）。今天的会议将讨论和制定明年的各项经济指标和生产计划。蓝先生，请把去年的各项经济指标和计划完成情况给大家通报一下。
蓝　天：好，经理。
查尔斯：万先生，请把今年的各项经济指标和生产计划的讨论稿给大家宣读一下。
万　海：好吧，先生。
查尔斯：让简先生先给我们谈谈自己对这一计划的看法。
简　丹：谢谢！咱们来看看工程项目总的计划吧。
查尔斯：现在咱们开始讨论这个方案吧。谁想谈一谈？
蓝　天：让我说几句吧，经理。
查尔斯：好吧，请讲。
蓝　天：我认为这个计划比上个计划更实际，毫无疑问，一定能完成。
查尔斯：说吧。还有谁要说吗？
简　丹：这个方案体现了多快好省，是个不错的计划。我没别的要说，先生。
万　海：对。那正是我想要说的话，我同意这个计划。
查尔斯：现在咱们举手表决吧。
万蓝简：好吧，请表决。
查尔斯：反对的，请举手。没反对的。赞成的，请举手。我们都一致通过。那么会就开到这，散会。

Explanatory Notes 注释:

1. manage 动词 (vt.) 管理；处理；经营
   例如: Manager Powell manages a Building Materials Market 鲍威尔经理管理一家建筑材料市场。

2. manager 名词 (n.) 经理，管理者
   例如: Sorry. I want to explain my thought to your manager himself.
   抱歉，我想把我的想法讲给经理本人听。

3. management 名词 (n.) 管理；处理；经营
   personnel management 人事管理   labour and management 劳资双方
   例如: The failure is caused by his poor management.
   失败是由于他的管理不当所造成的。
   例如: Modern Building Industry is under new management.
   现代建筑业应采用新的方式经营。

4. managing 形容词 (a.) 管理的；善于经营的
   例如: managing director 常务董事   managing consult 管理咨询
   managerial 形容词 (a.) 管理的；管理人的；管理上的；经营上的
   managerial talent 管理人才   managerial personnel 管理人员

Spoken Practice 口语练习

1. **Pair Work:**
   Imagine you're manager of a Construction Engineering Corporation, you're chairing a production meeting. Try to say how to chair it and what to say.

2. **Tell "true" or "false" in accordance with Learn to Speak English:**
   1) ( ) Everybody is absent, I'd love to say.
   2) ( ) They put their heads together to discuss what to do next year.
   3) ( ) They all disagree to this plan at last.
   4) ( ) This plan wastes both time and money, so I have nothing to say.
   5) ( ) The meeting is over means that's all for the meeting.

3. **Read & Interpret the Following Passage:**

   Professional Management in a Corporation

   The stockholders own a corporation, but they don't manage its daily basis. They elect a board of directors to deal with its affairs. The directors, in turn, employ professional managers to run its business. An individual stockholder has no right to participate in management unless he/she has been hired by the directors as a corporation manager.

4. **Try to Put the Following into English:**

   通　　知

   定于 2003 年 3 月 20 日，星期四，上午 8 点钟，所有部门经理在会议室开会。

   　　　　　　　　　　　总经理办公室
   　　　　　　　　　　　2003 年 3 月 19 日

5. **Substitute the Following Words & Expressions:**
   Use the following Terms about **Management Enterprises**（企业管理相关术语）to replace the black words in the following sentence:
   Charles: Mr. Wan, please read and talk over this year's **economic target figures** and **production plan**.
   查尔斯：万先生，请把今年的各项**经济指标**和**生产计划**的讨论稿给大家宣读一下。

Terms about Management of Enterprises [tə:mz əˈbaut ˈmænidʒmənt əvˈentəpraiziz] 企业管理相关术语

state-owned enterprises [steit ound ˈentəpraiziz] 国有企业

collective enterprises [kəˈlektiv ˈentəpraiziz] 集体企业

private enterprises [ˈpraivit ˈentəpraiziz] 私人企业

economic reckoning [ˌi:kəˈnɔmik ˈrekəniŋ] 经济核算

cost accounting [kɔst əˈkauntiŋ] 成本核算

reduction of cost [riˈdʌkʃən əv kɔst] 降低成本

circulating funds [ˈsə:kjuleitiŋ fʌndz] 流动资金

turnover of funds [ˈtə:nˌouvə əv fʌnds] 资金周转

profit rate [ˈprɔfit reit] 利润率

profit and loss [ˈprɔfit ənd lɔs] 盈利与亏损

gross/net profit [grous net ˈprɔfit] 毛/净利

capital goods [ˈkæpitl gudz] 生产资料

economic target figures [ˌi:kəˈnɔmik ˈta:git ˈfigəz] 各项经济指标

production investment [prəˈdʌkʃən inˈvestmənt] 生产投资

total value of output [ˈtoutl ˈvælju: əv ˈautput] 总产值

information feedback [ˌinfəˈmeiʃən ˈfi:dbæk] 信息反馈

raise/increase productivity [reis inˈkri:s ˌprɔdʌkˈtiviti] 提高生产率

state/ collective/individual ownership 国营/集体/个体所有制
[steit kəˈlektiv ˌindiˈvidjuəl ˈounəʃip]

system of reward and penalty 奖惩制度
[ˈsistəm əv riˈwɔ:d ənd ˈpenlti]

system of personal responsibility 岗位责任制
[ˈsistəm əv ˈpə:sənl risˌpɔnsəˈbiliti]

finished/semi-finished product 成/半成品
[ˈfiniʃd semi ˈfiniʃd ˈprɔdəkt]

budget of working drawing [ˈbʌdʒit əv ˈwə:kiŋ ˈdrɔ:iŋ] 施工图预算

regulations for technological operations 技术操作规程
[ˌregjuˈleiʃənz fə/teknəˈlɔdʒikəl ˌɔpəˈreiʃənz]

Situational Dialogic Unit 5
第五情景对话单元

Learn to Speak English

Talking about Making a Policy-decision

Gaoli: Hi. Mary. Please call chief engineer, chief accountant and deputy managers to my office. We're gong to have a short meeting.

Mary: OK. General Manager.

Gaoli: (after a while) Please sit down, everybody.

Mary: Thank you, sir. I'm anxious to know your decision.

Lizhe: I'm confident you have made the right choice.

Frank: I don't want to say anything to influence your decision.

Lixin: It's difficult for me to make a decision without knowing all the facts.

Boris: Let's invite our general manager to declare his decision.

M. L: Right. Please declare yours, general manager Gao.

Gaoli: OK. That's all right. I have spent more than ten days in investigating. Now I declare we can finalize the contract.

L. F.: We're very grateful for making nothing of hardship and investigating.

M. B.: We're sure to take coordinated activities with you and accomplish the task according to schedule.

Gaoli: Thank you for your trust and support.

学说英语

谈论作决策

高　立：喂，玛丽，请把总工程师、总会计师和副经理们叫到我办公室开个短会。

玛　丽：好的，经理。

高　立：(过了一会儿) 各位，请坐吧。

玛·丽：谢谢！先生。我急于想知道您的决定是什么？

栗　哲：我深信您已作出了正确的选择。

弗兰克：我不想说任何话来影响您的决定。

李　欣：不了解全部情况，很难做出决定。

鲍里斯：咱们还是请老总宣布吧！

玛　栗：对。您就宣布吧，高总。

高　立：是的，说得对。我花费了十多天的时间进行调查论证。现在，我宣布我们拍板这项合同。

李　费：我们为你不辞劳苦的调查而感激。

玛　鲍：我们一定配合您，如期完成这项任务。

高　立：谢谢大家的信任和支持。

Explanatory Notes 注释:

1. produce 动词 (vt. & vi.) 生产,制造

   例如: The workers produced 50 percent of the steel-iron quota in this year.

   工人们生产了今年钢铁定额的50%。

   例如: The factory is now able to mass-produce the new type of building materials. 这家工厂现在能批量生产这种新型的建筑材料。

2. producer 名词 (n.) 生产者,制造者

   product 名词 (n.) 产品,生产,产量

   industrial products 工业产品

   finished/semifinished product 成/半成品

   production 名词 (n.) 生产,产品,产量

   例如: These construction machines are put into mass serial production. 这些建筑施工机械投入成批生产。

   the relations of production 生产关系

   production cost 生产成本

   productivity 名词 (n.) 生产率,生产能力

   labour productivity 劳动生产率

   increase/raise productivity 提高生产率

3. productive 形容词 (a.) 生产的,生产性的

   the productive forces 生产力

   productive capacity 生产能力

Spoken Practice 口语练习

1. **Pair Work:**

   You're a duputy manager in charge of production in a Construction Engineering cooporation, you and your site directors, chiefs of division and factory directors are discussing a production task. Try to say how to make the decision.

2. **Tell "true" or "false" in accordance with Learn to Speak English:**

   1) ( ) Mary, please call students to my office and have a chat.
   2) ( ) Boris is too anxious to know the plan.
   3) ( ) Lizhe is confident the manager has made the correct choice.
   4) ( ) Frank wants to say anything to influence his leader's speech.
   5) ( ) It's so easy to make a decision with knowing all the facts.

3. **Read & Interpret the Following Passage:**

   Corporation High-ranking Officers and Their Responsibilities

   The top level of management usually includes a president/general manager or chief executive officer (CEO), a secretary, a controller and a treasurer. In addition, a vice-president oversees each functional department, such as personnel, production and business & sales.

   The secretary represents the corporation in many contractual and legal matters and maintains minutes of the meeting of directors and stockholders. The controller is responsible for the internal control and for preparation of accounting records and financial statements. The treasurer has custody of the corporation's funds and is generally responsible for planning and controlling its cash position.

4. **Try to Put the Following into English:**

   > 回 柬
   >
   > 约翰·史密斯先生愉快地接受中国建筑工程总公司总经理王海先生的盛情邀请，将出席1992年12月31日，星期四，晚上7时在希尔顿饭店大厅举行的除夕晚会。

5. **Substitute the Following Words & Expressions**:

Use the following **Deciding Items**（决定事项） to replace the black words in the following sentence:

Gaoli: OK. That's all right. I have spent more than ten days in investigating. Now I declare we can **finalize the contract.**

高立：是的，说得对。我花费了十多天的时间进行调查论证。现在，我宣布我们拍板这项合同。

Deciding Items［di'saidiŋ 'aitəmz］决定事项
offer ['ɔfə] 报价
tender ['tendə] 投/招标
contract [kən'trækt] 承包
inquire about price [in'kwaiə ə'baut prais] 询价
make a contract [meik ə 'kɔntrækt] 订立合同
sign a contract [sain ə 'kɔntrækt] 签署合同
annul a contract [ə'nʌl ə 'kɔntrækt] 取消合同
revise a contract [ri'vaiz ə 'kɔntrækt] 修改合同
terminate a contract ['tə:mineit ə 'kɔntrækt] 终止合同
inspect quality [in'spekt 'kwɔliti] 检查质量
inspect safety [in'spekt 'seifti] 检查安全
site test ['sait test] 现场试验
do quality supervision [du 'kwɔliti ˌsju:pə'viʒən] 进行质量监督
lay the foundation stone [lei ðə faun'deiʃən stəun] 奠基
do site investigation [du: sait in'vesti'geiʃən] 进行现场考察
purchase building materials ['pə:tʃəs 'bildiŋ mə'tiərəlz] 订购建材
start breaking up the ground [sta:t 'breikiŋ ʌp ðə graund] 破土动工
have an on-the spot meeting [hæv ən ɔn ðə spɔt 'mi:tiŋ] 召开现场会
carry out safety education 进行安全教育
['kæri aut 'seifti ˌedju'keiʃən]
hold a completion ceremony 举行落成典礼
[hould ə 'kəm'pli:ʃən 'serimən]

Situational Dialogic Unit 6
第六情景对话单元

Learn to Speak English

Talking about Consulting Tenderings

Jones: Mr. Xu, many companies have been invited to the tender for the construction of Greenland International Airport. Would your group corporation like to submit your tender?

Xujie: Yes, of course, but if we agree to send our tender, we want to know what we have to do?

Jones: As it stands, in addition to submission of tendering, you've to submit your information on cost, construction time and the volume of works concerning some big projects already constructed by you.

Xujie: I see. We'll do it as soon as possible. But we'd like to know the requirements of the tender committee.

Jones: OK. How do you assess the volume of work on the project?

Xujie: On the basis of data acquired. When will you register as tenderer for our corporation?

Jones: After we receive your data, I think.

Xujie: Which day is the tendering deadline, I'd love to know, miss?

Jones: Ten days before opening tender.

Xujie: When are you going to open the tender then?

Jones: On Jan. 1st., 2006.

Xujie: I've born in mind. How much is our chance of success as you see, miss?

Jones: Oh. That depends on your tender, but I know you have great experience and strong capacity in this field. You have a good chance of winning this tender, I think.

Zhou: Let's hope so.

Jones: Good luck!

Zhou: Thanks a lot. We're sure to seize the opportunity.

建筑企业管理人员英语情景会话

学说英语

谈论咨询投标事宜

琼　斯：徐先生，格林兰国际机场已经开始招标了，有好几家公司都要参与投标，难道贵公司不想参加这项工程的投标吗？

徐　杰：当然想，不过我们得了解一下这方面情况。如果我们打算投标的话，我们该做哪些准备工作呢？

琼　斯：通常的做法是，除了投标外，你们应该把你们所承建的一些大工程项目的造价，工期和工程量的相关资料都寄来。

徐　杰：我明白了。我们会尽快地寄来。不过我们想了解投标委员会的相关要求。

琼　斯：好吧。你们怎样确定工程项目的工程量呢？

徐　杰：根据已积累的相关资料来确定。何时能给我们公司办理投标注册登记？

琼　斯：我认为等到我们收到你们的相关资料后，才给办理投标注册登记。

徐　杰：我想知道哪天是投标的截止日期，小姐？

琼　斯：开标前十天。

徐　杰：那计划何时开标？

琼　斯：拟订2006年1月1日。

徐　杰：我记住了。您看我们成功的可能性有多大？

琼　斯：啊，那要根据你们的报价而定。不过我知道，你们在投标这方面富有经验，实力很强。我认为你们中标几率很高。

徐　杰：但愿如此。

琼　斯：祝你们好运！

徐　杰：多谢！我们会把握住这一时机。

Spoken Practice 口语练习

1. **Pair Work:**

   You're a vice-manager in charge of tender in the group corporation, you and your assistors are preparing the tender of International Hotel. Try to say what you must prepare before submitting the tender.

2. **Answer the following questions in accordance with Learn to Speak English:**

   1) What do you usually do before sending your tender?

   2) Must evey company be registered as tenderer?

   3) The tendering deadline is ten days before opening a tender, isn't it?

   4) Do you assess the volume of work on the project before submitting tender?

   5) Why do you have a good chance of winning the tender of Greenland bridge?

3. **Read & Interpret the Following Passage:**

   > **Reply to Submit Tender**
   >
   > Dear Sirs,
   >
   >   Having read the terms and conditions in the official form supplied by your Preparatory Department, we enclose our tender for the construction of **Tailai Guest House** in **Saibai Road** and trust that it will be accepted.
   >
   >   Your sincerely,
   >
   > Ecn. As stated

4. **Interpret and Change the Following Sentence Paterns according to the Requirements:**

   1) We found Chinese builders working on the construction site. (P. V.)

   2) Our party has given us so many construction tasks. (P. V.)

   3) Your construction plan must be worked out tomorrow. (A. V.)

4) Mr. Li will teach us engineering mechanics next term. (P. V.)

5) Electricity maks the building machines run faster than before. (P. V.)

6) These water supply and sewerage works were installed by Chinese builders last year. (A. V.)

7) Professor Smith is writing the book *Management of Enterprises* now. (P. V.)

5. Substitute the Following Words & Expressions:

Use the following **Terms about Submit Tender and Invite tender**（投标与招标相关术语）to replace the black words in the following sentence:

Xujie: On the basis of data acquired. When will you **register as tenderer** for our corporation?

徐杰：根据已积累的相关资料来确定，何时能给我们公司**办理投标注册登记**？

Terms about Submit Tender and Invite tender 投标与招标相关术语
[tə:mz ə'baut səb'mit 'tendə ənd in'vait 'tendə]

Tender Committee ['tendə kə'miti] 招标委员会

invite tenders/bids (Am.) [in'vait 'tendəz bidz] 招标

submit tender, bid (Am.) [səb'mit 'tendə bid] 投标

joint tender [dʒɔint 'tendə] 联合招标

tender/bid price ['tendə bid prais] 投标价格

tender/bid offers ['tendə bid 'ɔfəz] 投标开价

arbitrator [a:bi'treitə] 仲裁人

owner ['ounə] 业主

tenderer, bidder (Am.) ['tendərə 'bidə] 投标人，报价人

international tender/bid [ˌintə'næʃənl 'tendə bid] 国际招标

advertised bid/'tendə ['ædvətaizid bid 'tendə] 公开招标

competitive tender/bid [kəm'petitiv 'tendə bid] 竞争招标

tender /bid procedures ['tendə bid prə'si:dʒəz] 投标程序

tender /bid documents ['tendə bid 'dɔkjumənts] 投标文件，投标书

tender /bid deadline ['tendə bid 'dedlain] 投标截止日期

tender /bid guarantee ['tendə bid ˌgærən'ti:] 投标保证书

submit data ［səbˈmit /deitə］ 提供资料/数据

letter of enquiry/inquiry ［ˈletə əv ˈinˈkwaiəri］ 函询，投函询价

submission of tender ［səbˈmiʃən əv ˈtendə］ 投函、投标

pay dues /duties ［pei djuːz ˈdjuːtiz］ 纳税

give preference to ［geiv ˈprefərəns tu］ 给……特惠

volume of work(s) ［ˈvɔljuː məv wəːk(s)］ 工程规模(量)

commencement of work(s) ［kəˈmensmənt əv wəːk(s)］ 开工

completion of work(s) ［kəmˈpliːʃən əv wəːk(s)］ 竣工

opening a tender/bid ［ˈoupəniŋ ə ˈtendə bid］ 开标

winning a tender/bid ［ˈwiniŋ ə ˈtendə bid］ 中标

losing a tender/bid ［ˈluːziŋ ə ˈtendə bid］ 未中标

time of submission of tender ［taim əv səbˈmiʃən əv ˈtendə］ 投标日期

successful tenderer /bidder ［səkˈsesful ˈtendərə ˈbidə］ 中标人

submission of tender/bid 提标（提出承包书）

［səbˈmiʃən əv ˈtendə bid］

notification of tender of award 中标通知

［ˌnoutifiˈkeiʃən əv ˈtendə əv əˈwɔːd］

time of execution of work (s) 施工期

［taim əv ˌeksiˈkjuːʃən əv wəːk(s)］

Situational Dialogic Unit 7
第七情景对话单元

Learn to Speak English

Talking about Engineering Contract Negotiated

George: Let's discuss some concrete points in your contract now, Mr. Jin.

Jinxing: OK. That's just why I am here.

George: Why can't you do a good job with a competitive price?

Jinxing: Oh. There's a Chinese saying that you can't let a horse run fast without feeding it enough grass.

George: Yes. We've studied your offer carefully. Are you sure that your price is reasonable?

Jinxing: Personally, it should be.

George: The total price usually consists of ten items. Item 1 is labour cost. The total labour cost is US $7 million, about 10% of the total price. How many man-hours do you estimate to spend on this project?

Jinxing: About 9.5 million in minimum. The labour cost is only US $6 per day, which is rather low.

George: I think so. The item 2 is the cost of managerial personnel. It costs total up to US $2 million. What do you think of the cost?

Jinxing: Oh, It's medium.

George: But from our calculation, your managerial personnel cost is quite high. The monthly salary is about US $2,000. Is it higher than the average managerial personnel salary in your country?

Jinxing: Right. To tell truth, this amount isn't the actual salary of managerial personnel. In fact, only 60% becomes their net income.

George: Why? What about the other 40%?

Jinxing: Oh. The other is the cost for transportation, telecommunication, tax, insurance and so forth.

George: I see. There're something in what you say, but how about item 3?

Jinxing: Item 3 is the material cost that is the largest one, and nearly 55% of the total cost.

学说英语

谈论工程承包合同洽谈

乔 治：金先生，咱们现在讨论一下你们合同中的一些具体问题吧。
金 星：好。这正是我前来贵处的原因。
乔 治：你们为什么不采用一个有竞争力的价格来做好这项工作呢？
金 星：啊！中国人有句俗话"草不足，马不快"。
乔 治：是的。我们已经仔细研究了你们的报价。你能确定你们的价格合理吗？
金 星：就我个人而言，应该是。
乔 治：工程总价通常由10项组成。第一项是人工费，人工费的总价为700万美元，约占总价的10%。你们估计该工程能花费多少个工时？
金 星：最少为950万小时。每天人工费仅为6美元，这是相当低的。
乔 治：我想是。第二项是管理人员费用，总共为200万美元。你认为管理人员费用怎样？
金 星：啊！还比较适中吧。
乔 治：按照我们的计算，你们的管理人员费用太高。月薪高达2,000美元，与贵国管理人员平均薪水相比似乎有点过高吧。
金 星：对。但老实说吧，这个数目并不是管理人员的实际工资，而实际上这仅60%才是他们的纯收入。
乔 治：为啥？那另外的40%呢？
金 星：啊！其余40%为交通费，通讯费，税收，保险等费用。
乔 治：我明白了。说得有道理，但是第三项呢？
金 星：第三项是最大的一笔材料费用，几乎要占整个工程费用的55%。

George: We know the cement costs US $ 5 million. How much is the purchasing price for each tone of cement?

Jinxing: According to the investigation, the cement is US $ 80 per tone including the cost of material, transportation and other cost. The risk of inflation in next three years hasn't been considered yet.

George: That's right. It seems that 1,250 tones of cement, 500,000m^3 concrete is higher than usual, right?

Jinxing: Right. There're grades of concrete for different parts of the works and the mixture of each grade of concrete is different, too.

George: OK. We'd better have a detailed analysis for concrete, reinforcement bar and formwork in later step, right?

Jinxing: Right. We've spent a long time in talking today.

George: Yes. I agree to the other items of the draft contract. On the whole, it's acceptable, but we can't agree to your…

Jinxing: Never mind, I think. Negotiating contract, to some extent, talk over and exchange views. So it's a normal thing to have some different views.

George: I suppose so. As a matter of fact, we must seek common ground on major issues while reserving differences on minor one, the interest on both sides have not too much influence and that gets to our common view.

Jinxing: That's right. Negotiation is only way.

George: Yes. Cooperation is the sole purpose.

乔　治：我们知道水泥的造价是500万美元。那每吨的采购价是多少？

金　星：根据我们的调查，每吨水泥为80美元，包括材料费、运输费和其他费用在内。今后三年的通货膨胀风险因素还尚未考虑。

乔　治：那好。500,000立方米混凝土用掉1,250吨水泥似乎比一般的用量要高些，是吗？

金　星：是的。工程部位的不同而要使用的混凝土等级也就不同，每种混凝土的配料比也就不尽相同。

乔　治：对。就这样吧。我们最好下一步再对混凝土、钢筋和模板进行详细的单价分析，好吗？

金　星：这样也好。今天我们已经花费了很长时间讨论。

乔　治：是的。我们同意合同草案的其他款项，总的来说，可以接受，只不过我们不同意……

金　星：我认为没什么。洽谈合同，在某种程度上，就是讨论、磋商，所以有不同的意见才是正常的。

乔　治：我想也是这样。实际上，我们应求大同存小异，在各自的利益不受到太大的影响才能达成共识。

金　星：这就对了。洽谈只是一种形式。

乔　治：对，合作才是唯一目的。

Explanatory Notes 注释：

1. contract 动词（vt.）承办，承包，把（工程等）承包给（to）

   例如：Our company contracted to build a large bridge/ reservoir last year.

   我们公司去年承建了一座大桥/水库。

   例如：They have contracted a project to Huaqin Construction Company.

   他们已把工程包给了华秦建筑公司。

2. contract 动词（vi.）订契约；承办，承包

   例如：A foreign company contracts for the supply of raw materials to this big construction enterprise.

   一家外国公司长期承包这家大型建筑企业的材料供应。

3. contract 名词（n.）（个人、团体和国家间的）合同，合约，契约

   Make (enter into) a contract with sb. for sth.

   与某人（为某事）订立合同。

4. contractor 名词（n.）承包商（人），包工头

   engineering contractor 工程承包商（人）

Spoken Practice 口语练习

1. **Pair Work:**

   Suppose A acts as an engineering contractor, B acts as a building owner who wants to know something about his qualification and quoted price when they are negotiating a contract.

2. **Tell "true" or "false" in accordance with Learn to Speak English:**

   1) (　) There's a Chinese saying that you let a house run fast with feeding enough grass.

   2) (　) We've studied your offer carefully. The total price consists of 9 items.

   3) (　) The labour cost is only US $6 per day which is rather low.

   4) (　) Item 3 is the material cost that is the largest one, it makes up more than 5% of the total cost.

   5) (　) On the whole, it is acceptable, but we disagree to your total cost of contract.

3. **Read & Interpret the Following Passage:**

   Contract of Building the Friendship Hotel

   A contract is hereby concluded between the Huaxia Travel Service (hereafter to be called the first party) and the Tianshan Construction corporation (hereafter to be called the second party) for building the Friendship Hotel. The two contracting parties agree to the following terms:

   1. The first party entrusts the second party with building the Friendship Hotel, the designing drawing of which is to be submitted by the first party.

   2. Both contracting parties agree that the building cost is fixed at $6,000,000 only (six million U.S. dollars), thirty percent of which is to be paid by the first party to the second party within ten days after signing the present contract, all the rest to follow up two weeks after the completion of the hotel.

3. All the building materials to be used for building the hotel are to be supplied on time by the first party. But they must meet the agreed standards and specifications.

(To be continued)

4. Substitute the Following Words & Expressions:

Use the following **Contract Management**（合同管理）to replace the black words in the following sentence:

George: Yes. I agree to the other items of **the draft contract.** On the whole, it's acceptable, but we can't agree to your….

乔治：是的。我们同意**合同草案**的其他款项，总的来说，可以接受，只不过我们不同意……

Contract Management [ˈkɔntrækt ˈmænidʒmənt] 合同管理
negotiate a contract [niˈgouʃieit ə ˈkɔntrækt] 洽谈合同
initiate a contract [iˈniʃieit ə ˈkɔntrækt] 草签合同
hand over a contract [hænd ˈəuvə ə ˈkɔntrækt] 移交合同
consider a contract [kənˈsidə ə ˈkɔntrækt] 审查合同
terminate a contract [ˈtə:mineit ə ˈkɔntrækt] 终止合同
hold a contract [hould ə ˈkɔntrækt] 信守合同
make a contract [meik ə ˈkɔntrækt] 订立合同
revise a contract [riˈvaiz ə ˈkɔntrækt] 修改合同
sign a contract [sain əˈkɔntrækt] 签署合同
long-term contract [lɔŋ tə:m ˈkɔntrækt] 长期合同
void contract [vɔid ˈkɔntrækt] 失/无效的合同
annul/cancel a contract [əˈnʌl ˈkænsəl ə ˈkɔntrækt] 取消合同
infringe/break a contract [inˈfrindʒ breik ə ˈkɔntrækt] 违反合同
execute/perform a contract [ˈeksikju:t pəˈfɔ:m ə ˈkɔntrækt] 履行合同
terminal/fixed term contract [ˈtə:minl ˈfikst tə:m ˈkɔntrækt] 定期合同

Situational Dialogic Unit 8

第八情景对话单元

Learn to Speak English

Talking about Signing a Contract of Works

Yiran: This contract is valid for a period of two years from Jan. 1st. 2004 to Dec. 31st. 2005, right?

Denis: Right. This contract is made out in two originals, each in Chinese and English languages, both being equally legal effective. Each party holds original one.

Yiran: OK. I think that payment terms in the contract are also important, aren't they?

Denis: Yes. The contract contains basically all we have agreed upon during our negotiation. That's a copy of our contract. Would you please read it again before singing, Mr. Yi?

Yiran: I don't think it is necessary and I don't believe there're conflicts between this contract conditions and normal international contract documents. We've settled all the points under dispute.

Jingli: Good. If any problems arise in the process of work, we'll deal with them there and then.

Yiran: That's true enough! it should be. I think we'd better add one sentence here: "If one side fails to honour the contract, the other side has the right to cancel it."

Jingli: Clearly you're right, I think so.

Yiran: Some main points can be included in a contract supplement to the contract upon mutual agreement.

Denis: Fine. Everything is in order. Contract parties come and sit here, please.

Y. P: I think so. Please..

Denis: Please sign here. Exchange texts, please. Cheers (they drink)!

Yiran: I wish to cooperate closely with you——my honoured ladies and gentlemen.

Petrie: We must strictly abide by the contract, guarantee high quailty, have close coordination and increase friendship.

学说英语

谈论签订工程合同

毅　然：这份合同是从 2004 年元月 1 日开始到 2005 年 12 月 31 日终止，有效期两年，对吗？

丹尼斯：对。这份合同有两份原件，每份均用英汉两种文字打印，两种文本均有同等的法律效力，双方各持一份。

毅　然：好。我觉得合同中的付款条款也很重要，是吗？

丹尼斯：是的。这份合同基本上包括了在洽谈期间达成的所有款项。这是一份合同副本，请你在签署之前再审阅一次好吗，毅先生？

毅　然：我认为没有必要吧。我相信这本合同条款与一般国际合同文本没有任何矛盾之处。我们已经解决了所有有争议的问题。

经　理：那好。如果在工作运作中出现新问题的话，我们可随时解决。

毅　然：非常正确！应该这样。我觉得合同中最好加上这样一句："如果一方未履行本合同条款，另一方则有权终止该合同。"

经　理：显然你是对的。我也是这样认为的。

毅　然：一些原则性问题经双方同意后可以写入合同的补充文件中。

丹尼斯：好吧，一切就绪。请合同双方代表前来就座。

毅　皮：我想该这样了。请吧！

丹尼斯：请在此处签字。请互换文本。干杯！（喝酒）

毅　然：我希望同你们——尊敬的女士们，先生们密切合作。

皮特里：我们一定信守合同，保证质量，密切合作，增进友谊。

Spoken Practice 口语练习

1. **Pair Work:**

   Imagine A acts as an engineering contractor, B acts as a promote client. After both sides fully discuss and consult the contract terms, they decide to sign it. Try to talk something while they sign it.

2. **Answer the following questions accordance to Learn to Speak English:**

   1) Should the copy of our contract be read again before signing? Why?
   2) How shall we deal with contract if any problems arise in the process of work?
   3) What can be included in a contract supplement to the contract upon mutual agreement?
   4) The contract parties should exchange their signed contract texts, shouldn't they?
   5) What must second party of contract strictly do after signing the contract?

3. **Read & Interpret the Following Passage:**

   (continue from last unit)

   4. Building the hotel must be completed 12 months after signing the contract. The hand-over will take place on Oct. 1st, 1995.
   5. The said hotel is guaranteed for fifty years against collapse or leakage, for which, if found in any form, maintenance and repairs must be done gratis by the second party.
   6. Signed on Oct. 1st, 1994, at London, the present contract is made in duplicate in Chinese and English languages. Both texts being equally legal authentic.

Yang Ming	David Smith
(signed)	(signed)
For Huaxia Travel Service	For Tianshan Construction Corporation

   Supplements Omitted

4. **Try to Put the Following into English:**

鸡尾酒会

聚会有多种,例如(正式的)宴会、一般宴会、鸡尾酒会、招待会和茶(话)会,但为了商务和社交目的举行鸡尾酒会是很普通的事。酒会既可以是正式的,也可以非正式的,而且一般在晚上六点至八点钟之间举行。酒会上常以各种饮料、开胃小吃或点心款待各位来宾。

5. **Substitute the Following Words & Expressions:**

1) Use the following **Terms about Contract Clauses**(合同条款相关术语) to replace the black words in the following sentence:

Yiran: Some main points can be included in a **contract supplement to the contract** upon mutual agreement.

毅然:一些原则性问题经双方同意可以写入合同的补充件中。

Terms about Contract Clauses 合同条款相关术语
[tə:mz əˈbaut ˈkɔntrækt ˈklɔ:ziz]

contractual obligations [kənˈtræktjuəl ˌɔbliˈgeiʃənz] 合同的义务

talks under contract [tɔ:ks ˈʌndə ˈkɔntrækt] 根据合同谈判(洽谈)

defects liability period [diˈfekts ˌlaiəˈbiliti ˈpiəriəd] 保修期

appendix to contract [əˈpendiks tu ˈkɔntrækt] 合同附件

conditions of contract [kənˈdiʃənz əv ˈkɔntrækt] 合同条件

contract number [ˈkɔntrækt ˈnʌmbə] 合同编号

contract period [ˈkɔntrækt ˈpiəriəd] 合同期

contract sum [ˈkɔntrækt sʌm] 合同金额

bills of quantity [ˈbilz əv ˈkwɔntiti] 工程量表

date for possession [deit fə pəˈzeʃən] 施工日期

date for completion [deit fə kəmˈpli:ʃən] 竣工日期

2) Use the following **Contract Party**(合同当事人) to replace the black words in the following sentence:

Denis: Fine. Everything is in order. **Contract parties** come and sit here, please.

丹尼斯:好吧,一切就序。请合同双方代表前来就坐。

Contract Party ['kɔntrækt 'pa:ti] 合同当事人
contractor [kən'træktə] 承包人/商，订约人
engineering contractor [ˌendʒi'niəriŋ kən'træktə] 工程承包商/人
general contractor ['dʒenərəl kən'træktə] 总承包/订约人
sub-contractor ['sʌb kən'træktə] 分包商/人
first party [fə:st 'pa:ti] 甲方，第一方当事人
second party ['sekənd 'pa:rti] 乙方，第二方当事人
employer [im'plɔiə] 雇主，雇佣者
employee [ˌemplɔi'i:] 雇员，受雇者

Situational Dialogic Unit 9
第九情景对话单元

Learn to Speak English

Talking about Prolonging the Construction Contract Term

Jiaozi: You don't give any facts. I must know these.

Susan: What facts, sir?

Jiaozi: Prolong the contract term.

Susan: That's right. But why? Please make comments on it.

Jiaozi: OK. Until now there're so many people living on the site. How can we demolish the buildings and start breaking up the ground right now?

Susan: What you said is right. The conditions aren't suitable for you to start. I agree to your view. Anything else?

Jiaozi: No more up to the present, sir.

Susan: OK, I'll solve the problem at once. All the points are agreed upon after we discuss the clauses of contract.

Jiaozi: We're ready to accept the wording suggested by your side, and we hope that present negotiations will be successfully completed in the near future with the signing of a contract for the construction of a project on a "turn-key" basis.

Susan: Fine. In that case, we'll tell our experts and lawyers to prepare the contract for signing.

Jiaozi: OK. We've worked hard and fruitfully, so I think we deserve a good rest. I'd like to invite you to have a dinner in a restaurant, and then make a tour in our city.

Susan: I'm very happy to accept your invitation, sir.

Jiaozi: Let me once more thank you for the constructive way you have helped to settle all the problems and break the ice that were in the way of singing the contract.

Susan: Not at all, sir.

学说英语

谈论延长施工合同有效期

娇 紫：你不必开口，我便知何事。

苏 珊：是什么事，先生？

娇 紫：延长合同有效期。

苏 珊：正是此事。那为什么？请谈谈你的意见吧。

娇 紫：那好。直到现在，施工现场还有许多住户，我们怎能拆除现场的建筑物，又怎能立刻破土动工呢？

苏 珊：你说得对。我同意你的不具备动工条件看法。你还有什么要说明的吗？

娇 紫：到目前为止，没什么要说，先生。

苏 珊：没问题，我这就着手解决。自我们讨论合同条款后，所有的问题都会达成共识。

娇 紫：我们准备接受你方提出的条款，并且希望这次洽谈后，在最短时间内能签订一项"交钥匙"建设工程合同而圆满结束。

苏 珊：好吧。既然如此，我们现在即可委托我们的专家和律师准备好签字合同。

娇 紫：对。我们工作得很好，富有成效，所以我认为我们应好好休息一下，我想请你到餐馆就餐，然后进城逛逛。

苏 珊：我非常高兴接受你的邀请，先生。

娇 紫：你以建设性的、干练的方式解决了那些曾经拖延合同签字的问题，打破了僵局，对此我再次表示感谢。

苏 珊：不客气，先生。

Spoken Practice 口语练习

1. Pair Work:

Supposeing a building owner acts as first party. An engineering contractor acts as second party. After signing the contract, some new problems have taken place, second party wants to prolong the contract period. Try to talk something what they argue their cases in prolonging the contract term and give the explanation of each party.

2. Answer the following questions in accordance with Learn to Speak English:

1) Does the second party want to prolong the contract term? And why?

2) Why does the first party agree to the second party view of prolonging the contract term?

3) They hope to sign a construction contract in the near future, don't they?

4) Will the contract parties trust to prepare the construction contract for signing?

5) What would A like to invite B to do?

3. Read & Interpret the Following Passage:

Modifying Contract

Dear Sirs,

    We are very grateful for your letter of May 1st, 2001, and the enclosed draft contract.

    As regards Article No. 8 of the contract, we propose to make some modifications. The modified text reads:

    "Neither of the parties shall transfer to a third party any of the information, drawings, correspondence and other documents received from the other party. Either party may use the information, drawings and documents provided by the other party only in the construction, erection, maintenance and operation of the contracted project, as well as in the training of personnel, and neither party shall use the same for any other purposes or any other projects without the written consent of the other party."

> You will notice that the modified stipulation will fit in better with the actual needs and will prove workable and mutually beneficial in the days to come. We hope to have your confirmation by next mail.
>
> Your faithfully,

4. Put the Following into Chinese and Tell What Part of Speech the Underlined Part is：

1) Would you <u>hand</u> me your English-Chinese Dictionary?　(　)
   A clock usually has two or three <u>hands</u>.　(　)

2) "Please keep the <u>change</u>." I said to the taxi driver.　(　)
   <u>Change</u> the following passage into English.　(　)

3) Pronunciation & intonation is an important <u>step</u> for speaking English well.　(　)
   Why must you <u>step</u> on the tall water tower, young man?　(　)

4) You must <u>water</u> the bricks before laying.　(　)
   I have to drink more <u>water</u> after hard working.　(　)

5) We all have an electronic <u>watch</u> now.　(　)
   Some of builders are going to <u>watch</u> the football game if they finish their work on the worksite.　(　)

5. Substitute the Following Words & Expressions：

Use the following **Kinds of Contract**（合同的种类）to replace the black words in the following sentence：

Jiaozi: We're ready to accept the wording suggested by your side, and we hope that present negotiations will be successfully completed in the near future with the signing of a **contract for the construction** of a project on a "turn-key" basis.

娇　紫：我们准备接受你方提出的条文，并且希望这次洽谈后，在最短时间内能签订一项"交钥匙"**建设工程合同**而圆满结束。

Kinds of Contract [kaindz əv ˈkɔntrækt] 合同的种类

labour contract [ˈleibə ˈkɔntrækt] 劳动合同

economic contract [ˌiːkəˈnɔmik ˈkɔntrækt] 经济合同

construction contract [kənˈstrʌkʃən ˈkɔntrækt] 建设施工合同

risk contract [risk ˈkɔntrækt] 风险承担合同

cost-plus-fixed-fee contract 成本加固定利润合同
[kɔst plʌs ˈfikst fiː ˈkɔntrækt]

research-development contract 科研开发合同
[riːˈsəːtʃ diˈveləpmənt ˈkɔntrækt]

test-evaluation contract 分析试验与评估合同
[test iˌvæljuˈeiʃən ˈkɔntrækt]

contract awarded/gained 中标（投标优选结果签订）合同
[ˈkɔntrækt əˈwɔːdid geind]

contract for the supply of complete equipment 成套设备供应合同
[ˈkɔntrækt fə ðə səˈplai əv kəmˈpliːt iˈkwipmənt]

contract for the sending of specialists 派遣专家合同
[ˈkɔntrækt fə ðə ˈsendiŋ əv ˈspeʃəlists]

contract for the construction of engineering projects 建设工程项目合同
[ˈkɔntrækt fə ðə kənˈstrʌkʃən əv ˌendʒiˈniəriŋ ˈprɔdʒekts]

Situational Dialogic Unit 10

第十情景对话单元

Learn to Speak English

Talking about Completion Certificates Issued

Karen: Do you know when the Tailan Mansion is issued the section completion certificate, sir?

Liuyu: In my opinion, it's too early to issue it.

Karen: Why not? But I'm afraid I couldn't agree with you at this point, since we have finished 95% of the total works.

Liuyu: According to the calculation you have only finished 90% of the whole works.

Karen: I think we'd better stop arguing these.

Liuyu: Sound reasonable. What's to be done then?

Karen: Now I propose that you try your best to finish all the works within 20 days, after a further inspection to the whole works, the certification will be issued to you.

Liuyu: I see, sir. But does the retention period begin from the day of issuing the Certificate?

Karen: Naturally, you shouldn't forget an important thing during this period.

Liuyu: I know very well what you are referring to is the working-drawings. We'll have a thorough collection of all within 5 days.

Karen: That's all right. In addition to this, all the necessary information, such as QA/QC inspection forms, survey records, execution tracing files should be ready for submission.

Liuyu: No problem. (after one year) Usually, some defects will be found during the inspections. We'll be required to repair them within a period of time.

Karen: Yes, all the defects will be repaired very soon and the works will be kept perfect even after final handing over.

Liuyu: Surely. You must be satisfied with us. By the way, by whom do you set up jointly an inspection group?

谈论完工证书的颁发

卡　伦：先生，您知道何时将颁发泰蓝大厦的部分完工证书？

刘　誉：以我看，颁发该证书为时过早。

卡　伦：为什么不？可是我恐怕不能认同您这点，因为我们已经完成总工程的95%。

刘　誉：可是从统计报表上看，你们仅完成这项工程的90%。

卡　伦：我想我们最好不要争执这一问题。

刘　誉：言之有理。那可怎么办？

卡　伦：现在我建议你们尽最大的努力在20天内完成整个工程，我们将为你们颁发完工证书。

刘　誉：先生，我明白啦。那保修期是从颁发证书那天算起吗？

卡　伦：那自然是。在这期间有一件重要的事情你们可别忘了。

刘　誉：我非常清楚您想说什么：施工图，我们会在5天内彻底收集完施工图。

卡　伦：那就好。除了这点，所有必要的资料，如质保/质控的文件，测量记录，隐蔽工程记录等都应移交给我们。

刘　誉：那没问题。（一年后）通常说，在验收过程中，定会发现工程中的一些不足之处，我们会在一定的时间内修复完好。

卡　伦：是的，工程中所有不足之处应尽快修复完好，即使已经最后交工了，工程也应保持完好无损。

刘　誉：那是肯定的，你们一定会对我们的工程满意的。顺便问一句，由哪些部门的人联合组成验收小组？

Karen: The Employer, Contractor and representatives of relevant Government Departments.

Liuyu: What will the group do then?

Karen: The group will inspect all works in the scope of the Contract within 10 days and the inspection report will be issued to all relevant aspects.

Liuyu: I see. The Final Completion Certificate is issued after the procedure is fulfilled in accordance with the Condition of Contract, right?

Karen: That's right.

卡　伦：应由业主、承包商和政府有关部门联合组成验收小组。

刘　誉：验收小组随后还要做哪些工作？

卡　伦：在随后的 10 天内，验收小组就合同范围内所有工程项目进行检查。在对所有必要方面进行检查过后，将提出一份报告。

刘　誉：我明白了。依据合同条款，完成了这些程序后才颁发工程最后完工证书，对吗？

卡　伦：对。

Spoken Practice 口语练习

1. **Pair Work**:

   A acts as an inspector, B acts as a representative from a construction company who wants A to issue the completion certificate. Use the following expressions:

   A: Can I ... ?

   B: Certainly……but……

   A: Please show ……

   B: OK. It's... .

2. **Tell "true" or "false" in accordance with Learn to Speak English**:

   1) (   ) In my opinion Tailan Mansion is too early to issue the section completion certificate.

   2) (   ) In accordance with our calculation, you have only finished less than 90% of the whole works.

   3) (   ) The certificate will be issued to you before further inspection to the whole works.

   4) (   ) All the necessary information, such as QA/QC inspection forms, survey records, execution tracing files should be ready for submission except working-drawings.

   5) (   ) All the defects will be repaired very soon and the works will be kept perfect even after final handing over.

3. **Change the Following Sentence Paterns according to the Requirements**:

   1) They are students who learn architecture. (general question)

   2) Mr. Wang speaks English fluently. (exclamatory sentence)

   3) Engineers must have many reference books to read.

   (disjunctive question)

   4) <u>Teacher Sheng</u> teaches <u>you</u> English. (special question-S. O.)

   5) The constructors work on the day shift (night shift).

   (alternative question)

6) We study civil & industrial architecture in an Architectural Engineering College. (special question-O. Ad.)

4. Read & Interpret the Following Passage:

   The Examination, Taking Over and Defects Liability Period

   On the completion of every stage of the project, A and B sides should form an acceptance group to sign an acceptance certificate according to the drawings and specifications for the qualified works.

   If the works done is not conformable to the drawings, B side should remedy it up so as to reach the drawings, and all the expenditures are up to B side.

   The defects liability period of the project is one year from the date of the signing of taking over documents of the completion, the poor quality causing from the construction, B side will maintain it up to drawings at his own cost.

5. Substitute the Following Words & Expressions:

   Use the following **Building Appraisement**（工程评价）to replace the black words in the following sentence:

   Karen: That's all right. In addition to this, all the necessary information, such as **QA/QC inspection forms**, **survey records**, **execution tracing files** should be ready for submission.

   卡　伦：那就好。除了这点，所有必要的资料，如**质保/质控的文件，测量记录，隐蔽工程记录**等都应移交给我们。

   Project/Building Appraisememt 工程评价

   ['prɔjekt 'bildiŋ ə'preizmənt]

   acceptance check [ək'septəns tʃek] 验收
   judgement of quality ['dʒʌdʒmənt əv 'kwɔliti] 质量评定
   acceptance standard [ək'septəns 'stændəd] 验收标准
   acceptance procedure [ək'septəns prə'si:dʒə] 验收程序
   acceptance certificate [ək'septəns sə'tifikit] 验收合格证
   construction tolerances [kən'strʌkʃən 'tɔlərənsiz] 施工允许误差
   refer to working drawing [ri'fə:tu 'wə:kiŋ 'drɔ:iŋ] 参见施工图

inspection certificate ［inˈspekʃən səˈtifikit］检验合格证书
supply a complete equipment 提供成套设备
［səˈplai ə kəmˈpliːt iˈkwipmənt］
inspection of works progress 工序检查
［inˈspekʃən əv wəːks ˈprougres］
draw up a construction plan 制定施工方案
［drɔː ʌp ə kənˈstrʌkʃən plæn］
completion bond of building quality 工程质量保证书
［kəmˈpliːʃən bɔnd əv ˈbildiŋ ˈkwɔliti］
standardizational works of quality management 质量管理的标准化工程
［ˌstændədaiˈzeiʃnl wəːks əv ˈkwɔliti ˈmænidʒmənt］
technical sampling in quality management 质量管理中的抽样法
［ˈteknikəl ˈsaːmpliŋ in ˈkwɔliti ˈmænidʒmənt］
system of quality inspection and acceptance 工程质量检查验收制度
［ˈsistəm əv ˈkwɔliti inˈspekʃən ənd əkˈseptəns］
assurance system of quality control 质量管理的保证体系
［əˈʃuərəns ˈsistəm əv ˈkwɔliti kənˈtrəul］
quality control assurance during building 建设项目施工阶段的质量保证
［ˈkwɔliti kənˈtrəul əˈʃuərəns ˈdjuəriŋ ˈbildiŋ］

Situational Dialogic Unit 11
第十一情景对话单元

Learn to Speak English

Talking about Congratulations and Giving a Banquet

A. Congratulations on Completion Ceremony

Hoyt: I'm heard Sha River Bridge you constructed has been completed. Allow me to offer my heartiest congratulations!

Lilin: It's very nice of you to do so, Mr. Hoyt.

John: Let me congratulate you on your achievements, Manager Li.

Lilin: You're very kind, but really anyone else can do it.

Julia: Please accept my warmest congratulations, Mr. Li.

Lilin: Thank you. And the same to me, miss.

Arne: You really deserve to be congratulated, Mr. Lin!

Lilin: Thank you for coming.

Basil: I especially come to congratulate you, my close friend!

Lilin: I don't think you won't come, my old friend.

Kidd: May I offer you my congratulations on your complete success.

Lilin: I owe it all to my friends including you who have given me so much help. Thank you from the bottom of my heart for your coming, everybody. I propose a toast to our growing friendship and successful cooperation.

All: Cheers!

B. Giving a Banquet to Cooperative Partners

Yulin: Ladies and gentlmen: Welcome. Today is Chinese traditional day—Spring Festival. So we especially prepare the wine to thank you all for cooperation and support. Cheers!

All: Cheers!

Yulin: Now let's try Chinese dishes.

Kelly: OK. Very savoury, Chinese cooking is famous all over the world as well as Chinese wine.

Yulin: Yes. Help yourself to this. Would you like to use chopsticks or a knife and folk?

学说英语

谈论祝贺与宴请

A. 祝贺工程落成庆典

霍伊特：我听说你们承建的沙河大桥已竣工，请允许我向你们表示衷心的祝贺！

李　林：谢谢您这么说，霍伊特先生。

约　翰：请允许我为你们的成就，向你们祝贺，李经理。

李　林：谢谢你！不过别人也都能办到的。

朱莉亚：李先生，请接受我最热烈的祝贺。

李　林：谢谢你！我也一样，小姐。

阿　恩：你们的确应得到祝贺，李先生！

李　林：谢谢你光临。

巴兹尔：知友，我是专程前来祝贺你的！

李　林：我的老朋友，我想你不会不来的。

基　德：请允许我祝贺你们的圆满成功！

李　林：多亏了朋友们，包括在座的各位，给了我如此多的帮助。我衷心感谢大家的光临，并提议为我们日益增进的友谊与成功的合作干杯！

所有人：干杯！

B. 宴请合作方

余　林：女士们，先生们！欢迎光临！今天是中国的传统佳节——春节，特备薄酒以感谢各位的合作与支持，干杯！

所有人：干杯！

余　林：尝点中国菜吧！

凯　利：好吧，很有味道。中国烹调技术和中国酒一样名扬世界。

余　林：是的，请随便吃吧！您是用筷子还是用刀叉？

Black: I think I'll try chopsticks and see if I can manage.
Kelly: Me too.
Black: All the dishes have good flavour, are colourfull and very tasty. They're neither rare nor well done, just medium.
Yulin: To be precise. They're all well-known Chinese dishes and especially cooked for you, but I wonder if they are good for you to eat.
K. B.: Nice, very nice. This is the best Chinese food for me to have in my lifetime.
Yulin: Thank you for you to say so, Would you prefer some wine or spirits?
Black: Spirits. Chinese Liquor is very strong, right?
Yulin: Right, but it doesn't go to head. Wouldn't you like to try some?
K. B.: No. We'll try a little.
Yulin: Let me propose a toast to our everlasting friendship!
Kelly: Thank you. Let's drink to our future!
Y. K. B: May it bring us happiness! Cheers!
Yulin: Would you like some dumplings?
K. B: No, thanks. I've had enough.
Yulin: Would you like to try some fruits?
K. B: OK, that's sweet and juicy.
Black: I must say it was a lovely meal. It really wasn't half bad.
Kelly: It's said that Chinese are very hospitable. I've see it with my own eyes today and made a deep impression on me.
Yulin: I'm glad you enjoy it.
Kelly: Yes. It's really nice but I'm afraid it's getting late. We must be going now. Thank you for your hospitality. Bye!
Black: I'm also highly pleased, and have no alternative to say good-bye!
Yulin: Thank you for your coming! Bye!

布莱克:我想试试用筷子,看看我行不行。
凯　利:我也想试试。
布莱克:这些菜真是色、香、味俱全。(烧得)不嫩又不老,正好适中。
余　林:确切地说,这些都是中国的名菜,也都是特意为你们做的,但不知是否可口?
凯　利:好吃,非常好吃。这是我有生来吃得最可口的中餐。
余　林:谢谢你们这样说。你们喜欢喝葡萄酒还是白酒?
布莱克:白酒。中国的白酒很烈,是吗?
余　林:是的,但不上头,难道你们不想尝点吗?
凯　布:是的,尝点吧。
余　林:我提议为我们的永久友谊干杯!
凯　利:谢谢您。咱们为我们的未来干杯吧!
余凯布:但愿它给我们带来幸福!干杯!
余　林:再吃些饺子吧!
凯　布:不用啦,谢谢,我已吃饱了。
余　林:吃些水果好吗?
凯　布:那好吧。这些水果香甜多汁。
布莱克:我得说今天的酒席太丰盛了,真不错。
凯　利:都说中国人非常好客,今天我已亲眼目睹,感受颇深。
余　林:饭菜合你们的口味,我很高兴。
凯　利:是的,确实不错。但恐怕时间太晚了,我们该告辞啦。谢谢您的盛情款待。再见!
布莱克:我同样很高兴,但万般无奈,只好再见吧!
余　林:感谢你们的赏脸。再见!

Spoken Practice 口语练习

1. **Pair Work**:

   Imagine that you have been invited to a tea party. Discuss with your partners how to give your congratulations on the achievements each other.

2. **Tell "true" or "false" in accordance with Learn to Speak English**:

   1) (   ) Andy offered his heartiest congratulations as you have completed Sha River Bridge.

   2) (   ) John congratulates his manager on his failures.

   3) (   ) Thanks to your help, we can accomplish the bridge construction ahead of schedule.

   4) (   ) People have always told me Chinese are very miserliness.

   5) (   ) All the dishes have good flavour, are colourfull and very tasty.

3. **Read & Interpret the Following Passage**:

   > **Congratulations**
   > **on Completion of Foster Bridge**
   >
   > Your Excellency Mr. Wang,
   >
   >   My wife and I learned that Chinese builders have completed Foster Bridge.
   >
   >   My wife and I would like to add our congratulations to the many you must be receiving. We aren't surprised at all because Chinese builders under your leadership overcame all the difficulties and worked very hard from beginning to end.
   >
   >   My wife and I sincerely hope your staff and you meet greater success in the future.
   >
   >   Cordilly yours,
   >   Signature (Name in full)
   >   London, U. K. Dec. 26. 1996

4. Substitute the Following Words & Expressions:

1) Use the following **Congratulation on Something**（祝贺某事）to replace the black words in the following sentence:

Hoyt: I heard Sha River Bridge you constructed has been completed. Allow me to offer my heartiest **congratulations**!

霍伊特：我听说你们承建的沙河大桥已竣工，请允许我向你们表示衷心的祝贺！

Congratulation on Something [kən'grætjuleiʃən ɔn 'sʌmθiŋ] 祝贺某事
complete ahead of schedule [kəm'pli:t ə'hed əv 'ʃedju:l] 提前竣工
achieve complete success [ə'tʃi:v kəm'pli:t sək'ses] 取得圆满成功
open the road ['oupən ðə roud] 开通道路
winning tender ['winiŋ 'tendə] 中标
start breaking up the ground [sta:t 'breikiŋ ʌp ðə graund] 破土动工
Spring Festival [spriŋ 'festəvəl] 春节
Lantern Festival ['læntən 'festəvəl] 元宵节
Dragon-boat Festival ['drægən bout 'festəvəl] 端午节
Mid-Autumn Festival [mid 'ɔ:təm 'festəvəl] 中秋节
National Day ['næʃənl dei] 国庆节
Christmas Day ['krisməs dei] 圣诞节
Thanksgiving Day ['θæŋks͵giviŋ dei] 感恩节
New Year's Day/January 1st 元旦/一月一日
[nju: jiəz dei 'dʒænjuəri fə:st]
International Labour Day/May 1st 国际劳动节/五月一日
[͵intə:'næʃənl 'leibə dei mei fə:st]
promote mutual understanding and friendship 增进理解和友谊
[prə'mout 'mju:tjuəl ͵ʌndə'stændiŋ ənd 'frendʃip]

2) Use the following **Banquet, Wines and Drink**（宴会及其酒、饮料）to replace the black words in the following sentence:

Yulin: To be precise. They're all **well-known Chinese dishes.** Would you prefer some **wine** or **spirits**?

余林：确切地说，这些都是中国的名菜。你们喜欢喝葡萄酒还是白酒？
Banquet, Wines and Drink 宴会及其酒、饮料
['bæŋkwit wainz ənd driŋk]
brandy ['brændi] 白兰地酒
spirits; liquor ['spirits 'likə] 烈性酒
cocktail ['kɔkteil] 鸡尾酒
Maotai (spirits) ['maotai 'spiritz] 茅台
vodka ['vɔdkə] 伏特加
Red/white wine [red hwait wain] 红/白葡萄酒
XO [eks ou] 人头马
bamboo leaf [bæm'bu: li:f] 竹叶青
beer [biə] 啤酒
champagne [ʃæm'pein] 香槟酒
rum [rʌm] 朗姆酒
Fen Wine [fen wain] 汾酒
whisky ['hwiski] 威士忌酒
Vermouth ['və:məθ] 苦艾酒
sherry ['ʃeri] 雪利酒
gin [dʒin] 杜松子酒
drink [driŋk] 饮料
fruit juice [fru:t dʒu:s] 果汁
cocoa ['koukou] 可可
iced coffee ['aisid 'kɔfi] 冰咖啡
milk [milk] 牛奶
lemonade [ˌlemə'neid] 柠檬水
jasmine tea ['dʒæsmin ti:] 花茶
Longjing tea ['longjing ti:] 龙井茶
mineral water ['minərəl 'wɔ:tə] 矿泉水
soda water ['soudə 'wɔ:tə] 汽水/苏打水
state dinner [steit 'dinə] 国宴
dinner-party ['dinə 'pa:ti] 聚餐会

cocktail party ［'kɔkteil 'pɑːti］鸡尾酒会
informal dinner ［in'fɔːməl 'dinə］便宴
reception party ［ri'sepʃən 'pɑːti］招待会
tea party ［tiː 'pɑːti］茶（话）会

3）Use the following **Chinese Food**（中餐）to replace the black words in the following sentence：

Black： All the **dishes** have good flavour, are colourful and very tasty. They're neither rare nor well done, just medium.

布莱克：这些菜真是色、香、味俱全。（烧得）不嫩又不老，正好适中。

Chinese Food ［'tʃaiˈniːz fuːd］中餐
roast crab ［roust kræb］烤螃蟹
fried prawns ［fraid prɔːnz］炒大虾
pork meat patties ［pɔːk miːt 'pætiz］狮子头
spiced beef ［spaist biːf］五香牛肉
grilled chicken ［grild 'tʃikin］烧鸡
fried crisp chicken ［fraid krisp 'tʃikin］香酥鸡
Beijing roast duck ［beijing roust dʌk］北京烤鸭
instant boiled mutton ［'instənt bɔild 'mʌtn］涮羊肉
sweet and sour fish ［swiːt ənd 'sauə fiʃ］糖醋鱼
fish in brown sauce ［fiʃ in braun sɔːs］红烧鱼
bean curd in casserole ［biːn kəːd in 'kæsəroul］沙锅豆腐
braised pork tendons ［'breizd pɔːk 'tendənz］红烧蹄筋
stir-fried pork and eggs ［stəː fraid pɔːk ənd egz］炒木须肉
cold dish ［kould diʃ］冷盘
shrimp balls clear soup ［ʃrimp bɔːlz kliə suːp］上汤虾丸
sweet bird's nest soup with egg-white 甜芙蓉燕窝
［swiːt bəːdz nest suːp wið eg hwait］
wax gourd with assorted meats in soup 白玉藏珍
［wæks guəd wið ə'sɔːtid miːts in suːp］
thick soup of snake, cat and chicken 龙虎凤浓汤

[θik suːp əv sneik kæt ənd 'tʃikin]

4) Use the following **Parts of Staple Food**（部分主食）to replace the black words in the following sentence:

Yulin: Would you like some **dumplings**?

余林：再吃点饺子吧！

Parts of Staple Food ['steipl fuːd] 部分主食

sandwich ['sændwiʃ] 三明治（夹火腿面包片）

hamburger ['hæmbəːgə] 汉堡包（夹牛肉面包）

hot dog [hɔt dɔg] 热狗（夹香肠面包）

babao rice ['babao rais] 八宝饭

steamed stuffed bun [stiːmd stʌft bʌn] 包子

dumpling soup ['dʌmpliŋ suːp] 馄饨

sesame seed cake ['sesəmi siːd keik] 烧饼

crisp moon cake [krisp muːn keik] 酥泥月饼

instant (quick-served) noodles ['instənt kwik 'səːvid nuːdlz] 方便面

deep-fried twisted dough sticks [diːp fraid 'twistid dou stiks] 油条

dumpling (with meat and vegetable stuffings) 饺子
['dʌmpliŋ wið miːt ənd 'vedʒitəbl 'stʌfiŋz]

Part Two
English Situational Conversations with Building Engineering and Technical Personnel
(Situational Dialogic Unit 12-24)

第二部
建筑工程技术人员英语情景会话
（第十二至二十四情景对话单元）

Situational Dialogic Unit 12
第十二情景对话单元

Learn to Speak English

Talking about Introduction of Building Engineering and Technical Personnel

Jones: Hello, sir. May I introduce myself?

Liude: Yes. Please.

Jones: I'm Carl Jones from England (U. K.). Carl is my given name and Jones my surname.

Liude: How do you do, Mr. Jones?

Jones: How do you do? Happy to meet you.

Liude: Let me introduce myself to you. My given name is De and surname Liu. I come from China (P. R. C.).

Jones: Oh! Mr. Liu, a Chinese. Glad to know you. And what's your job?

Liude: I'm a resident engineer and a site director in charge of this worksite, too.

Jones: I've often heard about you. I'm a senior designer of the Royal Institute of British Architects.

Liude: I know you well by reputation, Mr. Jones. This project is designed by yourself, right?

Jones: Yes. It's my meticulous in design, but it depends upon your careful construction.

Liude: Yes, I could. Painstaking construction is our duty. Hope your mind at the rest, please.

Jones: The project of the best quality not only needs excellent designing, but also painstaking construction, so building engineering and technical personnel is key to the superfine project.

Liude: Precisely. Thank you for your trust. We'll do our utmost.

建筑技术与管理英语情景会话

学说英语

谈论建筑工程技术人员介绍

琼　斯：喂，先生。请允许我作个自我介绍好吗？

刘　德：好啊！请吧！

琼　斯：我是来自英国的卡尔·琼斯。卡尔是我的名字（第一名字），琼斯是我的姓（第二名字）。

刘　德：您好，琼斯先生！

琼　斯：您好！很高兴见到你。

刘　德：我也作个自我介绍吧。我姓刘，名德。我来自于中国（中华人民共和国）。

琼　斯：啊！是刘先生，中国人。很高兴结识您。那你是做什么工作的？

刘　德：我是一位驻地工程师，也是主管这个工地的工地主任。

琼　斯：久仰，久仰！我是英国皇家建筑师学会的一位高级设计师。

刘　德：琼斯先生，久闻大名。这项工程就是你亲自设计的，对吗？

琼　斯：对。是我精心设计的，但还得靠你们精心施工才是。

刘　德：精心施工是我们的职责。请你放心吧。

琼　斯：是的，我会。精品工程不仅需要精心设计，而且还需要精心施工，所以建筑工程技术人员才是建造精品工程的关键。

刘　德：正是这样。多谢你的信任。我们一定会竭尽全力精心施工。

Explanatory Notes 注释:

  build vt. 建筑，建造，建设等意思。例如：By 2050, we shall have built our country into one of the medium developed countries in the world. 到 2050 年，我们将把我国建设成为世界上中等发达国家。也可用作 vi. 建造，从事营造业。常用的短语有：build up to 增加；build up 振兴，改建，建成；build on/upon 建立在…上，指望，build in 嵌/砌/装入。build 是建筑英语中最普通而又最常用的单词之一，除了学好它的用法外，还应学好它的其他形词。例如：build 同样是一个不规则动词，其形式是 build, built, built；build 也可用作名词，意思是构造，造型。builder n. 建筑工人，施工人员，建设者等；还有 builder's labourer（施工）力工，小工；builder's handyman（施工）零杂工；building（既是 build 的现在分词形式，也是一种名词形式）n. 建筑物，房屋，营造，建造等。例如：building area 建筑面积，building codes and standards 建筑法规和标准，building centre 建筑中心，building permit（建筑）施工执照，building site 建筑场地、building line 建筑界线，building standards 建筑标准等。

Spoken Practice 口语练习

1. Pair Work:

A acts as an engineer of a building company, B acts as a visitor who wants to know something about A. Use the following expressions:

——Can you give . . . ?

——Yes, I'd like to. . .

——What's your. . . ?

——I'm. . .

2. Tell "true" or "false" in accordance with Learn to Speak English:

1) (　) May I give introduction yourself to me?

2) (　) Jones comes from America, Liu Canada.

3) (　) Liude is a resident engineer and a site director in charge of this construction site.

4) (　) Jones is a senior architect of the Royal Institute of British Architects.

5) (　) The project of the best quality not only needs excellent designing, but also careful construction.

3. Read & Interpret the Following Passage:

A Turning Building

The turning building looks so different that many people can't believe their eyes when they see it for the first time. This building has 54 storeys including ten storeys of offices, 147 apartments and meeting-rooms on the two top floors. It turns 90° from the bottom to the top, so every apartment can get enough light. With a height of 190 meters, it is the highest building in Sweden and one of the highest residential buildings in Europe. Many people think it is a wonder made by man. Don't you want to see it with your eyes?

4. Make Sentences after the Given Patterns:

1) George is taller than Robert.

(1) Mary, before, now, make few mistakes

(2) good, mine, her pronunciation, be.
2) Mr. Smith works hardest in our construction site, everybody knows him.
 (1) I've never seen, this is, a large and beautiful bridge over Huang River.
 (2) run across China like a huge dragon, the Great Wall of China, long wall in the world.
3) Young bricklayer is laying brick wall as fast as his master now.
 (1) be tall, the Great Hall of the People, the History Museum.
 (2) my pronunciation, foreigner, is not really and truly good.
4) The new railway station is one of the most magnificent buildings in Beijing.
 (1) in the world, be one of long rivers, the Yellow River.
 (2) of all the students in Northwest Construction Institute, clearly, Zhuxin speaks English.

5. Substitute the Following Words & Expressions:
Use the following **Building Engineering and Technical Personnel**（建筑工程技术人员）to replace the black words in the following sentence:
Jones: Mr. Liu. Glad to know you. And what's your job?
琼斯：刘先生，很高兴认识您。那你是做什么工作的？
Liude: I'm a **resident engineer** and a **site director** in charge of this worksite, too.
刘德：我是一位驻地工程师，也是主管这个工地的工地主任。

Building Engineering and Technical Personnel 建筑工程技术人员
[ˈbildiŋ ˌendʒiniəriŋ ənd ˈteknikəl ˌpəːsəˈnel]
chief designer　[tʃiːf diˈzainə]　总设计师
chief architect　[tʃiːf ˈaːkitekt]　总建筑师
chief engineer　[tʃiːf ˌendʒiˈniə]　总工程师
chief inspector　[tʃiːf inˈspektə]　总监（理）
department chief designer　[diˈpaːtmənt tʃiːf diˈzainə]　主任设计师
department chief engineer　[diˈpaːtmənt tʃiːf ˌendʒiˈniə]　主任工程师

section engineer ['sekʃən ˌendʒi'niə] 工段工程师
technician [tek'niʃən] 技术员
foreman ['fɔːmən] 工长；领班
inspector [in'spektə] 监理员
supervisor ['sjuːpəvaizə] 监督员，监督人
assistant engineer [ə'sistənt ˌendʒi'niə] 助理工程师
designer [di'zainə] 设计师
architect ['aːkitekt] 建筑师
engineer [ˌendʒi'niə] 工程师
civil engineer ['sivl ˌendʒi'niə] 土木工程师
material engineer [mə'tiəriəl ˌendʒi'niə] 材料工程师
resident engineer ['rezidənt ˌendʒi'niə] 驻地工程师
supervising architect ['sjuːpəvaiziŋ 'aːkitekt] 监理建筑师
supervising engineer ['sjuːpəvaiziŋ ˌendʒi'niə] 监理工程师
senior designer ['siːnjə di'zainə] 高级设计师
senior architect ['siːniə 'aːkitekt] 高级建筑师
senior engineer ['siːnjə ˌendʒi'niə] 高级工程师
expert/specialist ['ekspəːt 'speʃəlist] 专家
adviser/advisor in technology [əd'vaizə in tek'nɔlədʒi] 技术顾问
technologist [tek'nɔlədʒist] 技术专家
civil engineering expert ['sivl ˌendʒi'niəriŋ 'ekspəːt] 土木工程专家
qualified technician /engineer 合格的技术员/工程师
['kwɔlifaid tek'niʃən ˌendʒi'niə]

Situational Dialogic Unit 13
第十三情景对话单元

Learn to Speak English

Talking about Building Investigation Abroad

Lynd: Are you Chinese, sir?

Liao: Yes. As matter of fact, we're all the members of Chinese investigation Delegation. I'm Mr. Li, the head of the delegation.

Lynd: I'm Lynd and specially come to welcome you all. Welcome to London, England.

Liao: Thank you. We're glad to come to your country and are warmly received by you.

Lynd: Not at all. Did you have a pleasant trip?

Liao: Yes, indeed. This is our first time to London.

Lynd: Oh. Please say something about your investigation plan if you don't mind.

Liao: Certainly not, sir. But this is only rough one. You know London likes the back of your hand. Would you please give us some good idea?

Lynd: All right. As you know London is one of the most ancient cities in the world and now it's developing rapidly as others in the world, so there're many places worthing of visiting.

Liao: Yes, there're so many beautiful, unique style ancient buildings and magnificent modern to be visited. What's your suggestion?

Lynd: If you like, you may visit ancient buildings first and then the modern. How about this suggestion?

Liao: That's very nice. Then we'll take three days to visit ancient buildings first.

Lynd: I believe three days are enough. How to arrange your rest time sir?

Liao: The rest time is for us to pay a visit to the modern buildings and in the meantime we have to find out some information about the building situation and talk with a few local engineering contractors of the same trade or occupation.

Lynd: Good! Designer Glyn, Architect Scott and senior engineer Lynd are going to accompany you to do so.

学说英语

谈论国外建筑考察

林　德：先生，你们是中国人吗？

李　敖：是的。事实上我们都是中国建筑考察团的成员。我是李先生，也是团长。

林　德：我叫林德，是专程前来迎接你们的。欢迎你们光临英国、伦敦。

李　敖：谢谢！我们很荣幸光顾贵国并受到你们热情的接待。

林　德：没什么，你们旅途愉快吗？

李　敖：是的，的确如此。这也是我们首次远程来到伦敦。

林　德：啊。你不介意的话，请谈谈你们的考察计划吧。

李　敖：当然不介意，先生。但这只是一个粗略打算。你们对伦敦了如指掌，请给我们提供一个切实可行的计划好吗？

林　德：那好吧。正如你们所知，伦敦是世界上最古老的城市之一，而且如今和世界上其他城市一样发展得如此之快，所以有许多地方值得参观。

李　敖：是的。这儿有许多美丽、别具一格的古代建筑和宏伟壮观的现代建筑值得观赏。那您的建议呢？

林　德：如果你们乐意的话，可以先参观古代建筑，然后再参观现代建筑。你们认为如何？

李　敖：这个建议很好。那我们花费三天时间先参观古（代）建（筑）。

林　德：我相信三天时间就够了。先生，怎样安排这剩余时间呢？

李　敖：我们利用剩余的时间参观现代建筑。在此期间我们还得了解些建筑行情，并同一些建筑同行进行交谈。

林　德：那好。设计师格林，建筑师斯高特以及高级工程师林德将陪同你们一道参观。

Liao: Thank you for showing so much care. We believe that through this investigation, we must learn from your advance science and technology and running experience.

Lynd: We should help and learn from each other, to make up each other's deficiencies, and improve the friendly relations between the building engineering and technical personnel of our two countries.

Lynd: Yes, I think we can make progress side by side. Let's go sightseeing now, shall we?

Liao: OK, sir. Let's go.

李　敖：多谢你们的关照。我们深信通过这次考察，一定能学到贵国先进的科学技术和管理经验。

林　德：我们应相互学习、互相帮助、取长补短。这样做还能增进我们两国建筑工程技术人员之间的友好关系。

林　德：对呀，我认为我们会携手共进。咱们现在就去参观，好吗？

李　敖：好啊，先生，咱们走。

Explanatory Notes 注释：

　　architect（n.）建筑师，architecture 是由 architect 派生的另一个名词，其意思是 art and science of building; design or style building(s) 建筑学；建筑术；建筑之设计或式样。例如：civil and industry architecture 工业与民用建筑；architecture sketch 建筑草图；architecture of China (Asia, Europe, America) 中国（亚洲、欧洲、美洲）建筑。architectural（a.），of architecture 建筑上的；建筑学(术)的，建筑设计的。例如：architectural engineering 建筑工程(学)；the architectural beauties of a city 某一城中的设计优美的建筑物，architectural complex 建筑群，建筑总体；architectural section 建筑剖面图，architectural style 建筑风格，建筑式样。architectonics（n.）（是形式上的复数，意义上的单数，使用上应注意）建筑学，建筑原理；构造设计。

Spoken Practice 口语练习

1. **Pair Work:**

    Suppose your partner who is a civil engineer, and will be sent to a large modern country to do his investigation for some days, he asks you to help him make an investigation plan. Try to say how to investigate well during the short time.

2. **Answer the following questions in accordance with Learn to Speak English:**

    1) Who is the head of Chinese Investigation Delegation?

    2) What plan does Lynd want to know?

    3) There're so many beautiful ancient buildings and magnificent modern in London, aren't there?

    4) Does Chinese Investigation Delegation take seven days or three to see the modern buildings?

    5) Why does Chinese Delegation investigate London?

3. **Read & Interpret the Following Passage:**

    ### One of the Seven Wonders of the World
    ### ——The Great Wall of China

    The Great Wall, the masterpiece of human beings, the soul of China, the longest Wall in the world, winds across China like a huge dragon over mountains, through valleys, and starts the desert on the west and finally reaches to the sea on the east. It has history of over twenty centuries. The Great Wall, which is called in Chinese "The Ten Thousand Li Great Wall" is actually more than 9,000 kilometers long, 6~7 meters high and 4~5 meters wide. It is not only one of the Seven Wonders of the World, but also a man-made Wonder of the World, was rated in the 'List of the World Cultural Heritages' by UNESCO in 1978.

4. **Put the Following Sentences into Chinese and Pay attention to the Use of Changing the Negative Position（否定转移）:**

    1) I don't think you are right.

2) John wasn't late because he was ill.
3) It isn't probable that petrol price will fall this year.
4) It doesn't seem that Xiao Ming can get his money back.
5) I don't suppose Wang Hai cares, does he?

Explanatory Notes 注释:

　　否定转移是一种最常用的翻译技巧,要把这类英语句子翻译成汉语,决不能按照句子中词排列先后顺序按部就班的翻译,而要把否定的位置加以改变(即:把本该否定主句谓语的否定转移到否定从句谓语处);要把这类汉语翻译成英语,同样否定的位置也得改变。这样译出的句子才符合英汉两种语言表达的特点,因此掌握这一技巧很有必要。

5. Substitute the Following Words & Expressions:

Use the following **Terms about Ancient Architecture**(古代建筑相关术语) to replace the black words in the following sentence:

Lynd: If you like, you may visit **ancient buildings** first and then the modern. How about this suggestion?

林德: 如果你们乐意的话,可以先参观**古代建筑**,然后再参观现代建筑。你们认为怎样?

Terms about Ancient Architecture [tə:mz ə'baut'einʃənt 'a:kitektʃə]
古代建筑相关术语

Chinese style architecture [tʃai'ni:z stail 'a:kitektʃə] 中式建筑
landscape architecture ['lændskeip 'a:kitektʃə] 庭园建筑
pavilion [pə'viljən] 亭;阁
hall/ palace [hɔ:l 'pælis] 殿/宫
archway ['a:tʃwei] 牌楼
temple ['templ] 寺庙
pagoda [pə'goudə] 佛塔
church [tʃə:tʃ] 教堂,礼拜堂
bell/ drum tower [bel drʌm 'tauə] 钟/鼓楼
pyramid ['pirəmid] 金字塔

corner tower ['kɔːnə 'tauə] 角楼
parapet ['pærəpit] 女儿墙
column ['kɔləm] 柱
queen posts [kwiːn pousts] 双柱架
arch [aːtʃ] 拱
abutment [ə'bʌtmənt] 拱座
bracket ['brækit] 托架，斗拱（中腿）
flooring ['flɔːriŋ] 地板/面
plank floor [plæŋk flɔː] 木板地面
ceiling ['siːliŋ] 天花板，顶棚
eaves [iːvz] 屋檐
upturned eaves [ʌp'təːnd iːvs] 飞檐
sheathing ['ʃiːðiŋ] 望板
rafter ['raːftə] 椽子
angle rafter ['æŋgl 'raːftə] 角椽
purlin(e) ['pəːlin] 檩（木桁）
ridge [ridʒ] 屋脊
flat roof [flæt ruːf] 平屋顶
shed roof [ʃed ruːf] 单坡屋顶
gable roof ['geibl ruːf] 人字屋顶
overhanging roof ['ouvəhæŋiŋ ruːf] 大屋顶
upturned roof [ʌp'təːnd ruːf] 飞檐屋顶
arched roof [aːtʃd ruːf] 拱形屋顶

Situational Dialogic Unit 14
第十四情景对话单元

Learn to Speak English

Talking about Studying Building Working Drawings

Jordan: Hi. Can you do me a favor, engineer Gao?

Gaolin: OK. If I can, Jordan, but what?

Jordan: I've a question to ask.

Gaolin: What question, please?

Jordan: I don't know the switchboard's exact position. Please scratch it on the wall.

Gaolin: OK. But it must be scratched in accordance with your drawing. Where is yours?

Jordan: Here it is, engineer Gao.

Gaolin: Sorry. You have got a wrong drawing.

Jordan: Why! Isn't this drawing?

Gaolin: Yes. It's a plane and not an elevation. It's very clear on an elevation. Would you please get it?

Jordan: OK. Here you are, miss?

Gaolin: Oh. This drawing isn't clear enough. Let's check it up on the detailed drawing. Look, it's here, chap.

Jordan: Right! It's near the corner of the walls. You're very observant.

Gaolin: You'd have done the same in my position, I'm sure.

Jordan: That's true. But how high is the switchboard to the floor?

Gaolin: It's 1.5m.

Jordan: How do you know the size?

Gaolin: As it's a dimensioned drawing. If you don't believe it, please get a drawing scale and measure it yourself.

Jordan: No. Reading and studying drawing carefully is an essential prerequisite for construction well, I suppose.

Gaolin: Naturally. For every drawing is meticulously designed by designers, sizes and figures on the drawing are also calculated by themselves. Thus we should regard drawings as the norm and the guide for our construction.

学说英语

谈论研究建筑施工图

乔　丹：喂，高工程师，您能帮我个忙吗？

高　琳：可以。乔丹，假如我能的话，但不知要帮什么忙？

乔　丹：我有个问题要请教。

高　琳：什么问题，请说吧？

乔　丹：我不清楚配电控制板安装的具体位置，请给我在墙上画出来吧。

高　琳：好吧。但要根据图纸的尺寸来画。图纸在哪儿？

乔　丹：这就是，高工。

高　琳：抱歉，图纸拿错了。

乔　丹：怎么！难道这不是图纸吗？

高　琳：不，这只是一张平面图而不是立面图。配电控制板的位置在立面图上标注得一清二楚，请拿一张立面图好吗？

乔　丹：好。小姐，给你图纸。

高　琳：哦，这张图标注得还不够清楚，咱们在详图上再查一下，瞧！就在这儿，小伙子。

乔　丹：对呀，靠近两道墙夹角处。你观察得很仔细。

高　琳：我相信如果你处在我的地位，也会这样做。

乔　丹：那是肯定的。但配电控制板距离地面有多高？

高　琳：1.5米高。

乔　丹：你是怎么知道尺寸的？

高　琳：因为这是一张标有尺寸的图纸。如不信的话，请拿把比例尺，亲自量一下。

乔　丹：不用了。看来识图并认真钻研图纸才是搞好施工的必要前提。

高　琳：那自然是。因为每一张图纸都是由设计师精心设计出来的，图纸上的尺寸和数据也都是设计师们计算出来的。因此我们一定要把图纸看作我们施工的指南和准则。

Jordan: Yes. Construction is the translation of design into reality.
Gaolin: Right. By the way, I don't think you can read the drawing well.
Jordan: Oh. Just so-so.
Gaolin: But how to say that? Personally, I think you should read the drawing well, and then you can do your work well.
Jordan: Sure. I must follow your instructions.
Gaolin: Right. If you've any drawing problem in your work, please raise it at any time, I must try to solve it for you.
Jordan: You're very kind. Thank you for your help.
Gaolin: Not at all. That's my duty.

乔　丹：对。施工就是把设计变成现实。
高　琳：对啦。顺便问一句，我想你不识图吧。
乔　丹：啊，马马虎虎吧。
高　琳：怎能这样讲。就我个人认为你应该识好图，这样才能搞好本职工作。
乔　丹：确实是这个理。我一定遵照您的旨意去做。
高　琳：对。如果以后工作中再遇到有图纸问题，请随时提出来，我一定尽力解答。
乔　丹：你太好啦！多谢你的帮助。
高　琳：不必客气。这是我应尽的职责。

Explanatory Notes 注释：

　　drawing 的意思是 [U] the art of representing objects, scenes, ect., by lines, with a pencil, chalk, ect; [C] sth. made in this way; a sketch, plan, ect. 绘图；制图；图画；图案；图样。画图常用的图板是 drawing board，但 drawing-room 的意思是客厅。还有一点与 drawing 有关需要说明：in drawing 制图准确，out of drawing 制图不准确。

Spoken Practice 口语练习

1. **Pair Work:**

   Imagine A wants to do his work well without a working drawing, B thinks that it is impossible. They're arguing about it.

2. **Tell "true" or "false" in accordance with Learn to Speak English:**

   1) (   ) Jordan has a drawing problem to ask.
   2) (   ) Reality is the translation of design into construction.
   3) (   ) The position of the switchboard is unclear on a plane.
   4) (   ) Right! The switchboard is far away from the corner of the walls.
   5) (   ) A prerequisite for construction well must be studying drawings carefully.

3. **Reading & Interpreting the following Passage:**

   ### Building Drawings

   Building drawings involve a variety of drawings such as plan, elevation, cross section, layout, bird's-eye view, worm's-eye view, standard drawing, working drawing.... Drawings play an important part in construction. Therefore they are regarded as the norm and the guide of the construction. Construction is the translation of design into reality.

4. **Put the Following Sentences into Chinese and Pay attention to the Use of Dual Negation（双重否定）:**

   1) **Don't** touch the paint **until** it is dry.
   2) There is **no** work **unless** there is motion.
   3) **No** living thing could exist **without** air.
   4) There is **no** one **but** has his weak side.
   5) They **never** work **without** helping each other.
   6) **But** for your help, I would **not** make such good progress in my Architectural English study.

Explanatory Notes 注释:

双重否定：如果在英语句中出现 no, not, never 等否定词，再加上一个否定词或词组,这种句子就变成了双重否定。否定加否定等于肯定,因此在翻译时应根据上下文具体情况和英汉两种语言的表达习惯,既可译成肯定句也可译成双重否定句,应视具体语景而定。

5. **Substitute the Following Words & Expressions**:

1) Use the following **Kinds of Drawing**(图纸的种类)to replace the black words in the following sentence:

Gaolin: Yes. It's a **plane** and not an **elevation**. It's very clear on an elevation. Would you please get it?

高琳:不,这只是一张**平面图**而不是**立面图**。配电控制板的位置在立面图上标注得一清二楚,请拿一张立面图好吗?

Kinds of Drawing [kaindz əv 'drɔːiŋ] 图纸种类

master plan ['mɑːstə plæn] 总体规划

general layout ['dʒenərəl 'leiaut] 总图

draft [drɑːft] 草图

layout ['leiaut] 布置图

cross section [krɔs 'sekʃən] 剖面图

ground/first floor plan [graund/fəːst flɔː plæn] 一/二层平面图

roof/foundation plan [ruːf/faun'deiʃən plæn] 屋面/基础平面图

standard drawing ['stændəd 'drɔːiŋ] 标准图

building drawing ['bildiŋ 'drɔːiŋ] 建筑图

typical drawing ['tipikəl 'drɔːiŋ] 定型图

installation drawing [ˌinstə'leiʃən 'drɔːiŋ] 安装图

service drawing ['səːvis 'drɔːiŋ] 设备图

process drawing ['prouses 'drɔːiŋ] 工艺图

formwork drawing ['fɔːmwəːk 'drɔːiŋ] 模板图

reinforcement drawing [ˌriːin'fɔːsmənt 'drɔːiŋ] 配筋图

dimensioned drawing [di'menʃənd 'drɔːiŋ] 标有尺寸的图纸

legend [ˌ'ledʒənd] 图例

notes on drawing [nouts ɔn 'drɔːiŋ] 图注

read a drawing [riːd ə 'drɔːiŋ] 识图

2) Use the following **Verify Drawing**(审阅图纸)to replace the black

words in the following sentence:

Jordan: No. **Studying drawing** carefully is an essential prerequisite for construction well, I suppose.

乔丹：不用了。看来认真钻研图纸才是搞好施工的必要前提。

Verify Drawings ['verifai 'drɔːiŋz] 审阅图纸
approve drawings [ə'pruːv 'drɔːiŋz] 批准图纸
sign drawings [sain 'drɔːiŋz] 签署图纸
correct drawings [kə'rekt 'drɔːiŋz] 改正图纸
modify drawings ['mɔdifai 'drɔːiŋz] 改动图纸
scale of a drawing [skeil əv ə 'drɔːiŋ] 图纸的比例
copy of a drawing ['kɔpi əv ə 'drɔːiŋ] 图纸的副本
omissions in drawings [ou'miʃənz in 'drɔːiŋz] 图纸中的遗漏
departure from a drawing [di'paːtʃə frɔm ə 'drɔːiŋ] 与图纸不符
errors (mistakes) in drawings 图纸中的错误
['erəz mis'teiks in 'drɔːiŋz]
be responsible for drawings [biːris'pɔnsəbl fɔː 'drɔːiŋz] 对图纸负责

3）Use the following **Drawing Instruments**（绘图仪器）to replace the black words in the following sentence:

Gaolin: As it's a dimensioned drawing. If you don't believe it, please get a **drawing scale** and measure it yourself.

高　琳：因为这是一张标有尺寸的图纸。如不信的话，请拿一把绘图比例尺，亲自量一下。

Drawing Instruments ['drɔː in'instrumənts] 绘图仪器

drawing pen ['drɔːiŋ pen] 绘图笔
drawing-compasses ['drɔːiŋ 'kʌmpəsiz] 绘图圆规
T-square [tiː 'skwɛə] 丁字尺
drawing scale ['drɔːiŋ skeil] 绘图比例尺
drawing paper ['drɔːiŋ 'peipə] 绘图纸
tracing paper ['treisiŋ 'peipə] 描图纸
French curve [frentʃ kəːv] 曲线板

Situational Dialogic Unit 15
第十五情景对话单元

建筑技术与管理英语情景会话

Learn to Speak English

Talking about Inquiring Price of the Building Materials

Mark: Can I do anything for you, old chap?

Liwei: Certainly, young fellow. I came here to inquire the price of some building materials.

Mark: Oh. You're a Chinese, right?

Liwei: Right, I work in CSCEC. As you know Oscar Bridge has issued tenders already and after a few days it'll be invited tenters.

Mark: Really? Does your company want to tender?

Liwei: Yes. We do.

Mark: I see. You came to inquire price, but what material price do you want to know?

Liwei: Oh! Mainly some common materials such as cement, steel bar and some timber and so on. They're all in the bill and read it yourself, please.

Mark: Oh, let me have a look, we sale them all. Cement is 1 dollar per kilogram, steel bar is 500 dollars per ton and timber is 650 dollars per cubic meter...

Liwei: That's good. Please show me your quotation of materials.

Mark: OK. Here it is. Our materials are of the best quality, good and inexpensive, orders welcome, old chap.

Liwei: Is that true? I'll talk with you after reading it.

Mark: Truly. You can go to other materials stores if you don't believe.

Liwei: OK. We're sure to compare with the materials price at least three stores and then choose a suitable price.

Mark: Chinese are clever.

Liwei: Thank you for your praise. See you again, young fellow.

Mark: See you again, old chap.

建筑工程技术人员英语情景会话

学说英语

谈论询问建筑材料价格

马　克：老兄，我能为您效劳吗？

李　威：当然能，老弟。我前来贵处是询问一些材料价。

马　克：啊，那您是中国人，对吗？

李　威：对，我在中建公司工作。正如所知，奥斯卡尔大桥已发标，再过几天就要招标了。

马　克：真的吗？那贵公司也想投标吧？

李　威：是呀，我们想。

马　克：我明白啦。你来询价，你想了解哪些材料价？

李　威：啊！主要是些大众材料，像水泥、钢筋、木材等，都写在单子上，请自己看吧。

马　克：哦，让我看一看，这些材料我们店都经销。水泥每公斤1美元，钢筋每吨500美元，木材每立方米650美元……

李　威：好吧。请给我一份材料价目表看看吧。

马　克：好啊，这就是材料价目表。我们的材料品质优良、价廉物美，欢迎订购，老兄。

李　威：是吗？还是看过再说吧。

马　克：真的。假如不信的话，你可到别的店再打听一下。

李　威：是的，我们会货比三家，求出一个适中价位。

马　克：中国人就是精明。

李　威：多谢你的夸奖！再见，老弟。

马　克：再见，老兄。

Spoken Practice 口语练习

1. **Pair Work**:

   A acts as an assistant in a Materials Supermarket. B acts as a material customer who wants to inquire the price of some building materials such as cement, steel bar, timber, installation and decorative materials... Use the following expressions:

   ——Can I..., sir?

   ——Yes, I'd like to...

   ——How much...

   ——It's...

2. **Tell "true" or "false" in accordance with Learn to Speak English**:

   1) (   ) I came here to inquire the price of some building materials.

   2) (   ) Mark works in China State Construction Engineering Corporation.

   3) (   ) Inquiring the price of some materials in short supply are cement, steel bar, timber and so on.

   4) (   ) Our materials are good and the price is cheap, too.

   5) (   ) You can't go to other materials stores if you believe so.

3. **Read & Interpret the Following Passage**:

   Enquiry of Building Materials

   Dear Sir,

     We learn that you have been engaged in building materials many years.

     At present, we are interested in enquirying the price of some building materials, and enclosing the name of the materials needed for your information.

     If you are in a position to sell the materials needed, kindly advise us and we shall be glad to have a talk with you in the near future.

                 Yours faithfully,

   Encl.: a/s

4. Put the Following into English:

壁　纸

聚氯乙烯壁纸是目前在建筑装饰行业中广泛使用的一种具有防水功能的新型塑料壁纸。它克服了一般塑料壁纸湿度底、易霉烂的缺点，并且表面去污可擦性能大大提高，有防水、阻燃等特点。除此之外，还有一种无机颗粒为面层的蛭石壁纸。

5. Substitute the Following Words & Expressions:

1) Use the following **Kinds of Building Materials**（建筑材料种类）to replace the black words in the following sentence:

Mark: I see. You came to inquire price, but what **material** price do you want to know?

马克：我明白啦。你来询价，你想了解哪些**材料**价？

Liwei: Mainly some **common materials** such as **cement**, **steel bar** and some **timber** and so on. They're all in the bill.

李威：主要是些**大众材料**像**水泥**、**钢筋**、**木材**等，都写在单子上。

Kinds of Building Materials ['kaindz əv'bildiŋ mə'tiəriəlz] 建筑材料种类

installation materials [ˌinstəˈleiʃən məˈtiəriəlz] 安装材料
decorative materials [ˈdekərətiv məˈtiəriəlz] 装饰材料
import materials [imˈpɔːt məˈtiəriəlz] 进口材料
export materials [eksˈpɔːt məˈtiəriəlz] 出口材料
foreign materials [ˈfɔrin məˈtiəriəlz] 外来材料
artificial materials [ˌɑːtiˈfiʃəl məˈtiəriəlz] 人造材料
additional materials [əˈdiʃənl məˈtiəriəlz] 附加材料
defective materials [diˈfektiv məˈtiəriəlz] 残次材料
explosive materials [iksˈplousiv məˈtiəriəlz] 爆破材料
insulating materials [ˈinsjuleitiŋ məˈtiəriəlz] 绝缘材料
fire-proof materials [ˈfaiə pruːf məˈtiəriəlz] 耐火材料
cementing materials [siˈmentiŋ məˈtiəriəlz] 粘结材料
substitute materials [ˈsʌbstitjuːt məˈtiəriəlz] 代用材料
roofing materials [ˈruːfiŋ məˈtiəriəlz] 屋面材料

local materials ['loukəl mə'tiəriəlz] 地方材料
rust-resisting materials [rʌst ri'zistiŋ mə'tiəriəlz] 防锈材料
road (building) materials [roud 'bildiŋ mə'tiəriəlz] 筑路材料
materials in short supply [mə'tiəriəlz in ʃɔːt sə'plai] 短缺材料
reject materials [ri'dʒekt mə'tiəriəlz] 剔除（报废）材料
plastic materials ['plæstik mə'tiəriəlz] 塑性材料；塑料
structural materials ['strʌktʃərəl mə'tiəriəlz] 结构（建筑）材料
注：这里仅列举了部分笼统的建筑材料名称，详细的材料名称请参见各工种用料。

2）Use the following **Exchange Tables of Weights and Measures**（度量衡换算表）to replace the black words in the following sentence：

Mark：Oh, let me have a look, we sale them all. Cement is 1 dollar per **kilogram**, **steel** bar is 500 dollars per **ton** and timber is 650 dollars per **cubic meter.**

马克：哦，让我看一看，这些材料我们店都销售。水泥每**公斤**1美元，钢筋每**吨**500美元，木材每**立方米**650美元。

Exchange Tables of Weights and Measures
度量衡换算表（一）

中国市制 China system	公　制 The metric system	英　美　制 U. K. & U. S. system
1 尺（chi）	1/3 米（metre）	1.0936 英尺（feet）
1 里（li）	1/2 公里（kilometre）	0.3107 英里（mile）
1 亩（mu）	1/15 公顷（hectare）	0.1644 英亩（acre）
1 两（liang）	50 克（grammes）	1.7637 两（ounces）
1 斤（jin）	1/2 公斤（kilogramme）	1.1023 磅（pounds）
1 担（dan）	50 公斤（kilogrammes）	0.984 英担（CWT） （hundred-weight）
1 担（dan）	1/20 吨（metric ton）	0.0492 英吨（long ton） 0.0551 美吨（short ton）
1 升（sheng）	1 公升（litre）	0.22 加仑（British gallon）
1 斗（dou）	10 公升（litres）	2.2 加仑（British gallons）

Situational Dialogic Unit 16
第十六情景对话单元

Learn to Speak English

Talking about Quoting Building Materials

Grant: Hello, Madam! I don't think I disturb you.

Linda: Hello, sir! Don't worry about that. What can I do for you, sir?

Grant: Certainly. Can you direct me to your Material Supply Department?

Linda: Yeah. Here it is. Why don't you sit down!

Grant: Oh. Thank you. Who is in charge of the department, I'd love to know?

Linda: It's me, Lao Lin.

Grant: That's good. It's said that you are preparing to tender. I'd like to supply you some materials.

Linda: OK. But which materials can you supply?

Grant: Mainly electrical and water materials.

Linda: How much is one ton electrical wires, please tell me?

Grant: About 600 dollars. Oh, this's a catalogue of materials and quotation of prices, of course, including delivery charges.

Linda: Thanks a lot. We ergely need such information and let me read your quotation, OK?

Grant: OK. These materials of catalogue are for you, please read them. Our price of materials compares favorable with anything in markets today.

Linda: Let's hope so. The amount of our offer depends largely on your price. But you've to wait a few days, and then I shall call you.

Grant: All right. I'm awaiting your favourable reply.

Linda: We accept your price if you take the quantity we offer.

Grant: Here's my visiting card. Please ring me up as soon as you make your decision.

Linda: Please wait one or two days. I'm sure.

学说英语

谈论建筑材料报价

格兰特：夫人，你好！我想没打扰你吧。

林　达：先生，你好！没关系！我能为你做些什么吗？

格兰特：当然能。你能给我指一下材料供应部吗？

林　达：能，这就是。怎么不坐呢！

格兰特：啊，谢谢！我想知道谁负责这个部门？

林　达：是我，老林。

格兰特：这就好。据说你们正准备投标，我乐意为你们提供些材料。

林　达：好啊。但不知你们能提供哪些材料？

格兰特：主要是电料和水料。

林　达：请告诉我1吨电线多少钱？

格兰特：大约600美元。哦，这是材料目录和报价单，当然也包括运费在内。

林　达：多谢！我们急需这方面的信息，我看一看你们的报价可以吗？

格兰特：可以。这些就是送给你的材料目录，请看看吧。我们的材料价格与当今材料市场价相比很实惠。

林　达：但愿如此。要订购的材料数量在很大程度上取决于你方的价格，不过你得等些日子，然后我打电话与你联系。

格兰特：好吧。我一定恭候你们的佳音。

林　达：如果你方能确保我方的数量，我们就接受你方的价格。

格兰特：这是我的名片。你一旦作出决定的话，请给我打电话。

林　达：肯定会的。请稍等一两天吧。

Spoken Practice 口语练习

1. **Pair Work:**

   Suppose you are a material-man. Talk with a material engineer of a construction company and try to persuade her into purchasing your building materials.

2. **Tell "true" or "false" in accordance with Learn to Speak English:**

   1) (　) Grant thinks he doesn't bother you is a correct sentence structure.

   2) (　) Grant works in the Material Supply Department.

   3) (　) This's a material catalogue and quotation, of course, without delivery charges.

   4) (　) You've to wait few days, and then I can give you my plan of materials.

   5) (　) If you decided, please phone me.

3. **Read & Interpret the Following Passage:**

   ### Quotation for Installation Materials

   Dear Sirs,

   　　Seeing your advertisement in the newspaper, we now ask you to send us as soon as possible your latest-list of installation materials with the lowest quotation, together with an illustrated catalogue.

   　　We shall be pleased to have you inform us of best terms and conditions, and also your references.

   　　Looking forward to receiving your immediate reply.

   Yours truly,

   ---

4. **Put the Following into English:**

   一种新材料——塑料

   人们发现塑料不仅在我们的日常生活中得到广泛的应用,而且在现代工程中也得到广泛的应用。例如:在新建的大楼中使用了塑料地板和塑料窗框、塑料水管和配件。在机械工程中使用了塑料零件，而且在电气工程中也被用作为良绝缘体。

　　由于塑料有许多不同的特性，所以非常有用。塑料既轻便又坚固，而且根本不生锈，除此以外我们还以不同目的把塑料制作成许多形状各异的产品。

5. Substitute the Following Words & Expressions：

1) Use the following **Exchange Tables of Weights and Measures**（度量衡换算表）to replace the black words in the following sentence：

Linda：How much is one **ton** electrical wires？

琳　达：**1 吨**电线多少钱？

Exchange Tables of Weights and Measures
度量衡换算表（二）

公　制 The metric system	中国市制 China system	英　美　制 U. K. & U. S. system
1 米（metre）	3 尺（chi）	3.2808 英尺（feet）
1 公里（kilometre）	2 里（li）	0.6241 英里（mile）
1 平方公里（sq. km.）	4 平方里（sq. li）	0.3861 平方英里（sq. mile）
1 平方米（sq. metre）	9 平方尺（sq. chi）	10.7636 平方英尺（sq. feet）
1 公顷（hectare）	15 亩（mu）	2.471 英亩（acres）
1 公斤（kilogram）	2 斤（jin）	2.2046 磅（pounds）
1 吨（metric ton）	2000 斤（jin）	0.9842 英吨（long ton）
1 立方米（cubic metre）	27 立方尺（cubic chi）	353166 立方英尺（cubic feet）
1 公升（litre）	1 升（sheng）	0.22 加仑（英）（British gallon） 0.264 加仑（美）（U.S. gallon）

2) Use the following **Management of Materials**（材料管理）to replace the black words in the following sentence：

Linda：OK. But which **materials** can you supply？

林　达：好啊。但不知你们能提供哪些**材料**？

Grant：Mainly **electrical** and **water materials.**

格兰特：主要是**电料**和**水料**。

Management of Materials [ˈmænidʒmənt əv məˈtiəriəlz] 材料管理

list of materials ［list əv mə'tiəriəlz］ 材料目录（单）
quality of materials ［'kwɔliti əv mə'tiəriəlz］ 材料质量
bill of materials ［bil əv mə'tiəriəlz］ 材料单
material purchase ［mə'tiəriəl 'pə:tʃəs］ 材料采购
material testing ［mə'tiəriəl 'testiŋ］ 材料实验
material record ［mə'tiəriəl 'rekɔ:d］ 材料登记
check of materials ［tʃek əv mə'tiəriəlz］ 材料检查
material statistics ［mə'tiəriəl stə'tistiks］ 材料统计
damage to materials ［'dæmidʒ tu mə'tiəriəlz］ 材料的损坏
consumption of materials ［kən'sʌmpʃən əv mə'tiəriəlz］ 材料消耗
reclamation of materials ［ˌreklə'meiʃən əv mə'tiəriəlz］ 废料利用
economy of materials ［i:'kɔnəmi əv mə'tiəriəlz］ 节约材料
material transportation ［mə'tiəriəl ˌtrænspɔ:'teiʃən］ 材料运输
material appropriation ［mə'tiəriəl əˌproupri'eiʃən］ 材料调拨
acceptance of materials ［ək'septəns əv mə'tiəriəlz］ 材料验收
building materials schedule ［'bildiŋ mə'tiəriəlz 'ʃedju:l］ 建筑材料表
system of inspection materials 材料检验制度
［'sistəm əv in'spekʃən mə'tiəriəlz］
quota of materials consumption 材料消耗定额
［'kwoutə əv mə'tiəriəlz kən'sʌmpʃən］
material requirements planning 材料需用量计划
［mə'tiəriəl ri'kwaiəmənts 'plæniŋ］
classification of building materials 建筑材料分类
［ˌklæsifi'keiʃən əv 'bildiŋ mə'tiəriəlz］
field instruments and tools management 现场料具管理
［fi:ld 'instrumənts ənd tu:lz 'mænidʒmənt］

Situational Dialogic Unit 17
第十七情景对话单元

Learn to Speak English

Talking about Purchasing Building Materials

Gule: Hi, boss!

Boss: We haven't seen each other for a long time and I miss you very much, Chinses friend. But what can I do for you?

Gule: Our corporation has won another tender. It includes two dams in all and the total cost is five million Kroner.

Boss: Chinese, Great! You came to give me a big business. I really don't know how I can thank you enough. It's very luck for me to meet you, Chinese brothers.

Gule: Not worth mentioning. Let's return to the subject. Here's the list of materials.

Boss: OK. Strictly speaking, the price of materials has been rising lately, but I should give you a good price.

Gule: How much is per kilogram cement and per ton steel bar?

Boss: Original price. Cement is 1.5 dollars per kilogram and steel bar 500 dollars per ton.

Gule: A little higher by comparison, we can accept it, but keep your words and supply them according to the bill on time. Be sure not to cause delay in work!

Boss: Please set your mind at rest, my good brother. I must go all out, pledge to supply you with the materials and certainly deliver them to your site on time. If necessary, we start delievering at once.

Gule: Frankly speaking, they must be on time. By the way, do you know where the brick works is?

Boss: Yes. I'll show you where it's on the map.

Gule: I see. I've a lot of work to do and must go now, boss. See you again.

Boss: OK. See you again, brother.

学说英语

谈论订购建筑材料

古 乐：老板，你好！

老 板：中国朋友，我们好久未曾相见，很想你呀！但不知我能为你做些什么？

古 乐：我们公司又中了一个标。这个标共有两座水坝，总造价500万克朗。

老 板：中国人了不起！您是专程前来给我送生意，我真不知道该怎样感谢您才好。结识中国兄弟太幸运啦！

古 乐：不足挂齿。咱们还是言归正传吧，这是材料目录表。

老 板：好的。严格地说，建材价格近来又涨了，但我还应给您个优惠价，这样才对得起你。

古 乐：每公斤水泥和每吨钢筋多少钱？

老 板：原价嘛。每公斤水泥是1.5美元，每吨钢筋是500美元。

古 乐：和原价相比略高点儿，可以接受，不过你们一定说话算数，按料单如期供货。可千万别误事！

老 板：请放心吧，我的好兄弟，我一定会全力以赴，优先保证你们，按时把货送到工地。如果有必要的话，马上就可送货。

古 乐：坦率地说，只要准时送到就万幸。顺便问一下，你知道砖瓦厂在哪儿吗？

老 板：知道。我给你在地图上指一下它所处的方位。

古 乐：我知道了。老板，我还有许多事要办，我该告辞啦。再会。

老 板：好吧，兄弟，再会！

Spoken Practice 口语练习

1. **Pair Work**:

   One acts as a shop assistant, the other acts as a material customer who wants to buy some building materials such as electric wires, water pipe, paints... Use the following expressions:

   ——Can I help you, sir?

   ——Yes, I'd like to...

   ——How much...

   ——It's...

2. **Tell "true" or "false" in accordance with Learn to Speak English**:

   1) (　) The tender we have won includes two dams in all, the total cost is more than five million Kroner.

   2) (　) The price of materials has been rising lately, but I'll give you a reasonable price.

   3) (　) Boss said that I certainly delivered them to your site on time.

   4) (　) You want some local materials, don't you?

   5) (　) Right! I've a lot of work to do. I must be off now, boss.

3. **Read & Interpret the Following Passage**:

   What's an Alloy?

   　　If you melt two or more metals together, you can get a new metal. Such a metal is called an alloy. Of course, the alloy is completely different from the original metal.

   　　If you mix a metal with even a small percentage of another metal, its properties can be changed. For instance, Nickel can increase the strength and hardness. If you add nickel to steel, you will get nickel steel and nickel steel is useful for making cutting tools. Similarly, aluminum alloy has the strength of structural steel and is only one-third as heavy. Stainless steel has eliminated the danger of rust. The different alloys have different properties, therefore we adopt them for various purposes in Building Industry.

4. **Substitute the Following Words & Expressions:**

1) Use the following **Exchange Tables of Weights and Measures**(量衡换算表) to replace the black words in the following sentence:

Boss: Cement is 1.5 dollars per **kilogram** and steel bar 500 dollars per **ton**.

老板:每公斤水泥是1.5 美元,每吨钢筋是 500 美元。

Exchange Tables of Weights and Measures
度量衡换算表(三)

英 美 制 U. K. & U. S. system	公 制 The metric system	中国市制 China system
1 英尺(foot)	0.304 米(metre)	0.9144 尺(chi)
1 码(yard)	0.914 米(metre)	2.7432 尺(chi)
1 英里(mile)	1.6093 公里(kms.)	3.2187 里(li)
1 平方英里(sq. mile)	2.59 平方公里(sq. kms.)	10.36 平方尺(sq. chi)
1 英亩(acre)	0.405 公顷(hectare)	6.07 亩(mu)
1 磅(pound)	0.4536 公斤(kg.)	0.9072 斤(jin)
1 英吨(long ton)	1.016 公斤(kgs.)	2.032 斤(jin)
1 美吨(short ton)	907 公斤(kgs.)	1.814 斤(jin)
1 加仑(British gallon)	4.546 公升(litre)	4.546 升(sheng)

2) Use the following **Building Materials Enterprises**(建材企业) to replace the black words in the following sentence:

Gule: Frankly speaking, they must be on time. By the way, do you know where **the brick works** is?

古乐:坦率地说,只要准时送到就好。顺便问一下,你知道砖瓦厂在哪儿吗?

Building Materials Enterprises 建材企业
[ˈbildiŋ məˈtiəriəlz ˈentəpraiziz]
Aluminium Alloy Factory 铝合金厂
[ˌæljuːˈminjəm ˈæləi ˈfæktəri]
Steel Tubing Plant [stiːl ˈtjuːbiŋ plɑːnt] 钢管厂

Enamel Plant ［i'næməl plɑːnt］搪瓷制品厂
Plywood Factory ［'plaiwud 'fæktəri］胶合板厂
Glass Works ［glɑːs wəːks］玻璃厂
Ceramic Factory ［si'ræmik 'fæktəri］陶瓷厂
Plastics Factory ［'plæstiks 'fæktəri］塑料厂
Felt Roofing Factory ［felt 'ruːfiŋ 'fæktəri］油毡厂
Brick & Tile Works ［brik ənd tail wəːks］砖瓦厂
Cement Plant ［si'ment plɑːnt］水泥厂
Crushing Stone Mill ［'krʌʃiŋ stoun mil］碎石厂
Paint Factory ［peint 'fæktəri］油漆厂
Valve Factory ［vælv 'fæktəri］阀门厂
Asbestos Tile Works ［æz'bestɔs tail wəːks］石棉瓦厂
Fibre-board Plant ［'faibə bɔːd plɑːnt］纤维板厂
Steel Window Factory ［stiːl 'windou 'fæktəri］钢窗厂
Glass-fibre Factory ［glɑːs 'faibə 'fæktəri］玻璃纤维厂
Metal Products Plant ［'metl 'prɔdəkts plɑːnt］五金厂
Metal-structure Works ［'metl 'strʌktʃə wəːks］金属结构厂
Electric Bulbs Factory ［i'lektrik bʌlbz 'fæktəri］电灯泡厂
Timber Processing Plant ［'timbə 'prousesiŋ plɑːnt］木材加工厂
Concrete Parts Factory ［'kɔnkriːt pɑːts 'fæktəri］混凝土构件厂
Electrical Appliance Factory ［i'lektrikəl ə'plaiəns 'fæktəri］电器厂
Construction Materials Company 建筑材料公司
［kən'strʌkʃən mə'tiəriəlz 'kʌmpəni］
Building Materials Supermarket 建材超市
［'bildiŋ mə'tiəriəlz 'sjuːpəˌmɑːkit］

Situational Dialogic Unit 18
第十八情景对话单元

Learn to Speak English

Talking about Construction Plan

York: As far as I know, Mr. He, your company has won the tender for Queen Mansion, right?

Heze: Yes, it's true as touching, York.

York: Have you worked out your construction plan?

Heze: Yes, of course. Do you want to know anything about it?

York: Surely. Please say something about it if you don't mind.

Heze: With pleasure. Queen Mansion has a building area of 57,840 square metres. And it's an important works for our company.

York: I see. It's also one of the biggest works in our city. How long can it be completed according to the contract?

Heze: It can be completed within twelve months.

York: It means that the construction period is twelve months, right?

Heze: That's right. It takes us twelve months to complete it.

York: And what time are you going to ground breaking?

Heze: Oh. It's to start on 1st. Jan. next year.

York: When are you going to finish the foundation and main structure, sir?

Heze: We're going to finish them at end of Oct. That is to say, within ten months.

York: And installation and decoration?

Heze: Installation and decoration should be interpenetrated.

York: Good way. Are you sure you will be able to complete it within construction period?

Heze: Sure. We plan to be ahead of half a month, but we must complete it at end of next year. Otherwise we will be punished.

York: I can feel your full of determination and confidence by your introducetion, I fully believe you.

Heze: Credit is a lifeline of our company, if there're so many and so complex difficulties in our work, we must overcome them all.

学说英语

谈论建筑施工计划

约　克：贺先生，据我所知，贵公司中了皇后大厦的标，对吗？

贺　泽：对，一点没错，约克。

约　克：那你们制定施工计划了吗？

贺　泽：当然制定了。你想了解施工计划方面相关情况吗？

约　克：对。你不介意的话，请谈谈这方面情况好吗？

贺　泽：很乐意。皇后大厦有57840平方米的建筑面积，是我们公司的重点工程之一。

约　克：我明白啦。这项工程也是我市的最大的工程之一。依照合同，多长时间能竣工？

贺　泽：十二月就能竣工。

约　克：那就意味着施工期是十二个月，对吗？

贺　泽：对。要花费我们十二个月才能完工。

约　克：那你们计划何时破土动工？

贺　泽：哦，明年元月一日开始。

约　克：先生，计划何时完成基础和主体工程？

贺　泽：计划在十月底，也就是说十个月内完成。

约　克：那安装工程和装饰工程呢？

贺　泽：安装工程和装饰工程应同步穿插进行。

约　克：好方法。能肯定在施工期内完工吗？

贺　泽：肯定能。我们计划提前半个月，但必须在明年底完工，否则会受罚。

约　克：通过你的介绍，我能感到你们的决心很大，信心很足。我完全相信你们。

贺　泽：信誉是我们公司的生命线，所以在我们的工作中有再多、再大的困难，都必须克服。

York: What you said is nice and done is well, too. Is this your progress schedule, sir?

Heze: Yeah. It's a concrete schedule and working data in detail marks clearly on it. How do you think of it?

York: Let me have a read it first and then express my opinion. Very nice, but I think. Your advanced and practical shedule has made a deep impresssion on me and I pin all my hope on you, sir.

Heze: Thank you for your praise. We'll never let you down.

York: That's all right.

约　克：说得好干得也好，先生。这是你们的工程进度表吗？
贺　泽：是呀。具体的施工进度，详细的工作数量都标得很清楚。你觉得咋样？
约　克：我先看看再说。不过我想一定很不错。先生，贵公司的计划很先进，很实际，给我留下了很深刻的印象，我对你们寄予厚望。
贺　泽：谢谢你的夸奖，我们决不辜负你们的希望。
约　克：这就好。

Explanatory Notes 注释：

　　construct 也是建筑英语中最常用的词之一。用作动词时，它有建筑，建造，建筑施工等意思。在很大程度上，可以和 build 互换，例如：Chinese constrctors construct/ build a new dam/road/ house, etc.（中国建筑施工人员们建造一座新坝/一条新道路/一栋新房子等）。但 construct / construction 着重强调建筑施工，正如人们常说的 construction company 建筑施工公司，而 building company 只是建筑公司。construct 有两种名词形式：contructor 指人，表示建筑施工人员，建设者；而 construction 则指建造方法，建筑物，建筑施工等，如 construction site 建筑（施工）工地，construction plan 施工布置图。短语 be under construction 正在施工中；constructional/constructive 是形容词形式，其意思为建设的，建设性的。

Spoken Practice 口语练习

1. **Pair Work:**

   Work in groups or pairs. Suppose you have won a tender. Ask your partner to tell you what your construction schedule is and how to be completed the project on time.

2. **Answer the following questions in accordance with Learn to Speak English:**

   1) How much building area does Queen Mansion have?
   2) How many months can you complete Queen Mansion according to the contract?
   3) Do you plan to finish the main structure in eight months or ten?
   4) You must complete Queen Mansion next year, mustn't you?
   5) Why does York pin all his hope on Heze?

3. **Read & Interpret the Following Passage:**

   ### The Classification of Beams

   Beams are horizontal member used to support vertically applied loads across an opening. In a more general sense, they are structural members that external loads tend to bend or curve. According to ways of support, beams are commonly classified as simply supported beam, cantilever, beam with overhangs and continuous beam.

   Beams can be constructed of wood, steel and reinforced concrete in construction. For heavy-duty beams, especially railway bridge girdles and large span cross beams, reinforced concrete is widely used.

4. **Put the Following Sentences into Chinese and Pay Attention to the Uses of "and":**

   1) Read the working drawing **and** you will see how to construct.
   2) Because I'm a civil engineer **and** he's a economist.
   3) Let's go **and** inspect the water supplying works that you've completed just now.
   4) Our teacher gave many examples to explain the usage of 'and' **and**

we all understood well.

5) Li Ming was a little boy **and** stopped strong horse from running away.

6) Wish the fraternal Chinese people prosperity **and** happiness

Explanatory Notes 注释：

这里要说明的是'and'连接两个动词或两个并列分句是在一般书籍常讲到的，但'and'究竟怎样翻译却不常见。'and'不仅只有"和"的意思，而实际上'and'表示着各种不同的内在关系，翻译时首先要弄清其内在的关系，再反复推敲、灵活处理，不能言不搭意、生搬硬套。请参考下列解释：

1) 表示条件或结果，译为"就"或"便"。
2) 表示转折，近似but，可译为"而"、"却"、"可是"或不译。
3) 表示目的，常不译。
4) 表示因果关系，可译为"所以"或"因此"。
5) 表示让步，可译为"尽管……却"。
6) 表示递进，可译为"并且"、"还"或不译。

5. Substitute the Following Words & Expressions：

1) Use the following **Execution Program(me) of Works**（施工程序）
   to replace the black words in the following sentence：

York：Have you worked out your **construction plan**?

约克：那你们制定施工计划了吗？

Execution Program(me) of Works 施工程序
[ˌeksˈkjuːʃən ˈprougræm əv wəːks]

earthworks [ˈəːθwəːks] 土方工程

piling [ˈpailiŋ] 打桩

concreting [ˈkɔnkriːtiŋ] 浇筑混凝土

precast concrete parts [ˈpriːkaːst ˈkɔnkriːt paːts] 预制混凝土构件

brickwork and partitions [ˈbrikwəːk ənd paːˈtiʃənz] 砌砖墙及隔墙

drainage and sewage [ˈdreinidʒ ənd ˈsjuːidʒ] 排水及污水管敷设

roofing [ˈruːfiŋ] 屋面工程

asphalt [ˈæsfælt] 沥青工程

timbering ['timbəriŋ] 木工活

structural steel works ['strʌktʃərəl 'sti:l wə:ks] 钢结构工程

metal works ['metl wə:ks] 金属工程

plastering & brushing walls 墙面抹灰与粉刷
['pla:stəriŋ ənd 'brʌʃiŋ wɔ:lz]

tiling walls and floors ['tailiŋ wɔ:lz ənd flɔ:z] 贴地面与墙壁面砖

sheet metal [ʃi:t 'metl] 白铁工程

water supply & sanitary 供水及卫生设备工程
['wɔ:tə sə'plai ənd 'sænitəri]

gas & water mains [gæz ənd 'wɔ:tə meinz] 煤气及供水的干管工程

heating ['hi:tiŋ] 供暖设备安装工程

ventilating [ˌventi'leitiŋ] 通风设备安装工程

electrical [i'lektrikəl] 电气设备安装工程

painting ['peintiŋ] 油漆工程

hardware ['ha:dwɛə] 五金安装

glazing ['gleiziŋ] 安装玻璃

paving ['peiviŋ] 路面工程

masonry ['meisnri] 砖石工程

specialist works ['speʃəlist wə:ks] 专业工程

2) Use the following **Schedule of Works** (工程计划/进度表) to replace the black words in the following sentence:

York: What you said is nice and done is well, too. Is this your **progress schedule**, sir?

约克：说得好，干得也好，先生。这是你们的**工程进度表**吗？

Schedule of Works ['ʃedju:l əv wə:ks] 工程计划/进度表

detailed schedule ['di:teild 'ʃedju:l] 详细计划/进度表

production plan [prə'dʌkʃən plæn] 生产计划

consider a schedule [kən'sidə ə 'ʃedju:l] 磋商进度/计划

draw up a schedule [drɔ:ʌp ə 'ʃedju:l] 制订计划/进度表

maintain a schedule [men'tein ə 'ʃedju:l] 保持进度/计划

be ahead of schedule [bi ə'hed əv 'ʃedju:l] 超进度/计划

revise a schedule [ri'vaiz ə 'ʃedju:l] 修订进度/计划
run on schedule [rʌn ɔn 'ʃedju:l] 按进度/计划施工
keep to schedule [ki:p tu 'ʃedju:l] 遵守进度/表
schedule of construction ['ʃedju:l əv kən'strʌkʃən] 施工计划
be behind of schedule [bi: bi'haind əv 'ʃedju:l] 落后于原计划
compliance with a schedule [kəm'plaiəns wið ə 'ʃedju:l] 与计划一致
fulfilment of schedule [ful'filmənt əv 'ʃedju:l] 进度/计划的完成
schedule of earthwork(s) ['ʃedju:l əv 'ə:θwə:k(s)] 土方工程计划
departure from a schedule 与计划/进度不符
[di'pa:tʃə frɔm ə 'ʃedju:l]
schedule of erection work(s) 安装工程计划
['ʃedju:l əv i'rekʃən wə:k(s)]
schedule of delivery of materials 材料交付计划/进度表
['ʃedju:l əv di'livəri əv mə'tiəriəlz]
schedule of delivery of equipment 设备交付计划/进度表
['ʃedju:l əv di'livəri əv i'kwipmənt]

Situational Dialogic Unit 19
第十九情景对话单元

Learn to Speak English

Talking about Kind of Buildings

Peter: Excuse me, miss. I don't know anything about construction. Can you tell me what buildings you are going to build here?

Laya: Yes, sir. A multi-storey building.

Peter: A multi-storey building. How high is it?

Laya: It's very, very high. Maybe more than eighty metres and there should be so many storeys.

Peter: What's the difference between high-rise building and low-rise one, I'd like to know?

Laya: High-rise building is more than ten storeys (includes ten storeys), and low-rise building less than four (one-three) storeys, and also can be divided into multistoreys (4-6 storeys), and medium-high storeys (7-9 storeys).

Peter: Oh. I know it. The classification belongs to dwellings. How about public buildings?

Laya: Less than twenty-four metres belong to a single storey/ multi-storey building and more than twenty-foure metres high-rise building, and over one hundred metres belong to superhigh building.

Peter: I see. Thank you for your detailed explanation. How many storeys does this bulding have?

Laya: It has thirty-two or so.

Peter: Naturally it belongs to high-rise building. But what's the usage of this building?

Laya: As likes as not, some storeys are for the usage of business, and others for the living.

Peter: Which storeys are for the usage of department stores or shops?

Laya: Lower part, that is to say, ground and first floor, I think.

Peter: Why do you think so?

Laya: Because there aren't any partitions in these two storeys. The big rooms are usually for the usage of offices and department stores or shops...

学说英语

谈论建筑物种类

彼　得：小姐，对不起。我对建筑一窍不通，您能告诉我在这儿你们要建什么楼房？

拉　雅：能，先生。要建一栋多层楼房。

彼　得：多层楼房。有多高？

拉　雅：非常，非常高，也许有80多米高，有很多层楼。

彼　得：我想知道高层建筑和低层建筑究竟有什么不同？

拉　雅：高层建筑是指10层（包括10层）以上的高楼，而低层建筑则是指不足4层（1~3层）的矮楼，4~6为多层，7~9为中高层。

彼　得：哦，我现在才明白它们之间的区别。这种分类只限于住宅建筑，那公共建筑呢？

拉　雅：公共建筑则是24米高度以下为单层或多层，大于24米高度则为高层。100米高度以上的则称之为超高层。

彼　得：我清楚了，多谢你详细的讲解。那这栋楼有多少层？

拉　雅：大约有32层。

彼　得：那自然属于高层建筑。但用作什么？

拉　雅：十之八九，几层作为商业用，而剩下的则用作住宅。

彼　得：哪几层作为商业用的店铺？

拉　雅：我想低层，也就是一层和二层吧。

彼　得：你为什么这样认为呢？

拉　雅：因为这两层隔墙少，大房间常用作办公室和店铺……

Peter: What about the others?

Laya: However, there're many partitions in the others, so they become many small rooms, for the small rooms are usage of bedrooms, sitting room, bathroom...

Peter: Right, miss, but does the building belong to Chinese style architecture or western one?

Laya: It's just like that one over there. I think it belongs to western style architecture without a overhanging roof. With a overhanging roof, it belongs to Chinese style, or ancient architecture.

Peter: It's a modern architecture. The different between modern architecture and ancient architecture has a overhang roof, right?

Laya: I surppose it should be. But there're so many differents between modern architecture and ancient architecture, for example, using materials, adopting structures, choosing types, etc., overhang roof is a typical different at least.

Peter: I don't quite clear. Pleas give me some examples about ancient architecture, OK?

Laya: OK. the Forbidden City (is also called Imperial Palaces) in Beijing and Bell tower and Drum Tower in Xi'an, etc. are all the glaring examples.

Peter: Nice. Please show me some examples about modern architecture?

Laya: OK. So many examples for the modern ones, too numerous to mention, the People's Hall in Beijing and Orient Pearl in Shanghai.

Peter: I rearly understand. So modern architecture is buildings big and small, high and low along both sides of every street.

彼　得：其他楼层呢？

拉　雅：然而其他层却有很多隔墙，所以就变成小房间。小房间常用作卧室、客厅、浴室……诸如此类。

彼　得：对呀，小姐。那么这栋建筑物属于中式建筑还是西式建筑？

拉　雅：正如那栋楼一样，没有大屋顶，我想它属于西式建筑，而有大屋顶的建筑物则是中式的，古代建筑。

彼　得：这是一栋现代建筑。现代建筑和古代建筑的区别就是有没有大屋顶，对吗？

拉　雅：我认为应该是。不过现代建筑和古代建筑还有许多不同之处，比如用料、结构设计、选用式样等方面都有所不同，大屋顶只是一个起码的、典型的区别而已。

彼　得：我还不十分清楚，请给我举几个古代建筑的例子行吗？

拉　雅：行。例如北京的紫禁城（也称之为故宫）；西安的钟鼓楼都是突出的实例。

彼　得：很好。请再举几个现代建筑的实例可以吗？

拉　雅：好吧！现代建筑的实例太多啦，举不胜举，比如北京的人民大会堂、上海的东方明珠都属于现代建筑。

彼　得：我确实明白了。原来现代建筑就是大街两旁大大小小，高高低低的各种各样建筑物。

Explanatory Notes 注释：

1. storey 意思是表示房子高度的"层"，指的是空间。例如：a house of one storey 平房，平房也可说成 a single-storey house；又如：a building of twenty storeys 20 层大楼也同样是 a twenty-storey building. He lives in a five-storey building 他住在一幢五层的房子里。注意 storey 不是 story 的另一个拼写，而是两个不同意思的单词。story 的复数形式是 stories，意思是"故事，史话"等；storey 的复数形式则是 storeys

2. floor 常略作 fl. 意思是楼房的"第…层""每层"。第几层的算法，美国和英国的习惯不同，汉语的表达习惯与美语相同。例如：the first floor（美国说法）一楼，等于 the ground floor（英国说法）底层。The second floor（美国说法）二楼而（英国说法）三楼。Floor 的基本意思是地面，地板。所以 floor 指楼层是按地板层而分的，楼层地板是平的，因此一般用介词 on。例如 On which floor do you live? 你住在几楼? On second floor. 在二楼。

3. 还有一点需要强调，通常人们所说建筑物共有若干层时，是在建筑物外面看上去而言的，不用 floor，而用 storeyed；例如 our classroom is on the third floor of six-storeyed building. 我们的教室是在一幢六层楼的四楼（英语是三楼）上。因为 storey 也表示"第…层"，表示"在第…层上"时，用介词 in。第几层的算法英美英语是一致的。例如：our manager lives in the third storey. 我们的经理住在三楼。storeyed（常用以构成复合词）有…（层）楼的，如：a seven-storeyed building 七层楼的建筑。

Spoken Practice 口语练习

1. **Pair Work**:

   Suppose your partner lives in a small village and comes to a big modern city, You're walking along the street and try to talking about the houses on both sides of the streets what you see.

2. **Tell "true" or "false" in accordance with Learn to Speak English**:

   1) (　) We are going to build a low-rise building here.
   2) (　) High-rise building is less than six storeys and low-rise building more than six.
   3) (　) The multi-storey building belongs to Chinese style architecture with a overhanging roof.
   4) (　) The big rooms in ground and first floor are for the usage of offices and shops...
   5) (　) The other storeys are too small to use as dwelling.

3. **Read & Interpret the Following Passage**:

   ### Dwelling House

   There are many different kinds of houses in the world. They can be large or small, ancient or modern, Chinese style or western style. Many houses are square and a few are round. Some houses have only one floor, and others have two or more, even there are lots of multi-storey buildings, too.

   Many houses design similarly, with two or three bedrooms and bathroom upstairs, a dinner room, kitchen and living room downstairs, and a small garden at the back and in front of them.

   Most of houses are made of concrete, steel bar, wood, stone or bricks.

4. **Put the Following into English**:

房屋结构和配套设施	
结　构	钢筋混凝土框架，抗压、抗震、防火等性能
屋　顶	防水装置和隔热层

续表

外　墙	石头基础，高级墙砖
内　墙	建筑砖，环保油漆
电　梯	名牌电梯
楼　梯	公共楼梯使用实木扶手，防滑地砖和台阶
地　板	大理石地砖和复合地板
门　窗	彩色铝合金双层玻璃，双重开关式窗户。单元门有防火、防盗功能
主　卫	大理石墙面和地面，卫生设施，龙头
厨　房	整体橱柜和热水器
空　调	中央空调系统
供　电	独立电表，20kW/标准单元，30kW/套房
供　气	管道天然气（2.5 立方气表）
电　话	每家 3 条 ADSL 线路
有线电视	配备卫星和公共天线接收器
安全系统	配备中央监控室，每户装备智能管理系统，通过对讲机和监视器确定来访客人

5. **Substitute the Following Words & Expressions**：

1) Use the following **Terms about Modern Architecture**（现代建筑相关术语）to replace the black words in the following sentence：

Peter：OK. Please show me some examples about **modern architecture**?

彼　得：很好。请再举几个**现代建筑**的实例可以吗？

Terms about Modern Architecture 现代建筑相关术语
[tə:mz ə'baut 'mɔdən 'a:kitektʃə]

industrial architecture ［in'dʌstriəl 'a:kitektʃə］工业建筑

civil architecture ［'sivl 'a:kitektʃə］民用建筑

domestic architecture ［də'mestik 'a:kitektʃə］住宅建筑

western style architecture ［'westən stail 'a:kitektʃə］西式建筑

office building ［'ɔfis 'bildiŋ］办公大楼

teaching building ［'ti:tʃiŋ 'bildiŋ］教学大楼

business building ［'biznis 'bildiŋ］营业大楼

married quarters ［'mærid 'kwɔ:təz］家属楼

建筑技术与管理英语情景会话

apartment /flats ［ə'pɑːtmənt flæts］ 公寓，成套住房
multi-storey building ［'mʌlti'stɔri 'bildiŋ］ 多层建筑
skyscraper ［'skaiˌskreipə］ 摩天大楼
high-rise ［hai raiz］ 高层
lower-rise ［'louə raiz］ 低层
mansion ［'mænʃən］ 豪华宅第，大厦
villa ［'vilə］ 别墅
subway/ underground ［'sʌbwei 'ʌndəgraund］ 地下铁路
dam ［dæm］ 水坝，堤坝
tunnel ［'tʌnl］ 隧道
airport ［'ɛəpɔːt］ 机场
water tower ［'wɔːtə 'tauə］ 水塔
a single-storey house = a house of one storey 平房
［ə 'siŋgl 'stɔːrid haus ə haus əv wʌn 'stɔːr］

2) Use the following **Some Parts of Building**（建筑物一些部位）to replace the black words in the following sentence：

Laya： However, there're many **partitions** in the others, so they become many small rooms, for the small rooms are usage of **bedrooms**, **sitting room**, **bathroom**. ...

拉雅：然而其他层却有很多**隔墙**，所以就变成小房间。小房间常用作**卧室**，**客厅**，**浴室**……诸如此类。

Some Parts of Building ［sʌm pɑːts əv 'bildiŋ］ 建筑物一些部位
reception room ［ri'sepʃən ruːm］ 会客厅
living/sitting room ［'liviŋ 'sitiŋ ruːm］ 起居室
single/double bedroom ［'siŋgl 'dʌbl 'bedruːm］ 单/双人卧室
dressing room ［'dresiŋ ruːm］ 化妆间
study ［'stʌdi］ 书房
kitcken ［'kitʃin］ 厨房，灶房
dinning room ［'dainiŋ ruːm］ 餐厅
balcony ［'bælkəni］ 阳台
bathroom ［'bɑːθruːm］ 浴室

laundry ['lɔːndri] 洗衣间/房
toilet/watercloset ['tɔilit 'wɔːtə'klouzit] 厕所
basement ['beismənt] 地下室
staircase ['stɛəkeis] 楼梯间/房
garage ['gæraːdʒ] 汽车库

Situational Dialogic Unit 20
第二十情景对话单元

Learn to Speak English

Talking about Inspecting Construction Progress

Hegong: We haven't seen each other for a long time, I miss you very much. Why did you come here today, Mr. Newton?

Newton: Now I'm a statistician and in charge of statistical work in our group corporation. Naturally, I came to see how about the production progress on your site?

Hegong: The case as a whole is not bad, the production tasks finished very well. Please go to my office first, and then I'll report them to you, OK?

Newton: Unnecessarily. I know you had a production dispatching meeting. Every staff in all the companies tries his /her best to do so. I should go to see with my eyes on the site, right?

Hegong: Right. Let's go, shall we?

Newton: OK. Hear say that there're five companies on this site, which company shall we begin?

Hegong: Oh, just here. This is a construction area of No. 1 company.

Newton: Is that so? What about their construction tasks?

Hegong: Not bad. No. 1 company has finished 3 concrete foundations, 10 wooden roofs and other construction tasks.

Newton: Very good. How about No. 2 Company?

Hegong: Nice going! They've finished their tasks ahead of schedule this month.

Newton: What construction tasks have they finished?

Hegong: Five main structures.

Newton: Wonderful! How about other companies?

Hegong: Oh. They also have finished their tasks quite well. No. 4 Company is an installation company, the water & electrical installation tasks of No. 1~4 buildings have been finished already.

学说英语

谈论检查施工进度

何　工：我们好久都没见了，很想你！牛顿先生，你今来这儿有何贵干？

牛　顿：我现在是统计员，负责我们集团公司的统计工作，自然是来检查质量。你们工地生产进度怎样？

何　工：整体情况还好，生产任务完成得不错。请先到办公室，我再给你汇报好吗？

牛　顿：不必了。我知道你们召开了生产调度会议，各个公司的职工都很尽力，我应该到现场亲眼看一看对吧？

何　工：对。咱们走，好吗？

牛　顿：好吧，听说这个工地就有五个公司在施工。咱们先从那个公司开始统计？

何　工：啊！就从这儿开始吧。这是一公司的施工区。

牛　顿：是吗？他们的生产任务完成得怎样？

何　工：不错。他们完成了3栋楼的混凝土基础、10栋楼的木屋顶和其他施工任务。

牛　顿：很好。二公司怎样？

何　工：干得好！他们已提前完成了这月的施工任务。

牛　顿：都完成了哪些项目？

何　工：5栋主体工程。

牛　顿：好极了！其他公司完成得怎样？

何　工：哦，任务也完成得相当好。四公司是个安装公司，已经完成了1~4号楼的水电安装任务。

Newton: What a satisfying thing! I'd love to see the situation of No. 5 Decoration Company. Will you go with me?

Hegong: Naturally. No. 5 Decoration Company is a new company. The decoration task of Hilton Hotel is the first project to be contracted. Quality and progress are both satisfied.

Newton: Is it so? It's well said that well begun is half done. Let's go to congratulate them upon the great achievement.

Hegong: Yes, we should do so.

Newton: Decoration Company has done quite well. Let's go to see No. 3 Road & Bridge Company, shall we?

Hegong: Yes. No. 3 Company has built six kilometers road and a highway bridge.

Newton: The production tasks of every company are accomplished quite well. What I heard and saw maks me happy. By the way, are their monthly reports ready?

Hegong: Sorry, sir. Not yet.

Newton: It's not affect the situation as a whole. But these statistics throw a lot of light on the matter.

Hegong: Please watch the builders on the whole site are well doing and have made up their minds to overcome all kinds of hardships and difficulties in order to accomplish their tasks ahead of schedule.

Newton: Excellently. I was told they gave up their holidays and kept on working. Is that so?

Hegong: Yes, that's true.

Newton: Chinese builders are great! I'm deeply toutched.

牛　顿：多么欣慰呀！我还想看看装饰五公司施工情况，你能陪我一道去吗？

何　工：当然能。装饰五公司是一个新组建的公司，希尔顿饭店的装饰任务是他们承建的第一个工程项目。先生，进度都使人满意。

牛　顿：是啊！常言说得好啊"好的开始就是成功的一半"。咱们应去为他们所取得巨大成就而庆贺。

何　工：是的，应该庆贺。

牛　顿：装饰公司干得相当不错。咱们也去看看路桥三公司生产情况好吗？

何　工：好吧。三公司已修建好了6公里长的道路和一座公路桥。

牛　顿：各公司的生产任务都完成得很好，我所见所闻的一切真使我高兴。顺便问一下，他们的月报表都做好了吗？

何　工：抱歉，先生，还没呢。

牛　顿：这也无碍大局。不过我们统计的这些数据已说明问题。

何　工：请看，整个工地的广大职工干得多好，他们决心战胜各种艰难险阻，确保提前完成生产任务。

牛　顿：好极了。我得知他们放弃了节假日休息，坚持工作，是这样吗？

何　工：是的，那是真的。

牛　顿：中国建筑工人真了不起！我深受感动。

Explanatory Notes 注释：

1. statistics 名词（n.）统计学；统计，统计资料，统计数字
   capital construction statistics 基本建设统计
   例如：Statistics can tell some of story. 统计数字能说明一些问题。
   例如：According to incomplete statistics, all the companies have accomplished their production task of this year. 据不完全统计，所有公司已经完成今年的生产任务。
2. statistician = statist 名词（n.）统计员，统计学家
3. statistic = statistical 形容词（a.）统计的，统计学的
   statistical data 统计资料 statistical figure 统计数字
   statistical chart/table 统计图表

Spoken Practice 口语练习

1. **Pair Work:**

   A is a statist, B is a foreman. They are talking about the construction tasks what five companies have just finished on the site.

2. **Tell "true" or "false" in accordance with Learn to Speak English:**

   1) ( ) I have seen you for a long time. Where have you been, sir?
   2) ( ) The production tasks of No. 1 company finished not bad.
   3) ( ) No. 3 company have finished their tasks ahead of schedule this month.
   4) ( ) Their monthly schedule reports are ready.
   5) ( ) The builders on the whole site have made up their mind to have few days rest.

3. **Read & Interpret the Following Passage:**

   ### The Function of Columns

   The vertical members of a structural frame are called columns, and they transmit floor and roof loads to the foundation. Columns are often called posts, especially when made of timer. Truss members carrying compressive stresses are called struts, but their action is the same as that of columns.

4. **Put the Following Sentences into Chinese and Pay Attention to the Use of Meaning Negation（意义否定）:**

   1) He usually makes **few** mistakes in his spoken English as far as I know.
   2) I think the tool is **too** heavy for me **to** carry with one hand.
   3) She **failed** to keep her word before.
   4) John's operative skill is **little** better than mine now.
   5) Wang Lin is so tired that he can **hardly** walk, I'm afraid.
   6) We would **rather** learn architectural English **than** literature English, to tell the truth.
   7) Will you have tea **instead of** coffee today?

8) Mark writes the words several times **without** remembering them well.

9) **Seldom** have I met general manager, Mr. Huang recently.

10) Many builders **scarcely** know a word of special Engligh before learning Architectural English.

Explanatory Notes 注释:

　　意义否定就是形式上是肯定句,但句中却含有否定意义的词或词组,常见的否定意义的词或词组有 few, little, hardly, seldom, scacrely, barely, merely, too... to, be short of, be free from 等,实际上这些词或词组也是否定的,所以在翻译时应注意并表达清楚。

5. Substitute the Following Words & Expressions:

1) Use the following **Building Elements**(房屋构件)to replace the black words in the following sentence:

Hegong: Not bad. No. 1 company has finished 3 **concrete foundations**, 10 **wooden roofs** and other construction tasks.

何工:不错。他们完成了3栋楼的**混凝土基础**、10栋楼的**木屋顶**和其他施工任务。

Building Elements [ˈbildiŋ ˈelimənts] 房屋构件

foundation [faunˈdeiʃən] 基础,地基

footing [ˈfutiŋ] 基/底脚

retaining wall [riˈteiniŋ wɔːl] 挡土墙

external wall [eksˈtəːnl wɔːl] 外墙

internal wall [inˈtəːnl wɔːl] 内墙

bearing wall [ˈbɛəriŋ wɔːl] 承重墙

non-bearing wall [nʌn ˈbɛəriŋ wɔːl] 非承重墙

partition [paːˈtiʃən] 隔墙

gable [ˈgeibl] 山墙

girder [ˈgəːdə] 大梁

main beam [mein biːm] 主梁

ring beam [riŋ biːm] 圈梁

tie beam [tai biːm] 系梁

lintel ['lintl] 过梁

canopy ['kænəpi] 雨篷

2) Use the following **Building Codes and Standards**（建筑规范与标准）to replace the black words in the following sentence:

Newton: Unnecessarily. I know you had a **production dispatching meeting.** Every staff in all the companies tries his /her best to do so. I should go to see with my eyes on the site, right?

牛顿：不必了。我知道你们召开了**生产调度会议**，各个公司的职工都很尽力，我应该到现场亲眼看一看对吧？

Building Codes and Standards 建筑规范与标准
['bildiŋ koudz ənd 'stændədz]

standard specification ['stændəd ˌspesifi'keiʃən] 标准技术规范

standard building elements ['stændəd 'bildiŋ 'elimənts] 标准建筑构件

standard of construction ['stændəd əv kən'strʌkʃən] 建筑施工标准

code for constution [koud fɔ:kən'strʌkʃən] 施工规范

standard measurement ['stændəd 'meʒəmənt] 标准测量

code for soil and foundation 地基基础规范
[koud fɔ:sɔil ənd faun'deiʃən]

code for electrical installation 电气安装规范
[koud fə i'letrikəl ˌinstə'leiʃən]

codes for water supply and sewerage 给排水规范
[koudz fə 'wɔ:tə sə'plai ənd 'sjuəridʒ]

codes for heating and ventilating installation 供暖与通风装置规范
[koudz fə 'hi:tiŋ ənd ˌventi'leitiŋ ˌinstə'leiʃən]

Situational Dialogic Unit 21
第二十一情景对话单元

Learn to Speak English

Talking about Inspecting Quality of works

Gordon: Hello. Mr. Gao. I come here to inspect your engineering quality.

Gaohan: Welcome, Supervisor. Let's go and look around, shall we?

Gordon: OK. First I'd like to check up the size and the locating position of this building. Where're your theodolite and steel tape?

Gaohan: Here it is, sir. This is a new one.

Gordon: That's much better. According to designing requirements of the foundation plan, the size, the elevation and the locating position are accurate without any erro and diviation.

Gaohan: Thank you. We know the building location is very important. So we won't be the least bit negligent and not erro by a hair's breadth.

Gordon: What you thought is right. Let's go to check up the sewage and water supply pipes and see if there's any leak of water or not.

Gaohan: Oh, good. There isn't any leakage at all, please look.

Gordon: Do they put the concrete aggregate materials accurately?

Gaohan: Yes. Exactly, they put in the materials in property to their weight. These are concrete testing cubices and their pressure-testing records.

Gordon: What you've done is not bad. Thank you for your responsibility quality indeed.

Gaohan: Not at all. Let's go on, sir.

Gordon: The corner between the two walls isn't any steel rebars. Please put them down and redo them, and then you'll be punished if you are seen next time.

Zhuelin: Be extremely sorry, I can agree with you. This is my fault.

Gordon: I don't make thing difficult for you on purpose and don't finding your fault at all. No errors are to be treated tightly, look but see not and listen but hear not!

谈论检验工程质量

戈　登：你好，高工长。我前来贵地督查工程质量。

高　涵：欢迎，监督员。咱们去看一看，好吗？

戈　登：好吧。我想先检查一下这栋楼的定位和尺寸，你们的经纬仪和钢尺在哪儿？

高　涵：先生，给你。这是一台新仪器。

戈　登：这就更好些。根据基础平面图的设计要求，尺寸、标高和定位都准确无误，没有偏差。

高　涵：谢谢！我们知道楼房的定位的重要性，所以我们要做到一丝不苟，丝毫不差。

戈　登：这样认识是对的。咱们去检查排水管道和给水管子，看看是否有漏水现象。

高　涵：啊，很好。请看，一点都不漏（水）。

戈　登：他们把混凝土骨料投放准确了吗？

高　涵：是的，绝对准确，他们是按重量比投料的。这些是混凝土试块和试压记录。

戈　登：你们做得不错，确实该谢谢你们对质量的负责。

高　涵：没什么，这是应该的。咱们还是接着检查吧，先生。

戈　登：这两道墙的拐角处没放钢筋，请推倒，重砌。下次再被我发现，你就得受罚。

卓　霖：万分抱歉，我能认同，这是我的过失。

戈　登：这并非有意在刁难你，更不是挑你刺儿。对于错误决不能等闲视之，视而不见，听而不闻吧！

Zhuelin: Right. Because it's a rule that anything in the drawings can't be modified condition of the contract without a proval from the engineers.

Gordon: It's indisputable for this. It's mentioned in the contract.

Zhuelin: I know "a project of vital and lasting importance, quality is first". And I must vouch for the quality qualified from now on.

Gordon: Right. Any drawing queries on the site are to be clarified with the architect. Never act on one's own. Please help your staff workers further improve the sense of the engineering quality.

Gaohan: Sure. Quality is a lifeline for our enterprise. We'll do our best to do well.

Gordon: I agree with you. Maybe quality problems can make us unsatify temporarily, however, they can bring a penment loss to an enterprise.

Gaohan: Right. Quality problems bring the hidden danger for any buildings which can't be removed forever.

Gordon: Perfectly correct. Well and Fast means that guarantees both quality and quantity. Anyone must strictly keep the dialectical relation and never sight one's work.

Gaohan: There's an end of the words, but not to their message.

卓　霖：对。因为这是规定，未经工程师同意，不能改变设计图上任何东西。
戈　登：这在合同条款上已表明，对此无可争辩。
卓　霖：我懂得"百年大计，质量第一"，一定保证从今往后质量合格。
戈　登：对呀。现场的任何图纸问题均应与建筑设计师协商解决，决不能自作主张。请帮助你们的职工进一步提高工程质量意识。
高　涵：一定。质量是我们企业的生命线，我们会尽最大努力搞好的。
戈　登：我同意你的观点，也许质量问题会给我们带来暂时的不满意，然而却会给企业造成永久的损失。
高　涵：对，质量问题会给建筑物增添不可挽回的隐患。
戈　登：没错。又好又快就是要保质求量，任何人都必须严守这一辩证关系，决不能玩忽职守。
高　涵：言有尽，意无穷呀。

Spoken Practice 口语练习

1. **Pair Work:**

   A is a supervising engineer, B is a resident engineer. They're talking about quality of the construction works that B and his fellows are building.

2. **Tell "true" or "false" in accordance with Learn to Speak English:**

   1) (　) Gordon came to the worksite to inspect your production.

   2) (　) The sewage and water supply pipes aren't any leakage at all.

   3) (　) I'd like to check up the size and position of the location of this building with the level and steel tape.

   4) (　) Do you put the concrete aggregate materials in property to their weight, master?

   5) (　) It's a rule that anything in the drawings can't be modified without a proval from the engineer.

3. **Read & Interpret the Following Passage:**

   > **Replying to Complaint about Defects of Products Quality**
   >
   > Dear sirs,
   >
   > 　　Reference is made to your letter dated March 4th 2005, complaining that the steel trusses under contract No. 286 was found preliminary inspection that it is crack and wrinking and not smooth.
   >
   > 　　We would like to remind you that the steel trusses were purchased after the sample displayed in the showroom in your city, and therefore, the quality of the sample should serve as the standard for inspection. We have instructed by cable your showroom technicians to inspect the steel trusses in company with our surveyor and shall return to this matter when their reports come to hand.
   >
   > 　　　　　　　　　　　　　　　　　　　　　　　　Yours truly,

4. **Put the Following 'and' Phrases into Chinese and Learn Them by Heart:**

   1) day and night　　　　　　　　2) first and last

   3) over and over　　　　　　　　4) here and there

5) in(s) and out(s)   6) ways and means
7) day in and day out   8) near and dear
9) back and forth   10) now and then

Explanatory Notes 注释：

　　掌握 and 的习惯用法也很重要。这种惯用法就是把两个意思相近或相反的名词、形容词、动词、副词等用 and 连接起来，构成惯用词组，在日常生活中使用。但这些词组却有固定的译法，不能望文生义，所以一定要逐个记，以丰富自己英语词汇。

5. Substitute the Following Words & Expressions：

1) Use the following **Management of Quality** （质量管理）to replace the black words in the following sentence：

Gordon：Hello. Mr. Gao. I come here to inspect your **engineering quality.**
戈登：你好，高工长。我前来贵地督查工程质量。

Management of Quality [ˈmænidʒmənt əv ˈkwɔliti] 质量管理
quality of works [ˈkwɔliti əv wəːks] 工程质量
quality of products [ˈkwɔliti əv ˈprɔdəkts] 产品质量
standard of quality [ˈstændəd əv ˈkwɔliti] 质量标准
quality control [ˈkwɔliti kənˈtroul] 质量控制
quality inspection [ˈkwɔliti inˈspekʃən] 质量检验
quality supervision [ˈkwɔliti ˌsjuːpəˈviʒən] 质量监督
site inspection [sait inˈspekʃən] 现场监督
displacement [disˈpleismənt] 位移
resistance [reˈzistəns] 抗力
crack resistance [kræk reˈzistəns] 裂度
structural damage [ˈstrʌktʃərəl ˈdæmidʒ] 结构破坏
structural cracks [ˈstrʌktʃərəl kræks] 结构裂缝
limit error [ˈlimit ˈerə] 误差极限
deviation [ˌdiːviˈeiʃən] 偏差，偏离
correction [kəˈrekʃən] 校正，矫正
concrete curing [ˈkɔnkriːt ˈkjuəriŋ] 混凝土养护

below proof [bi'lou pru:f] 不合格
site investigation [sait in,vesti'geiʃən] 现场调查
limiting quality ['limitiŋ 'kwɔliti] 极限质量
acceptable quality [ək'septəbl 'kwɔliti] 合格质量
load test [loud test] 负荷试验
defective work(s) [di'fektiv wə:k(s)] 劣质工程
acceptance test [ək'septəns test] 验收试验（检验）
quality certification system ['kwɔliti ,sə:tifi'keiʃən'sistəm] 质量保证制度

2) Use the following **Instruments and Tools for Quality**（质量检测器具）to replace the black words in the following sentence：

Gordon: OK. First I'd like to check up the size and the locating position of this building. Where're your **theodolite** and **steel tape**?

戈登：好吧。我想先检查一下这栋楼的定位和尺寸，你们的**经纬仪**和**钢尺**在哪儿？

Instruments and Tools for Quality 质量检测器具
['instrumənts ənd tu:lz fə 'kwɔliti]

measuring tools ['meʒəriŋ tu:lz] 计量工具
theodolite [θi'ɔdəlait] 经纬仪
level ['levl] 水平仪
radius gauge ['reidjəs geidʒ] 半径规
plumb and level [plʌmb ənd 'levl] 垂直水平两用仪
steel tape [sti:l teip] 钢卷尺
feeler ['fi:lə] 厚薄规
steel protractor [sti:l prə'træktə] 量角规，半圆规
dividers [di'vaidəz] 分线规，两脚规
compasses ['kʌmpəsiz] 圆规
folding rule ['fouldiŋ ru:l] 折尺
stainless steel square ['steinlis sti:l skwɛə] 不锈钢直角尺
long-straight inspection bar [lɔŋ streit in'spekʃən ba:] 长直检查棒
universal bevel protractors 万能角度尺
[,ju:ni'və:səl 'bevəl prə'træktəz]

Situational Dialogic Unit 22
第二十二情景对话单元

Learn to Speak English

Talking about Inspecting Construction Safety

Ford: Hello, chap. Why are you working under the scaffolds without a safety helmet?

Lina: It's very hot today, so I just took it off and put it there.

Ford: I don't think what you have done is right. It's dangerous to work on the worksite without any safe measures. Have you ever seen anything dropping down from a height?

Lina: Never, but I know your meaning.

Ford: That's what can often happen. Especially small things like a head of brick, a piece of timber etc. drop down sometims.

Lina: I see. From now on I must keep safety in my mind all the time.

Ford: That's all right. I want to talk with your site director. Where's he?

Lina: He's out just now and hasn't been back yet. Why must you meet our site director himself, sir?

Ford: I'm an engineer in charge of safety. I saw many hidden troubles on your site and need to tell him about them and then take some measurements.

Lina: So that's how it is. I'm the site safety gard. What you tell me just as you tell our director.

Ford: Let's hope so. But your safety education isn't enough, safety hidden dangers can be seen anywhere.

Lina: It isn't like so. We had a meeting and told every one about it.

Ford: That's important, to be sure, but the key is how to remove the hidden dangers.

Lina: It looks as if we didn't carry them out very well.

Ford: OK. Please follow me to take a look around your site, OK?

Lina: OK. Let's go.

Ford: Look! The electrician fixing the bulbs and wires in the height isn't having any safety precautions. It's so dangerous.

学说英语

谈论检查施工安全

福　特：喂，小伙子。你在脚手架下干活怎么不戴安全帽呢？

林　纳：今天的天气太热，所以我刚把安全帽摘掉放在哪儿。

福　特：我认为你的做法不对，在建筑工地干活没有安全措施是危险的。你看见没看见过从高处掉下的东西？

林　纳：从未见过。不过我知道你的用意。

福　特：掉东西是常有的事，特别是像砖头、木块等小东西掉下来时有发生。

林　纳：我明白啦。从现在起我一定永远把安全牢记在心中。

福　特：这就对啦！我想同工地主任在一起聊一聊。他在哪儿？

林　纳：他刚出去，还没回来呢。先生，你为啥一定要见他本人？

福　特：我是主管安全的工程师，我发现你们工地有不少的安全隐患，有必要告诉他，并采取相应的防范措施。

林　纳：原来是这样，我是工地安全员，告诉我就等于告诉主任。

福　特：但愿如此。你们的安全教育不够，安全隐患随处可见。

林　纳：不会吧，我们开过会，给大家都讲过。

福　特：这固然重要，关键是怎样采取安全措施，消除安全隐患的问题。

林　纳：看来我们落实得不够好。

福　特：那好，请你带我在工地转一转，行吗？

林　纳：当然行。咱们走吧。

福　特：瞧！在高空安装灯泡、架电线的那位电工没有采取安全保障措施，这是很危险的。

Lina: Yes, he's without any safety measures. That doesn't conform to the operative rules.

Ford: Look! There isn't any safety net round the roof where the builders are doing their work on it. Please tell them to stop working and come down at once. Who bears the responsibility once something takes place.

Lina: OK. I'll stop them right now, and do the safety measures as quick as possible.

Ford: (a few minutes late) I'm sorry to stop your work. Do you know why?

Jemi: Yes. It's for our safety.

Ford: From now on, you should remember safety forever, and foster the ideal of safety first。

Jemi: Thank you for your remind. We must do.

Ford: Safety is for the production; however, production must be safe. Be sure and remember what I told you.

Jemi: Be sure. Take preventive measures. A case involving human life is to be treated with utmost case.

Ford: Please remember that merits uncited with not varish; safety undiscover may prove disastrous.

林　纳：是的，他没采取任何安全措施，这是不符合操作规范的。
福　特：看，工人们正在干活的屋顶四周都没围安全网，请叫他们停止工作，马上下来。万一出事谁负责？
林　纳：是，马上停工。我会尽快把屋顶围起的。
福　特：（几分钟之后）很抱歉停了你们的工。你们知道为什么吗？
杰　米：知道，是为了我们的安全。
福　特：从现在起，你们应永远记住安全，并树立安全第一的思想。
杰　米：多谢您的提醒。我一定记住。
福　特：安全为了生产；生产必须安全。千万要记住我对你讲的话。
杰　米：一定。防患于未然，因为人命关天。
福　特：请记住成绩不夸跑不了，安全不管不得了。

Spoken Practice 口语练习

1. **Pair Work:**

   A is a supervising engineer, B is a site director. They are talking about the construction safety regulations that B and his fellows are observing and safety measures that they have done on the construction site.

2. **Tell "true" or "false" in accordance with Learn to Speak English:**

   1) (   ) It's too safe to work on the worksite with any safe measures.

   2) (   ) From now on, the whole staff workers must keep safety in their minds all the time.

   3) (   ) The electricians fixing the bulbs and wires in the height take some safety measures.

   4) (   ) There should be a safety net round the roof where the builders are doing their work.

   5) (   ) Be sure and forget that safety is for the production; however production must be safe.

3. **Read & Interpret the Following Passage:**

   Expansion Joint

   Materials expand or contract with the change of temperature, so building materials also have different sizes at different temperatures. The expansion force of some building materials, to some extent with the change temperature, is very strong. It may cause a structure to break. That's why in all the large structures (the total length of a structure is over sixty metres) there must be an expansion joint between them.

4. **Put the Following Sentences into Chinese and Pay Attention to Two Expression Ways of "Negation":**

   1) We **don't** remember **all** the English words we have learned.

   Non of the English words we have learned don't remember.

   2) **Every** construction machine here is **not** made in China.

   No construction machine here is made in China.

   3) **Not both** these English text-books are suitable for us to learn.

Neither of these English text-books is suitable for us to learn.

4) Mr. Wang **doesn't** explain the technical problem **correctly** and **clearly.**

  Mr. Wang doesn't explain the technical problem correctly or clearly.

5) Many students **don't** interprete English **as well as** translate it.

  Many students don't interprete English or translate it.

Explanatory Notes 注释：

  部分否定和全部否定：对部分否定和全部否定的翻译练习很有必要，因为部分否定和全部否定实际上是两种不同的否定表达方式，决不能等同对待，一定要区别翻译。如果不清楚这一点，会在今后的翻译过程中出笑话，出差错。那么怎样识别部分否定和全部否定呢？如果句中只要有 all, every, both + not 或 not + all, every, both; not + a. / ad. and a. /ad. ; not + v. + as well as + v. 均属于部分否定；句中只有 not, no, non 便是全部否定。

5. Substitute the Following Words & Expressions：

1) Use the following **Safety in Production Management**（安全生产管理）to replace the black words in the following sentence：

Ford：Look! The electrician fixing the bulbs and wires in the height isn't having any **safety precautions.** It's so dangerous.

福特：瞧！在高空安装灯泡，架电线的那位电工没有采取**安全保障措施**。这是很危险的。

Safety in Production Mangement 安全生产管理

[ˈseifti in prəˈdʌkʃən ˈmænidʒmənt]

safety regulation　[ˈseifti ˌregjuˈleiʃən]　安全规则

total safety control　[ˈtəutl ˈseifti kənˈtroul]　全面安全管理

safety education　[ˈseifti ˌedju(:)ˈkeiʃən]　安全教育

safety inspection　[ˈseifti inˈspekʃən]　安全检查

safety apparatus　[ˈseifti ˌæpəˈreitəs]　安全设施

safety measures　[ˈseifti ˈmeʒəz]　安全措施

safety precautions　[ˈseifti priˈkɔːʃən]　安全保障措施

建筑技术与管理英语情景会话

safety code ['seifti koud] 安全操作规程
safety in operation ['seifti in ˌɔpə'reiʃən] 安全操作
labour safety ['leibə 'seifti] 劳动安全
labour protection ['leibə prə'tekʃən] 劳动保护
labour insurance ['leibə in'ʃuərəns] 劳动保险
site security [sait si'kjuəriti] 现场安全措施
construction sign [kən'strʌkʃən sain] 施工标志
safe and sound ['seif ənd saund] 安然无恙
labour protective supervision 劳动保护监督
['leibə prə'tektiv ˌsju:pə'viʒən]
construction safety regulations 施工安全规则
[kən'strʌkʃən 'seifti ˌregju'leiʃənz]
responsibility system of safety in production 安全生产责任制
[risˌpɔnsə'biliti 'sistəm əv 'seifti in prə'dʌkʃən]

2) Use the following **Labour Protection Appliances**（劳动保护用品）
to replace the black words in the following sentence:

Ford: Hello, chap. Why are you working under the scaffolds without a **safety helmet**?

福特：喂，小伙子。你在脚手架下干活怎么不戴安全帽呢？

Labour Protection Appliances 劳动保护用品
['leibə prə'tekʃən ə'plaiənsiz]
safety belt ['seifti belt] 安全带
safety helmet ['seifti 'helmit] 安全帽
safety lamp ['seifti læmp] 安全灯
safety catch ['seifti kætʃ] 安全挡
safety chain ['seifti tʃein] 安全链
protective clothing [prə'tektiv 'klouðiŋ] 安全服
gloves/mitten [glʌvz 'mitn] 手套；连指手套
sleevelets ['sli:vlits] 袖头
hazardous work ['hæzədəs wə:k] 危险性作业
hot-line work [hɔt lain wə:k] 带电作业

working on high ['wə:kiŋ ɔn hai] 高空作业
hydrant ['haidrənt] 消防龙头
fire extinguisher ['faiə iks'tiŋgwiʃə] 灭火器
remote control apparatus [ri'mout kən'troul ˌæpə'reitəs] 遥控装置
fire-extinguishing implement ['faiə iks'tiŋgwiʃiŋ 'implimənt] 消防用具
fire prevention measures ['faiə pri'venʃən 'meʒəz] 防火措施
working at high temperature ['wə:kiŋ ət hai 'tempəritʃə] 高温作业
working at low temperature ['wə:kiŋ ət lou 'tempəritʃə] 低温作业
health protection measures [helθ prə'tekʃən 'meʒəz] 保健措施
spraying of foam-agent solution 喷洒泡沫溶液
['spreiiŋ əv foum 'eidʒənt sə'lju:ʃən]

Situational Dialogic Unit 23
第二十三情景对话单元

Learn to Speak English

Talking about Visiting a Worksite

Visitor: Are you a builder, sir?

Builder: Yes, I'm a Chinese builder.

Visitor: I'm glad to see you on the site.

Builder: So am I, Can I help you, sir?

Visitor: Yes, of course. I'd like to visit your worksite. I called yesterday.

Builder: Welcome to our site, my friends!

Visitor: Thank you. I'm a civil engineer in a local building company and also in charge of construction, and they're all my foremen. We came here to learn from you.

Builder: I'm site director. We should learn from each other, make up each other's deficiencies.

Visitor: Right, We certainly do. Could you please give us a brief introduction to this project first?

Builder: All right. It's what I mean. The project is designed by Chinese designers, that we're building is a concrete reinforced structure with an area of 60,000 square metres.

Visitor: It's a large project. The designing is with a specific style and also with traditional style. When can you complete it?

Builder: In accordance with the contract period, it must be completed by end of this year.

Visitor: Time of executive work is too emergent! And then how about your construction progress?

Builder: Quite well. The main structure has been finished within nine months, two months ahead of schedule, meanwhile water-proofing and plastering works are to be finished by next month.

Visitor: How fast you're doing! Look at you with new eyes! And how too far behind to catch up with you!

建筑技术与管理英语情景会话

学说英语

谈论参观一家工地

参观者：先生，您是一位建筑工人吗？
建设者：是的，我是一位中国建筑工人。
参观者：我很高兴在这家建筑工地见到您。
建设者：我也一样。我能为你效劳吗？
参观者：当然能，我想参观一下你们的工地，昨天预约过。
建设者：欢迎你们光临，朋友们！
参观者：谢谢。我是当地一家建筑公司的土木工程师，也是搞施工的，他们都是我手下的工长。我们前来贵地是向你们学习的。
建设者：我是工地主任。我们应该互相学习，取长补短才对。
参观者：对，应该这样。你能先给我们把这一工程作一简单介绍吗？
建设者：那好吧，这也正是我的意思。正在建设中的这一工程是由中国设计师设计的，钢筋混凝土结构，有60,000平方米。
参观者：是项大工程。设计很独特，又具有传统特点。那何时能竣工？
建设者：根据合同期，必须在今年底竣工。
参观者：工期很紧呀！那么你们的施工进度怎样？
建设者：还行吧。主体工程在九个月内已完成，比原计划提前了两个月，同时防水工程以及抹灰工程预计在下月底也要完成。
参观者：你们的施工进度可真快呀！真叫人刮目相看，望尘莫及！

Builder: No, I wouldn't say that. As a few of then hasn't been finished yet, for example, eighty-five percent of the plumbing and electrical works has been finished and one-thirds of the interior decorative works has been finished, too.

Visitor: Don't worry. According to construction schedule, you're sure the whole project can be completed within eleven months, thirteen days ahead of schedule. But I don't understand what construction method you adopt, Chinese brothers?

Builder: Oh, flyover crossing construction method. Won't you go and see them with your eyes?

Visitor: Of course not. What's the flyover crossing construction, I'd love to know?

Builder: Follow me, please. To make a long story short, flyover crossing construction is that constructs alternately.

Visitor: Oh! Hit the nail on the head, I understand indeed.

Builder: Look! This office-building and those married quarters have been completed already for many months.

Visitor: Very good. And what building are you building there?

Builder: A Culture Palace, where we're going to pay a visit.

Visitor: Oh, great! The main structure is ready. And quality is quite nice, too. We've really learned a lot today and are very proud of Chinese builders.

Builder: Thank you for your praise. We came to construct in your country and to guarantee quality, quantity and progress of project is our repulation.

Visitor: Oh, I'm pleased to hear this and it's a pleasure to have an opportunity to visit your site and listen to your explanations. See you again, sir.

Builder: See you, brothers!

建筑技术与管理英语情景会话

建设者：不，我倒不这么想。因为还有一些工程量尚未完成，比如水电工程才完成 85%，室内装饰工程才完成三分之一。

参观者：别着急。按计划，整个工程肯定在 11 个月内能完成，还能提前 30 天。但我弄不明白你们究竟采用什么施工方法，我的中国兄弟？

建设者：啊，立体交叉施工法。你们难道不想亲眼看看吗？

参观者：那能不去呢。我还想知道什么是立体交叉施工？

建设者：请随我来。长话短说吧，立体交叉施工就是交叉施工。

参观者：啊！一语道破，我这才恍然大悟。

建设者：瞧！这些是在数月前已经完工的办公大楼和家属楼。

参观者：很不错！那儿正在建造的是什么建筑物？

建设者：文化宫，是我们就要去参观的工程。

参观者：啊，真棒！主体已经建起。而且质量也不错。我们今天的确学到许多东西，也为中国建筑工人而自豪。

建设者：多谢你们的夸奖。我们来贵国施工，保质、保量、保进度是我们的信誉。

参观者：哦，很荣幸有机会参观贵工地并聆听你的讲解。先生，再见！

建设者：再见，兄弟们！

Explanatory Notes 注释：

1. site 的意思是"（建筑）工地，现场"等，通常在 site 前面用介词 on，其原因是 site 表示一个较大而又宽广的地方。site 也可用作动词，意思是……的地点。

2. worksite 的意思是"工地，工作场地或工作现场"，是建筑英语中最常用的词语。注意：规范的英语把 work 和 site 连在一起拼写，即 worksite。

3. building site 表示"建筑工地"，也可解释为"工地"之意，也是最普通而又最常见建筑的词语。

4. construction site 一般译为"施工现场"或"建筑工地"均可。

5. 介词 on 用于 worksite，building site 和 construction site 前，因为这三个短语中都有 site。site 前用 on，所以这三个短语前也应用 on。这三个短语虽意思相似，但在使用时应根据其词意进行选择，这一点也必须说明。

Spoken Practice 口语练习

1. Pair Work:

Supposing A acts a foreman, B acts a visitor who is visiting a worksite. Try to say what A is introducing to B and what construction method B is anxious to know.

2. Tell "true" or "false" in accordance with Learn to Speak English:

1) ( ) Please give us a brief introduction of this project.
2) ( ) In accordance with the contract period, the whole project must be completed at end of next year.
3) ( ) Eighty-five percent of main structural works has been finished.
4) ( ) We adopt the method of flyover crossing construction.
5) ( ) To have an opportunity to visit your site is a pleasure.

3. Read & Interpret the following Passage:

A Busy Worksite

This is a construction site of Huashan Building Engineering Corporation. Materials here are in good order and the site is very clean.

Some tall tower-cranes are standing on the site. Many apartment houses have been completed already. A large multi-storey building is under construction.

Crane-drivers are operating their cranes to lift building materials. The mortar mixers are mixing sand mortar. Many groups of bricklayers on the tall scaffolds are laying concrete brick walls. Plumbers are laying water-pipes. All the builders on the worksite are busy with their work.

4. Put the Following into English:

工地上两种关键人物

施工现场最关键的两种人是承包商代理人和普通工人,但他们各自的职责有所不同。承包商代理人之所以重要是因为他拥有承包商的权利,并在现场代表承包商行使其职责。普通工人的重要则在于建筑工地上的绝大多数工作都是由数以百计的普通工人承担并完成的。

5. Substitute the Following Words & Expressions:

1) Use the following **Building Construction** (建筑施工) to replace the black words in the following sentence:

Visitor: Time of executive work is too emergent! And then how about your **construction progress**?

参观者：工期很紧呀！那么你们的**施工进度**怎样？

Building Construction ['bildiŋ kən'strʌkʃən] 建筑施工
construction technique [kən'strʌkʃən tek'niːk] 施工技术
building site ['bildiŋ sait] 建筑工地
site instruction [sait in'strʌkʃən] 现场指令
site organizations [sait ˌɔːgənai'zeiʃənz] 工地组织
ground breaking [graund 'breikiŋ] 破土（动工）
leveling of site ['levəliŋ əv sait] 工地抄平
survey of site [sə(ː)'vei əv sait] 工地测量
stake [steik] 放线桩
sitting ['saitiŋ] 定位，定线
site supervision [sait ˌsuːpə'viʒən] 现场管理
site selection [sait si'lekʃən] 选址
site exploration [sait ˌeksplɔː'reiʃən] 场地勘探，工地调查
specification [ˌspesifi'keiʃən] 施工说明
construction sign [kən'strʌkʃən sain] 施工标志
site facilities [sait fə'silitiz] 工地设备
site clean-up [sait kliːn ʌp] 工地清理
site installations [sait ˌinstə'leiʃənz] 工地设施
site road [sait roud] 施工道路
site office [sait 'ɔfis] 工地办公室
barracks ['bærəks] 工房
site canteen [sait kæn'tiːn] 工地食堂
field laboratory [fiːld lə'bɔrətəri] 工地试验室
completion [kəm'pliːʃən] 竣工
completion ceremony [kəm'pliːʃən 'seriməni] 落成典礼

2) Use the following **Construction Organization and Management** (施工组织与管理) to replace the black words in the following sentence:

Visitor: Don't worry. According to construction schedule, you're sure the whole project can be completed within eleven months, thirteen days ahead of schedule. But I don't understand what **construction method** you adopt, Chinese brothers?

参观者：别着急。按计划，整个工程肯定在 11 个月内能完成，还能提前 30 天。但我弄不明白你们究竟采用什么**施工方法**，我的中国兄弟？

Construction Organization and Management 施工组织与管理
[kənˈstrʌkʃən ˌɔːgənaiˈzeiʃən ənd ˈmænidʒmənt]

construction management ［kənˈstrʌkʃən ˈmænidʒmənt］施工管理

site test ［sait test］现场试验

site preparation ［sait ˌprepəˈreiʃən］现场准备

flow production / process ［flou prəˈdʌkʃən ˈprouses］流水作业

crossing construction ［ˈkrɔsiŋ kənˈstrʌkʃən］交叉作业

arrangement of construction ［əˈreindʒmənt əv kənˈstrʌkʃən］施工布置

preparation of construction ［ˌprepəˈreiʃən əv kənˈstrʌkʃən］施工准备

progress of construction ［ˈprougres əv kənˈstrʌkʃən］施工进度计划

flyover / overhead crossing construction 立体交叉施工法/作业
［flaiˈouvə ˈouvəhed ˈkrɔsiŋ kənˈstrʌkʃən］

supervision of works ［ˌsjuːpəˈviʒən əv wəːks］工程管理

treating obstacles and leveling the ground 处理障碍物与平整场地
［ˈtriːtiŋ ˈɔbstəklz ənd ˈlevəliŋ ðə graund］

Situational Dialogic Unit 24
第二十四情景对话单元

Do you know what items the claim mainly includes?

It mainly includes technical issues, financial problems, materials, machines, manpower and so forth.

Learn to Speak English

Talking about Claims of Works

David: I would like to know what claim is? Can you explain it to me, Mrs. Cao?

Caole: Surely. First of all, we would like to make it clear that the claim is quite normal things in construction field. It's just like a person who makes mistakes and they can be corrected from time to time.

David: So then. Claim is correcting mistakes of the loss fact which costs. Is my comprehension right?

Caole: Basic meaning is right, I think.

David: Do you know what items the claim mainly includes?

Caole: Let me think. It mainly includes technical issues, financial problems, materials, machines, manpower and so forth.

David: Please give me an example about technical issue, OK?

Caole: OK. Technical issues are delay of issuing working drawings, delay of reply technical clarification request, non-conformance between drawing and specification.

David: This's a technical claim. What about financial claim?

Caole: Oh. It belongs to delay of progress payment and the fluctuation of exchange rates between U. S. dollars and local currency.

David: I quite understand this. And what's the claim procedure?

Caole: The claim procedure is quite complex. Usually it has three steps.

David: What's the first, Mrs. Cao?

Caole: The claim has to be submitted within 14 days regulated in the condition of Contract.

David: First is time period. What's the second?

Caole: The bill for the cost of the claim should be submitted within 30 days after the first instruction.

David: Second is the bill for the claim cost. Third?

Caole: The further analysis of the claim must be submitted within 14 days.

学说英语

谈论工程索赔

大　卫：我想知道什么叫索赔，您能给我解释一下吗，曹女士？

曹　乐：当然能！首先，我们得清楚这点，对于建筑行业来说，索赔是一件很正常的事情，这就好比一个人，总会做错一些事，需要不时地加以纠正才能完善一样。

大　卫：原来是这么一回事。索赔就是对纠正过失产生费用的索取，这样理解对吗？

曹　乐：我觉得基本是这个意思。

大　卫：您知道索赔主要包括哪些项目吗？

曹　乐：让我想一想。索赔主要包括技术问题、财务问题、材料问题、机械问题、人工等方面的费用问题。

大　卫：请给我举一个技术方面的实例行吗？

曹　乐：行。技术问题就是延误颁发施工图纸，不及时回答技术核校单，以及图纸和规范相互矛盾等方面的问题。

大　卫：这就是技术索赔。什么是财务问题？

曹　乐：哦，财务问题属于延误拨发工程进度款以及因美元与当地货币的汇率差浮动所引起索赔方面的问题。

大　卫：我明白这点。而索赔的程序是什么？

曹　乐：索赔的程序比较复杂。通常分三步。

大　卫：第一步是什么，曹女士？

曹　乐：就是要把索赔通知书在合同规定的14天时间之内必须递交上。

大　卫：第一步是时间有效期限。第二步呢？

曹　乐：是在递交索赔通知书后，30天时间之内应递交索赔费用账单，并提出需要索赔的金额。

大　卫：第二步应该是索赔的金额。第三步？

曹　乐：是在14天内必须递交索赔更详细的分析资料。

David: Third is the further analysis of the claim. I think the three steps are very important.

Caole: Yes. The procedures and time period of the claim are very clear. I have one thing to be pointed out.

David: What's that, Mrs. Cao?

Caole: All the records and reports should be with signatures by both sides.

David: I see. This decision will be final. So it'll take a long time, perhaps two or three months.

Caole: Yes, it's in maximum and also normal case.

David: Oh, what a complex procedure it is!

Caole: Yes, It's a necessary regular procedure in the Contract.

David: Right. Only in this procedure may claim be success. What time can the total compensation of the claim entitled to be received?

Caole: In accordance with the Condition of Contract, within 60 days after receiving. The further material for convincing of the claim, the engineer informs the contractor of the final decision of the claim after consultant with the employer.

David: I see. And how about materials claim?

Caole: If your claim is reasonable, we'll effect a full settlement of yours.

David: I'm very glad to learn claims knowledge from you.

Caole: I'm deeply moved that you have got such knowledge.

David: Thank you for you instruction, Mrs. Cao.

Caole: Don't mention it!

大　卫：第三步是递交资料期限。这三步的确都很重要。
曹　乐：是的。索赔的程序和时效已讲清楚了,我还有一点要指出。
大　卫：这一点是什么,曹女士?
曹　乐：那就是所有的记录和报告都应该经双方人员验收签字。
大　卫：我明白啦。这才是最后结论。所以从开始提出索赔到作出结论总共要用很长时间,也许两三个月吧。
曹　乐：是的,这是按正常程序进行索赔的最长期限。
大　卫：啊,结论的确是一个复杂的程序呀!
曹　乐：是的,这是合同所规定的必要的程序。
大　卫：对。只有采用这种程序,索赔才能成功。什么时候才能收到此项索赔的总金额呢?
曹　乐：根据合同条款,在收到该项索赔的进一步证明材料后一般在60天内,工程师会同业主协商,待此项索赔的最后决定后才通知承包商。
大　卫：我明白了。那材料索赔呢?
曹　乐：假如你们的索赔是合理的,对于你提出的要求,我们将予以解决。
大　卫：我很高兴,从你们这里学到了索赔方面的知识。
曹　乐：你对索赔知识的虚心讨教,使我深感心慰。
大　卫：多谢你的教诲,曹女士。
曹　乐：没什么!

Spoken Practice 口语练习

1. **Pair Work:**

   Granting that A is a supervising engineer, B is a resident engineer. They are talking about how to solve the problem of manpower and materials claims.

2. **Tell "true" or "false" in accordance with Learn to Speak English:**

   1) (   ) The claim is just like a person who often makes mistakes and it needs to be corrected.

   2) (   ) The final decision will take less than 100 days from submitting claims.

   3) (   ) The fluctuation of exchange rates between US dollars and local currency belongs to financial claims.

   4) (   ) The claim procedure usually has five steps at least.

   5) (   ) All the records and reports should be without signatures by both sides except the essential claim procedures.

3. **Read & Interpret the Following Passage:**

   ### Claim for Damage by Fire

   Dear Sirs,

     I regret to report that a fire broke out in the site stores last night. The cause isn't known yet, but we estimate the damage of the stock to be about US＄85,989. Luckily, no records were destroyed so that there will be no difficulty in assessing the value of the loss.

     Please arrange for your representative to call as soon as possible and let me have your instructions regarding salvage.

   Yours faithfully,

4. **Read and Learn the Following Useful Homophones by Heart:**

homophone	Pronunciation	homophone	homophone	Pronunciation	homophone
are 是	[ɑː]	ah 啊	lesson 功课	[ˈlesn]	lessen 减少
air 空气	[ɛə]	heir 继承人	meet 遇见	[miːt]	meat 肉

续表

homophone	Pronunciation	homophone	homophone	Pronunciation	homophone
aunt 伯母	[aːnt]	ant 蚂蚁	no 不	[nou]	know 知道
be 是	[biː]	bee 蜜蜂	not 不是	[nɔt]	knot 结
buy 买	[bai]	by 靠近	pear 梨	[pɛə]	pair 一对
cell 细胞	[sel]	sell 卖	peace 和平	[piːs]	piece 一片
dear 亲爱的	[diə]	deer 鹿	right 右边	[rait]	write 写
father 父亲	[ˈfaːðə]	farther 更远	sale 出售	[seil]	sail 航行
flour 面粉	[ˈflauə]	flower 花	see 看见	[siː]	sea 海
four 四	[fɔː]	for 为	sun 太阳	[sʌn]	son 儿子
hear 听见	[hiə]	here 这里	tale 故事	[teil]	tail 尾巴
I 我	[ai]	eye 眼	there 那里	[ðɛə]	their 他们的
our 我们的	[ˈauə]	hour 小时	week 星期	[wiːk]	weak 弱的
night 夜间	[nait]	knight 骑士	whole 所有的	[houl]	hole 洞

5. Substitute the Following Words & Expressions：

Use the following **Claim Terms**（索赔术语）to replace the black words in the following sentence：

David：So then. **Claim** is correcting mistakes of the loss fact which costs. Is my comprehension right?

大卫：原来是这么一回事。**索赔**就是对纠正过失产生费用的索取，这样理解对吗？

Claim Terms ［kleim təːmz］ 索赔术语

claim for compensation ［kleim fɔːˌkɔmpenˈseiʃən］ 要求索赔
compensation ［ˌkɔmpenˈseiʃən］ 索赔费
cause for claim ［kɔːz fɔː kleim］ 索赔原因
quantity claim ［ˈkwɔntiti kleim］ 数量索赔
refusing / rejecting a claim ［riˈfjuːziŋ riˈdʒektiŋ ə kleim］ 拒绝索赔
waiving/dropping claim ［ˈweiviŋ ˈdrɔpiŋ kleim］ 放弃索赔
accepting a claim ［əkˈseptiŋ ə kleim］ 接受索赔
granting a claim ［ˈgraːntiŋ ə kleim］ 承诺索赔

meeting/satisfying a claim ['miːtiŋ 'sætisfaiiŋ ə kleim] 满足索赔
clearing up a claim ['kliəriŋ ʌp ə kleim] 清理索赔
claim for losses [kleim fɔː 'lɔːsiz] 索赔损失
settling a claim ['setliŋ ə kleim] 理赔
compensatory damages [kəm'penseitəri 'dæmidʒz] 损失的赔偿额
compensating fully/partly ['kɔmpenseitiŋ 'fuli 'paːtli] 全部/部分索赔
unreasonable claim [ʌn'riːznəbl kleim] 不合理的索赔
claim sheet [kleim ʃiːt] 索赔清单
notice of claim ['noutis əv kleim] 索赔通知
claim term of validity [kleim təːm əv və'liditi] 索赔时效
claimer/claimant ['kleimə 'kleimənt] 索赔人/者
compensator ['kɔmpenseitə] 赔偿人
claims adjuster [kleimz ə'dʒʌstə] 索赔理算人
claims settling agent [kleimz 'setliŋ 'eidʒənt] 索赔代理

Part Three
English Situational Conversations with Building Economic Managerial Personnel
(Situational Dialogic Unit 25-33)

第三部
建筑经济管理人员英语情景会话
（第二十五至三十三情景对话单元）

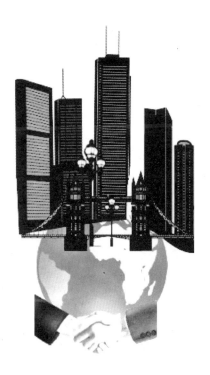

Situational Dialogic Unit 25
第二十五情景对话单元

Learn to Speak English

Talking about Accounting

Buddy: Can I ask you any questions about accounting, miss?
Kuaiji: Certainly. Go ahead, please.
Buddy: OK. Would you mind explaining what accounting is?
Kuaiji: There're a number of definitions of accounting at present.
Buddy: Is it true, miss?
Kuaiji: Yes. To some extent, accounting is a system to provide decision makers with information in business economic activities.
Buddy: What's the system, I don't know, miss?
Kuaiji: It is primarily financial information, stated in monetary terms.
Buddy: Well, so that's how it is! And what's the main purpose of accounting?
Kuaiji: Its main purpose is to provide and report financial information to interested users.
Buddy: Is this financial information so important to a user or an orgnization?
Kuaiji: Yes, of course. For instance, investors need financial data in order to compare protective investments. Especially computerized accounting system, it makes decision makers more and more rapid and efficient.
Buddy: I understand this kind of accounting definite. Could you give another example to me so as to understand accounting better?
Kuaiji: OK. Accounting, in the economic activity, using moneys as its main measurement and invoices and bills as its basis, applies variety of special methods to continuously, systematically and overall carry out economic calculation, and supply managing departments with requiring economic information in order to realize supervision and control in ecomomic moving course and an impotant way of the best management.
Buddy: I'm very delighted with your whole explaining. Thank you for your help.
Kuaiji: Not at all. If you need some help, please feel free to come as you like.
Buddy: Sure.

学说英语

谈论会计工作

巴　迪：小姐，能请教你有关会计方面相关问题吗？

会　计：当然能。请说吧。

巴　迪：那好吧。你能给我解释一下什么叫会计？

会　计：目前会计有多种定义。

巴　迪：小姐，是吗？

会　计：是的。在某种程度上讲，会计就是一种为决策者提供经济活动信息的系统。

巴　迪：小姐，我并不明白什么是系统？

会　计：用金融术语解释，系统就是基本的金融信息。

巴　迪：啊，原来如此。那会计的主要目的是什么？

会　计：会计的主要目的就是把金融信息提供并报告给感兴趣的用户。

巴　迪：这些金融信息对用户或团体至关重要吗？

会　计：那是自然的。比方说，为了比较，投资者们就需要金融数据，特别是电算化系统，使决策者越来越快捷，越有效。

巴　迪：我已清楚这种会计定义了。为了更好地了解会计，不知还能再列举一种定义吗？

会　计：能。会计是在经济活动中，以货币为主要量度，以凭证为依据，运用各种专门方法，连续地、系统地、全面地进行经济计算，提供管理所需要的经济信息，以实现对经济运行过程进行监督和最优化管理的一种重要手段。

巴　迪：对你的整个解释我非常满意。感谢你的帮助。

会　计：没什么。你有什么要帮助的话，请随时前来。

巴　迪：那是肯定的。

Explanatory Notes 注释：

1. account 动词（vt.）认为
   例如：They all account Xiao Wang a good young chap.
   他们都认为小王是个好小伙。
   account 动词（vi）account for 说出（钱的）用途
   例如：He accouted to his manager for the expenditure of this economic meeting. 他向经理汇报了这次经济工作会议的开支。

2. account 名词（n.）账；账目，账户，会计科目
   例如：Open / Close an account in the Construction Bank/ Bank of China.
   在建设银行/中国银行开立/结束账户
   a current account （略作 A/C 或 C/A）往来账户
   accounting 名词（n.）清算账目；会计学
   construction accounting 建筑企业会计
   accounting for joint ventures 合资企业会计
   accountant 名词（n.）会计
   accountant in charge 主管会计，会计主管员
   accountantship 会计职务
   I.O.U. 也可以写成 IOU，是"I owe you."的缩写，即"我欠你"的意思，相当于汉语"今借到""今欠"等意思。I.O.U. 用作名词，表示"欠条""借据""欠据"等。I.O.U. 的复数形式是 I.O.U.'S 或 IOU'S。

Spoken Practice 口语练习

1. **Pair Work:**

   Suppose A is a chief accountant of a Constrction Company, B is an accountant. They are talking about the accounting work that B and his fellows are doing.

2. **Tell "true" or "false" in accordance with Learn to Speak English:**

   1) (　) Accounting is one of the most important parts in Modern Building Industry.

   2) (　) Accounting is an information system that used in business economic activities.

   3) (　) The main purpose of accounting is to provide and report financial information to decision makers.

   4) (　) Computerized accounting systems are popular nowadays in the Building Industry.

   5) (　) Investors need financial data in order that they compare protective investments.

3. **Read & interpret the Following Passage:**

   ### What's Accounting?

   Accounting is the process of identifying, measuring and communicating economic information which permit the users (decision makers and businessmen) to make information judgements and decisions. This information is primarily financial, stated in monetary terms.

   Each profit seeking business organization that has economic resources, such as money, machinery and buildings, uses accounting information. For this reason, accounting is regarded as the language of business. During the twenty-first century, the globalization of world economy will spur the advance of accounting.

4. **Put the Following into English:**

今 借 到

公司财务科壹仟美元整。

郑浩

2002年6月8日

5. **Substitute the Following Words and Expressions:**

Use the following **Economic Managerial Personnel**（经济管理人员）
to replace the black words in the following sentence:

Kuaiji: Yes. To some extent, accounting is a system to provide **decision makers** with information in business economic activities.

会　计：真的。在某种程度上讲，会计就是一种为**决策者**提供经济
　　　　活动信息的系统。

Economic Managerial Personnel 经济管理人员
[ˌiːkəˈnɔmik ˌmænəˈdʒiəriəl ˌpəːsəˈnel]

chief economist [tʃiːfiː(ː)ˈkɔnəmist] 总经济师

economist [iː(ː)ˈkɔnəmist] 经济师，经济学家

chief accountant [tʃiːf əˈkauntənt] 总会计师

accountant-general [əˈkauntənt ˈdʒenərəl] 会计主任

certified public accountant [ˈsəːtifaid ˈpʌblik əˈkauntənt]（美）会计师

chartered accountant [ˈtʃaːtəd əˈkauntənt]（英）会计师

cashier [kæˈʃiə] 出纳员

accountant in charge [əˈkauntənt in tʃaːdʒ] 主管会计

budgeter/budgeteer [ˈbʌdʒitə ˌbʌdʒiˈtiə] 预算员

agent [ˈeidʒənt] 代理人/商

client [ˈklaiənt] 委托人

broker [ˈbroukə] 经纪人，中间人

quantity surveyor [ˈkwɔntiti sə(ː)ˈveiə] 估价（算）师

statist/statistician [ˈsteitist ˌstætisˈtiʃən] 统计员/学家

auditor [ˈɔːditə] 审计员，查账人

Situational Dialogic Unit 26
第二十六情景对话单元

Learn to Speak English

Talking about Opening a Bank Account

Lewis: May I help you, sir?

Jinxin: Yes, I hope so. I'd like to open a bank account.

Lewis: OK. Which category of accounts are you interested in opening?

Jinxin: I'm not sure. But can you tell me something about your banking facilities?

Lewis: Certainly. We usually accept deposits, handle variety of settling accounts, grant mortgages and provide services for letters of credit or credit card, etc.

Jinxin: I see, miss. I'm an accountant and work in CCIEC (the Chinese Construction Installation Engineering Corporation).

Lewis: An accountant! You want to open a bank account for your corporation, isn't that right?

Jinxin: That's right. Opening a current account for our corporation.

Lewis: No problem. Ours is an International Bank. We can do everything that customers want. Will you please fill out this signature card first?

Jinxin: OK. (a few minutes late) Here you are.

Lewis: Let me have a look and how you filled it out?

Jinxin: How do you think of it? Is it OK?

Lewis: It's OK. This is your account number and empty checking. Please look after them carefully.

Jinxin: Thank you for your reminding, I must.

Lewis: You're welcome.

学说英语

谈论开立银行账户

刘易斯：先生，我能为您效劳吗？

金　鑫：是的，希望如此。我想开立个银行账户。

刘易斯：好的。你想开那种账户？

金　鑫：我并不十分肯定。但你能告诉我贵行的相关服务项目吗？

刘易斯：当然能。我们通常的服务项目包括：接受存款，办理各种结算业务，发放抵押贷款，为信用证和信用卡提供服务等。

金　鑫：我明白啦。小姐，我是中建安司（中国建筑安装工程总公司）的一名会计。

刘易斯：一名会计！你想给贵公司开一个银行账户，对吗？

金　鑫：对呀！就是给公司开一个往来账户。

刘易斯：没问题。我们银行是一家国际银行，我们为客户所急，替客户所想。请先填写这份签字卡好吗？

金　鑫：好啊！（几分钟过后）给你签字卡。

刘易斯：让我看看填得怎样。

金　鑫：怎么样？可以吗？

刘易斯：很好。这是你的账号和空白支票，请妥当保管。

金　鑫：谢谢您的提醒，我一定保管得好。

刘易斯：没什么。

Explanatory Notes 注释：

1. 国际银行票据的金额一般先用文字表达，然后再用阿拉伯数字表示，例如：Pay to Dollars One hundred Eighty-five and Cents thirty-four Only（＄185,34/00）

2. 在日常生活中表示带有角、分零数的金额，一般用阿拉伯数字表示，例如：5 美元 89 美分，一般写作 US＄5.89，而不写为 five dollars and eighty-nine cents。

建筑经济管理人员英语情景会话

Spoken Practice 口语练习

1. **Pair Work:**

    A is a clerk in a bank, B is an accountant who wants to open a current account for his corporation. Use following expressions:

    A: *Can I help you...?*
    B: *Yes, I'd like to...*
    A: *What's your...?*
    B: *I'm... but...*

2. **Tell "true" or "false" in accordance with Learn to Speak English:**

    1) (　) I'd like to open a new savings account for my enterprise.
    2) (　) He's a manager and work in the Chinese Construction Installation Engineering Corporation.
    3) (　) You want to open a current account for your company.
    4) (　) Here is your account number and empty checking, sir.
    5) (　) Our bank is a Construction Bank, not a Bank of Communications.

3. **Read & interpret the Following Passage:**

    Opening an Account

    If you go to a bank to open an account, you would probably go through most of the following procedures. First you would go to the New Accounts Department and fill out a signature card. Then you would have to furnish proof of your identity in order to open an account. You would need to have a permanent address in the city, and you would also be asked to supply the name of a permanent resident who is willing to recommend you. And last but not least, you would need to bring some cash with you in order to open your account. Many banks require a minimum cash deposit of $100.

4. **Put the Following into English:**

今　收　到

郑浩先生交来壹仟美元整。

公司财务科
经手人 约翰·史密斯
2002 年 6 月 18 日

5. Substitute the Following Words and Expressions：

1) Use the following **Kinds of Bank**（银行种类）to replace the black words in the following sentence：

Lewis：No problem. Ours is an **International Bank.** We can do everything that customers want. Will you please fill out this signature card first?

刘易斯：没问题。我们银行是一家**国际银行**，我们为客户所急，替客户所想。请先填写这份签字卡好吗？

Kinds of Bank ［kaindz ɔv bæŋk］银行种类

The Bank of World ［ðə bæŋk ɔv wə:ld］世界银行

overseas bank ［'ouvə'si:z bæŋk］国外银行

The People's Bank of China 中国人民银行

［ðə 'pi:plz bæŋk ɔv 'tʃainə］

Import & Export Bank ［im'pɔ:t ənd eks'pɔ:t bæŋk］进出口银行

Bank of China ［bæŋk ɔv 'tʃainə］中国银行

China Construction Bank ［'tʃainə kən'strʌkʃən bæŋk］中国建设银行

Investment Bank ［in'vestmənt bæŋk］投资银行

Industrial & Commercial Bank of China 中国工商银行

［in'dʌstriəl ənd kə'mə:ʃəl bæŋk ɔv 'tʃainə］

Bank of Communications ［bæŋk ɔv kə,mju:ni'keiʃəns］交通银行

exchange bank ［iks'tʃeindʒ bæŋk］汇兑银行

local bank ［'loukəl bæŋk］地方银行

domestic bank ［də'mestik bæŋk］国内银行

branch bank ［brɑ:ntʃ bæŋk］银行分行

sub-branch bank ［sʌb'brɑːntʃ bæŋk］银行支行
self-service bank ［'self 'səːvis bæŋk］自助/无人银行
savings bank/bank of deposit ［'seiviŋz bæŋk bæŋk əv di'pɔzit］储蓄所
money market ［'mʌni 'mɑːkit］金融市场
credit cooperative ［'kredit kou'ɔpərətiv］信用合作社
trust company ［trʌst 'kʌmpəni］信托公司
stock market ［stɔk 'mɑːkit］证券市场

2）Use the following **kinds of Opening an Account**（开立账户种类）
   to replace the black words in the following sentence：
Jinxin：That's right. **Opening a current account** for our corporation.
金鑫：对呀！就是给公司开一个往来账户。

kinds of Opening a Banking Account 开立银行账户种类
［**kaindz əf 'oupəniŋ ə bæŋkiŋ ə'kaunt**］
government account ［'gʌvənmənt ə'kaunt］政府账户
clearance account ［'kliərəns ə'kaunt］清算账户
resident account ［'rezidənt ə'kaunt］居民账户
current account ［'kʌrənt ə'kaunt］活期账户
fixed account ［'fikst ə'kaunt］定期账户
savings deposit ［'seiviŋz di'pɔzit］储蓄存款
checking account ［'tʃekiŋ ə'kaunt］开支票账户
petty current account ［'peti 'kʌrənt ə'kaunt］小额活期存款
current savings account ［'kʌrənt seiviŋz ə'kaunt］活期储蓄存款
current account/ demand deposit 活期存款
　［'kʌrənt ə'kaunt di'mɑːnd di'pɔzit］
savings account/deposit account 定期存款
　［'seiviŋz ə'kaunt di'pɔzit ə'kaunt］
deposit by various institutions & social groups 机关团体存款
　［di'pɔzit bai 'vɛəriəs ˌinsti'tjuːʃənz ənd 'souʃəl gruːps］

Situational Dialogic Unit 27
第二十七情景对话单元

Learn to Speak English

Talking about Money Exchange

Charles: Excuse me, Please tell me which counter I can exchange my money, miss?

Cashier: At the foreign exchange counter, it's here.

Charles: Oh, What a happy coincidence! I'm very luck!

Cashier: What currency do you want to exchange, sir?

Charles: Britain Pound for American dollar.

Cashier: How much do you want to exchange?

Charles: Only one thousand. What's the exchange rate today?

Cashier: One moment, please. Let me check it for you. The rate today is 1.3 dollars to 1 pound.

Charles: OK. Please exchange it for me.

Cashier: How would you like it?

Charles: Let me think it over. Please give me 100 dollars in fives and 50 dollars in sevens and 10 dollars in tens and the others in 1 dollar.

Cashier: I see. Just a mimute, please. Here you are, sir. Please account them.

Charles: For you counted just now, I don't think it is necessary.

Cashier: Quite so. But money should be well counted as soon as you get it, otherwise it's irresponsible.

Charles: OK. Let me count it! It's just enough. Sorry to bother you. I wonder whether you could change me any coins?

Cashier: Certainly, you can. What's it for, I'd like to know?

Charles: It's for long distance phone call fee or by bus fare.

Cashier: Which do you prefer, copper or silver?

Charles: Silver is better.

Cashier: OK. Silver.

Charles: Thank you.

Cashier: Don't mention it. This is my duty.

建筑技术与管理英语情景会话

学说英语

谈论货币兑换

查尔斯：对不起，小姐，请告诉我在哪个柜台兑换钱？
出纳员：在外币兑换处，就在这儿。
查尔斯：啊，太巧啦！我可真幸运！
出纳员：先生，您想兑换哪种货币？
查尔斯：想把英镑兑换成美元。
出纳员：想兑换多少钱？
查尔斯：仅兑1,000英镑。今天的汇率是多少？
出纳员：请等片刻，我给您查查。今天的汇率是1:1.3（1英镑兑换1美元30美分）。
查尔斯：好吧。请给我把这些钱兑换了吧。
出纳员：您想要多大面值的现金？
查尔斯：我想想吧。请给我兑换成100美元的五张，50美元的七张，10美元的十张，其余的兑换成1美元一张的面值就可以了。
出纳员：我知道了。请稍等片刻。先生，这是给您兑换的钱，请点一下吧。
查尔斯：我想没有必要吧，你刚点过。
出纳员：是这样，但钱应该当面点清，过后不管。
查尔斯：好吧，我数一数。啊！正好无误。对不起麻烦一下。不知你能否给我兑换些硬币？
出纳员：当然可以，但我想知道你兑换硬币有何用？
查尔斯：是用来打长途电话或乘公交车。
出纳员：您喜欢哪种货币，铜币还是银币？
查尔斯：银币比较好。
出纳员：好吧，银币。
查尔斯：谢谢。
出纳员：不客气。这是我的职责。

建筑经济管理人员英语情景会话

Spoken Practice 口语练习

1. **Pair Work:**

    A is a woman teller in a bank, B is an accountant in a building company and wants to exchange some Pula for US $. B asks A what rate of exchange today is...?

2. **Tell "true" or "false" in accordance with Learn to Speak English:**

    1) (　) I want to convert pound into American dollar.

    2) (　) Please give me five-hundred dollars bill and others in 1 dollar.

    3) (　) The rate today is one dollars to 1.3 pound.

    4) (　) I wonder whether you could change me any notes?

    5) (　) I prefer copper coin to silver one.

3. **Read & interpret the Following Passage:**

    The Money Systems of United States and Great Britain

    Governments of different countries issue paper money and metal money. Each government decides on a money unit and its standard of value, usually this standard is gold or silver.

    In 1785, the Congress of the United States chose dollar as the unit of currency and the decimal system as the basic method of counting. One American dollar is equal to 100 cents or pennies. The word in the United States '**bill**' is used to refer to paper money.

    In 1971, Great Britain converted its currency to the decimal system. The pound is the basic monetary unit, it is made up of 100 pennies or pence (1 pound = 100 pennis). In Great Britain the word 'note' is used to refer to paper money.

4. **Substitute the Following Words and Expressions:**

    1) Use the following **Terms about Currency**（货币术语）to replace the black words in the following sentence:

    Charles: Only one thousand. What's **the exchange rate** today?

    查尔斯：仅兑1000英镑。今天的汇率是多少？

    Terms about Currency [tə:mz əˈbaut ˈkʌrənsi] 货币术语

foreign exchange ['fɔrin iks'tʃeindʒ] 外汇
exchange table [iks'tʃeindʒ 'teibl] 汇兑换算表
rate of exchange [reit əv iks'tʃeindʒ] 汇价/汇率
current exchange ['kʌrənt iks'tʃeindʒ] 现行汇率
buying rate ['baiiŋ reit] 银行买入价
selling rate ['seliŋ reit] 银行卖出价
floating rate ['floutiŋ reit] 浮动汇率
settlement of exchange ['setlmənt əv iks'tʃeindʒ] 结汇
balance of exchange ['bæləns əv iks'tʃeindʒ] 外汇收支
foreign exchange market ['fɔrin iks'tʃeindʒ 'maːkit] 外汇市场
exchange fluctuation [iks'tʃeindʒ ˌflʌktju'eiʃən] 外汇浮动
total foreign exchange ['toutl 'fɔrin iks'tʃeindʒ] 外汇收支总额
exchange quotations [iks'tʃeindʒ kwou'teiʃənz] 外汇行情（挂牌）
exchange surrender certificate 外汇转移证
[iks'tʃeindʒ sə'rendə sə'tifikit]

2）Use the following **Main Moneys of the World**（世界主要货币）to replace the black words in the following sentence：

Cashier：What **currency** do you want to exchange, miss?

出纳员：小姐，您想兑换哪种**货币**?

Charles：**Britain Pound** for **American dollar.**

查尔斯：想把**英镑**兑换成**美元**。

Main Moneys of the World [mein 'mʌniz əv ðə wɔːld] 世界主要货币

Symbol/Abbreviation	Name of Currency	Country or Place	货币名称	使用货币的国家或地区
RMB/¥	yuan [yuæn]	China	人民币元	中国
GBP/£	pound [paund]	U. K.	镑	英国
USD/$	dollar ['dɔlə]	U. S. A.	元	美国
FF	france [frɑːns]	France	（新）法郎	法国
DEM	mark [mɑːk]	German	马克	德国
HK $	dollar ['dɔlə]	Hong Kong	（港）元	香港

续表

Symbol/Abbreviation	Name of Currency	Country or Place	货币名称	使用货币的国家或地区
JP/¥	yen [jen]	Japan	日 元	日 本
Lit	lira [ˈlirə] /lire [ˈliri]	Italy	里 拉	意大利
F.（Fl）	florin [ˈflɔrin]	Netherlands	盾	荷 兰
Mex $	peso [ˈpeisou]	Mexico	比 索	墨西哥
R	rand [rænd]	South Africa	兰 特	南 非
KSH	shilling [ˈʃiliŋ]	Kenya	肯先令	肯尼亚
S/	sol [sɔl]	Peru	索 尔	秘 鲁
SEK	krona [ˈkrounə]	Sweden	克 郎	瑞 典
Rs	rupee [ruˈpiː]	India	印卢比	印 度
R	rouble [ˈroubl]	Russion	卢 布	俄罗斯
P	Pula [ˈpulaː]	Botswana	普 拉	博茨瓦纳
ID	dinar [ˈdiːnaː]	Iraq	第纳尔	伊拉克
EUR	Euro [ˈjuərou]	Europe	欧 元	欧 洲

Explanatory Notes 注释：

1. EUR（欧元）是欧盟的货币单位，现已在德国、法国、意大利等绝大多数欧洲国家通用。

2. $（元），美国元（US.$）、加拿大元（CA.$）、澳大利亚元（$A.）、新西兰元（NZ.$）等国的货币单位。

3. £（镑）是爱尔兰，马耳他，苏丹，英国等国的货币单位。

4. Din（第纳尔）是伊拉克、阿尔及利亚等国的货币单位。

5. F.（法郎）是法国，比利时（BF.），瑞士（SF.）等国的货币单位。

6. s 或 sh（先令）是坦桑尼亚，肯尼亚等国的货币单位；英国原货币单位；美国早期货币单位。

7. Kr（克郎），瑞典（SKr）、丹麦（DKr）、挪威（NKr）等国的货币单位。

Situational Dialogic Unit 28
第二十八情景对话单元

Learn to Speak English

Talking about Applying for and Using Credit Card

Jielun: May I get any information of the credit cards, miss?

Teller: Of courses, sir. You'd like to get a credit card, right?

Jielun: Yes. I work in a building company more than ten years, and I also have a steady income.

Teller: That's good. Anyone just like you have a good record and a steady income may apply for it.

Jielun: I see. But what's the use of it, I don't know clearly?

Teller: For the sake of convenience, if you buy whatever you need with it, don't carry any cash at all.

Jielun: That sounds quite good. But how can I pay for my expense if I use my card?

Teller: Well, There're three ways for you to be chosen.

Jielun: What's the first way to pay, miss?

Teller: You can pay for it as soon as you receive the bill.

Jielun: I see. That's first way to pay. Second?

Teller: The second way is that you can pay for your expenses a month later without any extra charge after you may receive a monthly bill.

Jielun: A month later without any extra charge. That's not bad. And third?

Teller: Third, you may even choose to make your payments over several months and pay only part of the total amount each month.

Jielun: OK. I see. I'd like to get a credit card, and how can I apply for it, miss?

Teller: Before you handle your application, there's one point to be emphasized.

Jielun: What's that, miss? Speak quickly, please.

Teller: A small service charge will be added to your total bill if you do third paying way. I think this point is very important for users to understand.

学说英语

谈论申请与使用信用卡

杰　伦：小姐，我可以了解些信用卡方面情况吗？
班克尔：当然可以。你想获得一张信用卡，对吗？
杰　伦：对。我在一家建筑公司工作了十年之久，有稳定的收入。
出纳员：那好。就像你这样有良好信誉记录和稳定收入的任何人都可以申请信用卡。
杰　伦：我明白了。但信用卡有何用处，我不十分清楚？
出纳员：是为了方便起见，如果你想用信用卡购买你所需的任何东西，根本无需携带现金。
杰　伦：那可真好。假如使用信用卡，我怎么支付我的消费？
出纳员：啊，有三种付款方式供你选用。
杰　伦：第一种方式是什么，小姐？
出纳员：你以收到你的消费账单后，即可支付。
杰　伦：我知道了。那只是支付消费的第一种方式。第二种呢？
出纳员：第二种方式则是在你收到每月消费账单后，你可以在一个月后支付它，不需额外交费。
杰　伦：一个月后支付消费还不需额外交费，那不错。第三种呢？
出纳员：第三种方式，你也可以几个月支付你的消费账单，每月只支付总额的一部分。
杰　伦：好，我清楚了。小姐，我想申请一个信用卡，但怎么申请呢？
出纳员：在你办理申请前，还有一点得强调。
杰　伦：是什么，小姐？请快点说吧。
出纳员：如果你以第三种方式消费的话，你的账单上就会加一笔数目不大的服务费。我觉得这一点对于用户来说很重要。

Jielun: Right. Thank you for giving me so much useful information.

Teller: With pleasure. I suggest you apply for a common one, the Great Wall card.

Jielun: OK. What should I do next, miss?

Teller: Fill in the application form first and then pay one thousand dollars as earnest money.

Jielun: OK. Angthing I should do?

Teller: Yes. If you get the card, you should be a guarantor together with your signed application form. This point must be emphrasised, too.

Jielun: I see. How much service fee should I pay?

Teller: For your common card, the yearly fee is US $ 20 dollars.

Jielun: OK. For the convience of consume, I'll apply for a common one.

Teller: Please wait a minute, I'll do it for you as quick as possible.

Jielun: Take your time, miss. I've patient in wait.

Teller: Thank you, sir. That's good.

杰　伦：对，感谢你给我提供了这么多有用的信息。

出纳员：很乐意。我建议你申请一种普通卡——长城卡就行了。

杰　伦：那好吧。小姐，下一步手续该咋办？

出纳员：先填写这份申请表，再交1,000美元的保证金。

杰　伦：好。还有什么手续要办的吗？

出纳员：是的。如果你领到信用卡，连同你签过字的申请书一起成为担保人。这点也必须强调。

杰　伦：知道了。我应付多少服务费？

出纳员：对于你申请的普通信用卡来说，每年的服务费仅收20美元即可。

杰　伦：好吧。为了消费方便起见，我就向你们申请长城普通信用卡。

出纳员：请稍等片刻，我尽快给你办理。

杰　伦：不着急，我会耐心等待，小姐。

出纳员：多谢！先生，这就好。

Explanatory Notes 注释：

1. 1-1. 名词economy 经济；经济实惠，例如：political economy 政治经济学；state-owned/ collective/ building/national economy 国营/集体/建筑/国民经济；1-2. 名词economics 经济学；1-3. 名词economist 经济学家；1-4. 名词economism 经济主义。

2. 动词economize 节约，节省

    例如：Modern industry must economize (in) raw materials. 现代工业一定得节约原料。例如：Managers should forever economize (on) man-power and material resouces 管理者们应该永远节省人力和物力

3. 形容词economic 经济学的，经济（上）的。例如：Economic Association 经济协会；European Economic Community (EEC) 欧洲经济共同体（欧共体）

Spoken Practice 口语练习

1. **Pair Work:**

   One acts as a teller in a bank, the other acts as a user who wants to apply for a credit card and doesn't know how to get it. Use the following expressions:

   ——Can I help you, sir?

   ——Yes, I'd like to...

   ——How...

   ——It's...

2. **Tell "true" or "false" in accordance with Learn to Speak English:**

   1) (　) User may use the credit card to pay for goods and services.
   2) (　) Everyone can apply for a credit card.
   3) (　) It's safer to bring credit card than bring cash or traveller's checks.
   4) (　) A small service charge will be added to your total bill if you do third paying way.
   5) (　) The yearly fee for a common card is less than $20 dollars.

3. **Read & interpret the Following Passage:**

   ### Banking Facilities

   Most banks in China are owned and run by the state. Banks engage in all kinds of Renminbi banking business. They manage international financial exchange, too. The function of banks is to raise, utilize, accumulate and manage domestic funds or foreign exchange funds.

   Banks perform many kinds of functions—opening saving accounts, drawing and cashing checks, granting mortgages. Now, on-line computer systems help banks give even more speedy and accurate services to custommers or users, credit card is a typical instance.

   In a word, people's life would be unimaginable without the services of banks.

4. Put the Following into English and Pay Attention to English Expressive Ways:

1) A > B 2) A < B
3) A ≈ B 4) A ≠ B

5. Substitute the Following Words and Expressions:

1) Use the following **Terms about Banking Facilities**（银行业务相关术语）to replace the black words in the following sentence:

Jielun: OK. I see. I'd like to get a **credit card**, and how can I apply for it, miss?

杰伦：好，我清楚了。小姐，我想申请一个**信用卡**，但怎么申请呢？

Terms about Banking Facilities ［təːmz əˈbaut ˈbæŋkiŋ fəˈsilitiz］银行业务相关术语

client's name ［ˈklaiəntz neim］户名

deposit ［diˈpɔzitə］储户，存款人

(annual) interest rate ［ˈænjuəl ˈintrist reit］（年）利率

letter of credit ［ˈletə əv ˈkredit］信用证

credit ［ˈkredit］信贷

trust ［trʌst］信托

mortgage ［ˈmɔːgidʒ］抵押

loan ［loun］贷款

principal ［ˈprinsəpəl］本金

security ［siˈkjuəriti］担保

deposit slip ［diˈpɔzit slip］存款单

bankbook ［ˈbæŋkbuk］存折

check/cheque book ［tʃek buk］支票簿

traveller's cheque/check ［ˈtrævləz tʃek］旅行支票

deposit receipt ［diˈpɔzit riˈsiːt］存款收据

lump deposit & draw ［lʌmp diˈpɔzit ənd drɔː］整存整取

one for all ［wʌn fə ɔːl］定期一本通

time/current ［taim/ˈkʌrənt］定/活期

earnest money ［ˈə:nist ˈmʌni］定金，保证金

service fee/charge ［ˈsə:vis fi: tʃa:dʒ］服务费用

without any extra charge ［wiˈðaut ˈeni ˈekstrə tʃa:dʒ］不额外收费

the total amount ［ðə ˈtoutl əˈmaunt］总金额

withdrawal order/form ［wiðˈdrɔ:əl ˈɔ:də fɔ:m］取款单

making a deposit ［ˈmeikiŋ ə diˈpɔzit］存入一笔款

odd deposit（De）& lump draw（Dr）零存整取
［ɔd diˈpɔzit ənd lʌmp drɔ:］

renewal & Interest（Int）draw（Dr）存本取息
［riˈnju:əl ənd ˈintrist drɔ:］

making a withdrawal of a deposit 提取一笔存款
［ˈmeikiŋ ə wiðˈdrɔ:əl əv ə diˈpɔzit］

2）Use the following **Cardinal Numeral**（基数词）to replace the black words in the following sentence：

Teller: For your common card, the yearly fee is US＄**20** dollars.

出纳员：对于你申请的普通信用卡来说，每年的服务费仅收 **20** 美元即可。

Cardinal Numeral ［ˈka:dinl ˈnju:mərəl］基数词

one	[wʌn]	1	eleven	[iˈlevn]	11	twenty-one	[ˈtwenti wʌn]	21
two	[tu:]	2	twelve	[twelv]	12	twenty-nine	[ˈtwenti nain]	29
three	[θri:]	3	thirteen	[ˈθə:ˈti:n]	13	thirty	[ˈθə:ti:]	30
four	[fɔ:]	4	fourteen	[ˈfɔ:ˈti:n]	14	forty	[ˈfɔ:ti]	40
five	[faiv]	5	fifteen	[ˈfifˈti:n]	15	fifty	[ˈfifti]	50
six	[siks]	6	sixteen	[ˈsiksˈti:n]	16	sixty	[ˈsiksti]	60
seven	[ˈsevn]	7	seventeen	[ˈsevnˈti:n]	17	seventy	[ˈsevnti]	70
eight	[eit]	8	eighteen	[ˈeiˈti:n]	18	eighty	[ˈeiti]	80
nine	[nain]	9	nineteen	[ˈnainˈti:n]	19	ninety	[ˈnainti]	90
ten	[ten]	10	twenty	[ˈtwenti]	20	one hundred	[wʌn ˈhʌndrəd]	100/百
one thousand	[wʌn ˈθauzənd]	1000/千		Ten thousand	[ten ˈθauzənd]		10000/万	
One hundred thousand	[wʌn ˈhʌndrəd ˈθauzənd]	100000 十万		million	[ˈmiljən]		1000000/ 百万	
One hundred million	[wʌn ˈhʌndrəd ˈmiljən]	10000000/ 千万		milliard(Br.)/ billion(Am.)	[ˈmiljɑ:d] / [ˈbiljəd]		1000000000/ 十亿	

建筑技术与管理英语情景会话

Explanatory Notes 注释：

1. 经济管理人员常与钱打交道，可钱数均用数字来表示，所以数字对于经济管理人员来说尤为重要。可以这样说，要把数字表达准确是经济管理人员不出工作差错的首要标准，因此在经济管理人员会话这一部中出现数词是笔者的初衷。

2. 英语数词的表达和汉语相比有着许多不同之处，用汉语的某些方式表达英语数词可能会出笑话，甚至会有误。为了准确无误使用好数词，首先必须掌握好数词，所以在相继的三个单元中均列举了英语数词及其构词法供在实际运用中参考：

   1) 13—19 均以 – teen [ti:n] 结尾，它们都有两个重音，特别提醒 thirteen, fifteen, eighteen 的发音和拼写与其他数字不同。

   2) 20—90 十位数的整数均以 – ty [ti] 结尾，它们的重音均在第一个音节上。注意 twenty、forty 的发音和拼写形式。

   3) 十位数和个位数之间一般须用连词符号 " – " 连接，例如：59 = fifty-nine.

   4) 十位数和百位数之间一般须用连词 "and" 连接。如：859 = eight hundred and fifty-nine.

   5) hundred, thousand, million, milliard 用作基数词时，一般不用复数形式。

Situational Dialogic Unit 29
第二十九情景对话单元

Learn to Speak English

Talking about Telegraphic Remittance

Caoni: Hello! I want to remit one million pounds to Shanghai, China. Can you give me a money order application?

Klaus: With pleasure. But how do you like to remit yours?

Caoni: This is my first remittance. I wonder what remittance business you have here?

Klaus: Several kinds, such as postal remittance, telegraphic remittance and so on.

Caoni: This is a remittance abroad. Which way is better?

Klaus: Either a regular or urgent cable would be faster than sending a mail transfer from our bank to China.

Caoni: OK. Telegraphic remittance. But how long will it take?

Klaus: About two minutes.

Caoni: Which is cheaper, the telegraphic remittance or the postal one?

Klaus: Of course, telegraphic remittance.

Caoni: How mush is the telegraph fee?

Klaus: 50 p for the telegraph fee is 1% of the remittance fee.

Caoni: Anything else, sir?

Klaus: Yes. The maximum limit for a remittance usually is 300,000 pounds with three pennies per word for the postscript. Which kinds of money are you going to remit, miss?

Caoni: It's U.K pounds

Klaus: How much?

Caoni: £ 1 million.

Klaus: Please show me your address, the name of payer and account number of China Bank. Fill out this remittance request and check the box that says "BANK TRANSFER BY CABLE".

Caoni: OK. Here you are.

Klaus: OK. Thank you.

学说英语

谈论电汇

曹　妮：喂！我想给中国上海汇 100 万英镑。您能给我一张汇款单吗？

克劳斯：很高兴为您服务。但你想用什么方式汇呢？

曹　妮：这是我首次汇款，不知道你们都有哪些汇款业务？

克劳斯：有好多种汇款业务，例如邮政汇款、电汇等。

曹　妮：这是向境外汇款，哪种方式较好？

克劳斯：从我们银行汇到中国银行，无论是普通的还是加急电汇，都比邮寄要快得多。

曹　妮：好吧！那就电汇吧。这种汇款需用多长时间才能收到？

克劳斯：大约两分钟就能收到。

曹　妮：电汇与邮汇相比，那种资费便宜些？

克劳斯：当然是电汇。

曹　妮：电汇的资费是多少？

克劳斯：每宗汇款电报费 50 便士，汇费是百分之一。

曹　妮：先生，还有什么费用吗？

克劳斯：有，通常每笔汇款最高限额为 300,000 英镑，附言每字 3 便士。小姐，你打算汇哪种货币？

曹　妮：是英镑。

克劳斯：汇多少？

曹　妮：1,000,000 英镑。

克劳斯：请出示你的地址，收款人和中国银行的账号。填写汇款申请书并显明"经银行电汇"字样。

曹　妮：好的，这就是。

克劳斯：好。谢谢！

建筑技术与管理英语情景会话

Spoken Practice 口语练习

1. **Pair Work:**

   Suppose your partner who is an accountant, and comes to a sub-branch bank, he asks a teller to give him some information how to send money by cable to the head office in Canada.

2. **Tell "true" or "false" in accordance with Learn to Speak English:**

   1) (　) Your money can be sent by air-mail if you like.
   2) (　) Either sending a check or mail transfer would be faster than a regular or urgent cable from our bank to yours.
   3) (　) You've to show me the name of payer and account number of China bank and address.
   4) (　) The telegraph fee is 1% of the remittance fee.
   5) (　) Less than 300 pounds is the minimum limit for a remittance.

3. **Read & interpret the Following Passage:**

   > **Informing Payment**
   >
   > Dear Sirs,
   >
   > 　　In settlement of your invoice No. 369, we enclose our bank cheque for US $ 13,120. We add that we are pleased with the way you executed the order. The goods arrived exactly on time by airplane of Air China and could be put on building without delay. We thank you for your immediate attention on this matter.
   >
   > 　　　　　　　　　　　　　　　　　　　　Your faithfully,
   >
   > Encl. a/

4. **Put the Following Chinese into English:**

> **通知已收到汇款**
>
> 敬启者：
>
> 　　很高兴收到贵方寄来的 13120 美元的银行支票，我们已将此款记入贵公司账户，如今已完全结清。只要我们力所能及，盼望能有机会再为贵公司服务。
>
> 谨上

5. **Substitute the Following Words and Expression**：

　1）Use the following **Remittance and Other**（汇款与其他）to replace the black words in the following sentence：

　　Klaus：Either a **regular** or **urgent cable** would be faster than **sending amail transfer** from our bank to China.

　克劳斯：从我们银行汇到中国的银行，无论是**普通的**还是**加急电汇**，都比邮寄要快得多。

Remittance and Other [riˈmitəns ənd ˈʌðə] 汇款与其他

postal remittance [ˈpoustəl riˈmitəns] 邮政汇款

postal order [ˈpoustəl ˈɔːdə] 邮政汇票

mail remittance [meil riˈmitəns] 信汇

telegraphic remittance [ˌteliˈgræfik riˈmitəns] 电汇

credit card [ˈkredit kaːd] 信用卡

letter of credit [ˈletə əv ˈkredit] 信用证

air-mail remittance [ɛə meil riˈmitəns] 航空汇

postal (money) order [ˈpoustəl ˈmʌni ˈɔːdə] 汇款单

remit [riˈmit] 汇出

postscript (PS) [ˈpoustskript] 附言

remittance fee [riˈmitəns fiː] 汇（款）费

remitter [rimiˈtiː] 汇款人

remittee [ˌriˈmitə] 收款人

　2）Use the following **Percent**，**Fraction and Decimal**（百分数，分数和小数）to replace the black words in the following sentence：

　　Caoni：How mush is the telegraph fee?

曹妮：电汇资费是多少？

Klaus: 50 p for the telegraph fee is **1%** of the remittance fee.

克劳斯：每宗汇款电报费50便士，汇费是**百分之一**。

Per cent / Percent [pə'sent] 百分数

one percent [wʌn pə'sent] 1%

sixty-five percent ['siksti faiv pə'sent] 65%

ninety-nine percent ['naiti nain pə'sent] 99%

Fraction ['frækʃən] 分数

a / one half [ə wʌn hɑːf] 1/2

a / one-third [ə wʌn θəːd] 1/3

a / one fourth / quarter [ə wʌn fɔːθ 'kwɔːtə] 1/4

three-fourths / quarters [θriː fɔːθs 'kwɔːtəz] 3/4

nine tenths [nain tenθs] 9/10

three and two-fifths [θriː ənd tu fifθs] $3\frac{2}{5}$

Decimal ['desiməl] 小数

zero point five ['ziərou pɔint faiv] 0.5

one point two four [wʌn pɔint tu fɔː] 1.24

sixty-five point seven ['siksti faiv pɔint 'sevn] 65.7

Explanatory Notes 注释：

1. 百分数中的百分号（%），拼写为 per cent 或 percent 均可。
2. 分数词中的分子用基数词，分母则用序数词构成。如果分子大于一，分母则用复数，即加 – s。

Situational Dialogic Unit 30
第三十情景对话单元

Learn to Speak English

Talking about Accounts

Jingji: Miss. Linda, you looked so busy right now, surrounded by so many statements and your calculating materials, didn't you?

Linda: Yes, of course. Mr. Jing, you know, it's the time of year again-year-end. The accountants are all very busy with totaling accounts. And I've to submit the report to my chief accountant.

Jingji: Sorry, I really don't know you're so busy。

Linda: It doesn't matter. Do you have any questions to ask?

Jingji: Yes. what's the different between financial accounting and management accounting, would you please explain them to me?

Klaus: With pleasure. Checking work for financial accounting is concerned in recording the day-to-day income and expenditure of the company—sales and purchases, wages and salaries, petty cash and expenses and so on.

Jingji: So many vocational work. Anything else?

Linda: Yes. It also deals with credit control and economic active analysis, etc.

Jingji: I see. And then what about management accounting? What does management accounting consist of?

Linda: Oh. It's concerned with supplying information to the Managerial departments and enable them to plan their objectives and control their budgets.

Jingji: And what's the purpose?

Linda: It helps them to measure the profitability of projects.

Jingji: I quite understand the defferents between them. Thank you for so much explanations.

学说英语

谈论会计科目

经 吉：琳达小姐，那么多财务报表和计算资料把你都围起来了，看起来你这会儿很忙，是吧？

琳 达：当然很忙。经先生，你是知道的，又到每年的这个时间——年终。会计们都非常忙于做年终决算。而我还得给总会计师递交报表呢。

经 吉：对不起，我确实不知道你这么忙。

琳 达：没什么。你有事吧？

经 吉：是的。请你给我讲一讲财务会计和管理会计之间的区别，可以吗？

琳 达：很乐意。财务会计的核算工作，涉及每天公司的收入与支出的账目——销售与购买，工资与薪金，零用钱与经费等项业务。

经 吉：那么多业务。还有其他业务吗？

琳 达：有。财务会计同样涉及信贷控制，经济活动分析等业务。

经 吉：我明白了。那管理会计是怎么一回事？管理会计由哪些业务组成的？

琳 达：啊，管理会计涉及向管理部门提供相关的信息，使其信息为制定，控制目标计划和控制预算。

经 吉：其目的是什么？

琳 达：有助于计算工程项目的收益。

经 吉：我对财务会计和管理会计之间的区别有一定了解。谢谢你所做的这么多解释。

Spoken Practice 口语练习

1. **Pair Work:**

   A acts as an accountat in a construction enterprise, B acts as a student whose major is economic management and who wants to know what kinds of an account A is in charge of. Use the following expressions:

   A: Can I help you, young man?
   B: Yes, I'd like to...
   A: What's your...?
   B: I'm...

2. **Tell "true" or "false" in accordance with Learn to Speak English:**

   1) (　) It's that time of year again-year-end. The accountants are too leisure to do totaling accounts.

   2) (　) Accountant has to hand in the report to her chief engineer.

   3) (　) Financial accounting is concerned with supplying information to the Managerial Departments.

   4) (　) Management accounting is dealed with recording the day-to-day income and expenditure of the company.

   5) (　) The purpose of management accounting helps them to measure the profitability of projects.

3. **Read & interpret the Following Passage:**

   ### Accountant and Bookkeeper

   Accountant can analyze and interpret financial information, prepare financial statements, conduct audits, design accounting systems, make forecasts and budgets and provide tax services. This person who specializes in this field is an accountant.

   Bookkeeper's job is to keep an accurate record of daily financial data, not to design or set up a record-keeping system. Financial records are frequently referred to as the books of account.

4. **Put the Following into Chinese and Pay Attention to the Expressive Ways of the Cardinal Numerals (基数词):**

1) How much is ten plus/minus five?
2) One hundren plus fifty-five equal one hundred and fifty-five.
3) Sixteen minus eight is/leaves eight.
4) How much is twelve divided by /times two?
5) Four times ninety is three hundred and sixty.
6) Thirty divided by five is six.
7) One hundred divided by twenty plus five times two minus six is nine.

5. **Substitute the Following Words and Expressions:**

Use the following **Classifications of Accountings**（会计分类）to replace the black words in the following sentence:

Jingji: Sorry, I really don't know you're so busy, but what's the differet between **financial accounting** and **management accounting**. Would you please explain them to me?

经吉：对不起，我确实不知道你这么忙，但还请你给我讲一讲**财务会计**和**管理会计**之间的区别，可以吗？

Classifications of Accounting [ˌklæsifiˈkeiʃənz əv əˈkauntiŋ] 会计分类

cost accounting [kɔst əˈkauntiŋ] 成本会计

industrial accounting [inˈdʌstriəl əˈkauntiŋ] 工业会计

public accounting [ˈpʌblik əˈkauntiŋ] 公共会计

business accounting [ˈbiznis əˈkauntiŋ] 商业会计

bank accounting [bæŋk əˈkauntiŋ] 银行会计

construction accounting [kənˈstrʌkʃən əˈkauntiŋ] 建筑企业会计

management accounting [ˈmænidʒmənt əˈkauntiŋ] 管理会计

computerized accounting [kəmˈpjuːtəraizd əˈkauntiŋ] 电脑化会计

accounting for joint ventures 合资企业会计 [əˈkauntiŋ fə dʒɔint ˈventʃəz]

Situational Dialogic Unit 31
第三十一情景对话单元

Learn to Speak English

Talking about Financial Budget Preparation

Williams: Sorry to interrupt you, miss.

Budgeter: No. What's up, sir?

Williams: Can you say anything about a financial budget in brief?

Budgeter: Financial budget. OK. Financial budget is a plan showing a company's objectives and proposed ways of attaining those objectives.

Williams: Oh, I see. The financial budget is to establish a financial framework for a company or a unit.

Budgeter: This is just my meaning, Mr. Williams.

Williams: And how is a budget created?

Budgeter: General speaking, it's done by means of separate budget which can then be combined into a master budget.

Williams: So a master budget is a comprehensive planning document of a company or a unit, right?

Budgeter: That's right. In other words, decision makers can control and monitor the business operations in accordance with the master budget.

Williams: So it's the purpose. What contents does it usually contain?

Budgeter: It contains two parts, as far as I know.

Williams: What's the concrete content, miss?

Budgeter: The first part is about providing a basis for projected income statement.

Williams: And second?

Budgeter: It's about providing a basis for projected balance sheet.

Williams: OK. What's the detailed item of the second part?

Budgeter: It contains capital expenditures budget and cash budget.

Williams: I see. Thanks a lot.

Budgeter: Not at all.

谈论财务预算编制

威廉姆斯：小姐，对不起，打断你说话了吧。

预 算 员：没什么。先生，有什么事吗？，

威廉姆斯：你能简单地解释一下财务预算吗？

预 算 员：财务预算，那好吧。财务预算就是表明公司的目标以及提出达到这种目标的计划。

威廉姆斯：啊，我明白了。财务预算也就是为公司或单位建起的金融框架。

预 算 员：正是此意，威廉姆斯先生。

威廉姆斯：那怎么编制预算呢？

预 算 员：一般来讲，它是先由各部门编制各部门的预算方式完成的，然后再把这些部门的预算汇编成总预算。

威廉姆斯：因此总预算就是公司或单位的综合计划文件，对吗？

预 算 员：对。换句话说，决策者就能根据总预算监控企业的经营运转情况。

威廉姆斯：原来是这一目的。那预算通常都包括哪些内容？

预 算 员：据我所知预算通常包括两部分内容。

威廉姆斯：具体内容是什么，小姐？

预 算 员：第一部分是提供相关计划收入报表的依据。

威廉姆斯：第二部分呢？

预 算 员：第二部分是提供相关计划平衡单的依据。

威廉姆斯：第二部分具体项目是什么？

预 算 员：第二部分具体项目是资本支出预算和现金预算。

威廉姆斯：我知道了。多谢！

预 算 员：没什么。

Explanatory Notes 注释：

1. estimate 动词（vt.）预算，估价，评价

    例如：Our company estimates its income at US. ＄6,000,000 this year and expenditure US. ＄3,000,000. 我们公司预计今年收入6,000,000美元，支出3,000,000美元。

2. estimate 动词（vi.）评价，估计，预算，估价

    例如：Manager invited an engineering contractor to estimate for the repair of our workshop.

    经理已邀请了一位工程承包商估算修理我们车间的费用。

3. estimate 名词（n.）估计数，预算，估价，评价

    例如：We hope the construction wouldn't exceed our estimates.

    我们希望施工不要超出我们的预算。

4. estimator 名词（n.）（人力，物力等的）估价者（师），评估人（师）

5. estimation 名词（n.）估计，预算，估价，评价

    例如：You should form a true, objective estimation of his work.

    你们应该对他的工作作出公正、客观的评价。

6. estimative 形容词（a.）被估计的，被判断的

    例如：estimative figure 估计数字

Spoken Practice 口语练习

1. **Pair Work:**

    Work in groups or pairs. Suppose you are budgeters and have won a tender. Ask your partners to tell me what the project budget is and how to be completed the master budget.

2. **Tell "true" or "false" in accordance with Learn to Speak English:**

    1) (　) Budgeters budget the separate budgets that can then be combined them into a master budget.

    2) (　) Budget is to set up a financial frame-work for users.

    3) (　) General budget usually is less than two parts.

    4) (　) The first part of a master budget contains capital expenditures budget and cash budget.

    5) (　) Managers can monitor the business operations according to the master budget.

3. **Read & Interpret the Following Passage:**

    ### Cost-volume-profit Analysis

    Let's choose the equation method to discuss the following example:

    Concrete Parts Factory sells concrete floor slabs. The selling price is £.48 per floor slab. The variable costs are £.8 per floor slab and the fixed expenses are £.24,800 per month. How many concrete floor slabs must be sold to break-even or make a profit?

    Sales = Variable Costs + Fixed Expenses + Profits.

    Assume X = Volume of units to be sold to break-even at the break-even point, profits will be zero. This equation would be:

    £.48 X = £.8 + £.24,800 + 0

    £.8X = £.24,800

    X = 620 concrete floor slabs.

    (or total sales £.29,760 at £.48 per concrete floor slab)

    This example tells us: in each month the Concrete Parts Factory must sell 620 concrete floor slabs to reach the break-even point. The Factory must sell more than 620 concrete floor slabs to make any profit.

4. Substitute the Following Words and Expressions:

Use the following **Terms about Budget** （预算术语） to replace the black words in the following sentence:

Budgeter: General speaking, it's done by means of **separate budget** which can then be combined into a **master budget**.

预算员：一般来讲，它是先由各部门编制各部门的预算方式完成的，然后再把这些部门的预算汇编成总预算。

Terms about Budget [tə:mz ə'baut 'bʌdʒit] 预算术语

master/general budget ['ma:stə 'dʒenərəl 'bʌdʒit] 总预算

budget statement ['bʌdʒit 'steitmənt] 预算书

making/preparing a budget ['meikiŋ pri'pɛəriŋ ə 'bʌdʒit] 编制预算

building job budget ['bildiŋ dʒɔb 'bʌdʒit] 单位工程预算

budget quota ['bʌdʒit 'kwoutə] 预算定额

additional budget [ə'diʃənl 'bʌdʒit] 追加预算

construction budget [kən'strʌkʃən 'bʌdʒit] 施工预算

direct labour budget [di'rekt 'leibə 'bʌdʒit] 直接人工预算

raw materials budget [rɔ: mə'tiəriəlz 'bʌdʒit] 原材料预算

production budget [prə'dʌkʃən 'bʌdʒit] 生产预算

budget control ['bʌdʒit kən'troul] 预算控制

budget surplus/deficit ['bʌdʒit 'sə:pləs 'defisit] 预算盈余/赤字

budgetary revenue/expenditure 预算收入/支出
['bʌdʒitəri 'revinju: iks'penditʃə]

revenue and expenditure in balance 收入与支出平衡
['revinju: ənd iks'penditʃə in 'bæləns]

budgetary/ extra-budgetary funds 预算内/外资金
['bʌdʒitəri 'ekstrə 'bʌdʒitəri fʌndz]

increasing/cutting down a budget 增加/削减预算
[in'kri:siŋ 'kʌtiŋ daun ə'bʌdʒit]

inspecting and approving budget of working drawing 施工图预算的审查
[in'spektiŋ ənd ə'pru:viŋ 'bʌdʒit əv 'wə:kiŋ drɔ:iŋ]

Situational Dialogic Unit 32
第三十二情景对话单元

Learn to Speak English

Talking about Computing the Unit Cost

Zhaolin: Excuse me, sir. May I disturb you?

Charley: No. It doesn't matter. What can I do for you?

Zhaolin: Yes. I'm very interested in cost accounting. Could you explain what cost accounting is?

Charley: OK. It provides timely unit product cost through the use of perpetual inventory procedures and predetermined factory overhead rates.

Zhaolin: I see. In a sense, any orderly method of developing cost information constitutes cost accounting, OK?

Charley: Exactly, I think.

Zhaolin: You said unit product cost above. But how do you analyze it?

Charley: Usually we do it by two basic types of cost accounting systems.

Zhaolin: What are the two types of systems?

Charley: Job order cost accounting and process cost accounting.

Zhaolin: What's the difference between the two?

Charley: No difference at all.

Zhaolin: Why not, sir?

Charley: Because their purpose is to allocate manufacturing cost to products and determine their unit costs.

Zhaolin: So that's how it is. How many parts is product manufacturing cost made up of?

Charley: Product cost is made up of prime cost (also known as manufacturing cost or factory cost), direct materials cost, direct labour cost and manufacturing overhead cost.

Zhaolin: What's the equation of unit cost?

Charley: Unit cost equal total manufacturing costs divides into the number of products manufactured.

Zhaolin: You expained it thoroughly. I learned a lot. Thank you, indeed.

学说英语

谈论计算单位成本

赵　林：抱歉，先生，打扰了吧？
查　利：不，没什么大不了的事。我能为你做些什么吗？
赵　林：是。我对成本会计很感兴趣，你能给我讲一讲什么是成本会计吗？
查　利：好吧。成本会计是通过使用永续存盘制和预定的制造费用分配率定期提供产品的单位成本。
赵　林：我明白了。从某种意义上讲，任何形成成本信息系统的方法都能构成成本会计，对吗？
查　利：我认为你表达得很确切。
赵　林：你上边讲过的'产品的单位成本'，那怎样分析呢？
查　利：我们通常用两种基本的成本会计体系分析。
赵　林：这两种基本体系分析是什么？
查　利：是分批成本会计和分步成本会计。
赵　林：这两种成本会计有什么不同之处吗？
查　利：没什么本质的不同。
赵　林：怎么没有不同之处呢，先生？
查　利：因为它们的共同目的都是要把制造成本分配于各种产品，以确定它们的单位成本。
赵　林：原来如此。产品制造成本由哪些部分组成？
查　利：产品制造成本由基本造价（同样认为是制造费用或出厂费）、直接材料成本、直接人工成本和制造管理费用组成的。
赵　林：单位成本的公式是什么？
查　利：单位成本等于全部制造费用除以制造的产品数量。即：

$$单位成本 = \frac{全部制造费用}{制造的产品数量}$$

赵　林：你讲得很透彻，我受益匪浅。真的谢谢。

Charley: Not at all.

Zhaolin: Now don't laugh at me. I'm an unprofessional. If calculating unit cost, you should use cardinal numeral and not ordinal numeral, right?

Charley: Right. Naturally cardinal numeral.

查　利：不客气。

赵　林：我是外行，你可别见笑。计算单位成本，通常应使用基数词而不使用序数词，对吗？

查　利：对。自然通用基数词。

Spoken Practice 口语练习

1. **Pair Work**:

   Suppose your partner who is an accountant of a Building Engineering Corporation and comes to your workshop, he asks you to show him your income account, expense account etc. Try to say how to compute the unit cost.

2. **Tell "true" or "false" in accordance with Learn to Speak English**:

   1) (　) I want to know how to settle accounts.
   2) (　) Construction accounting provides timely unit product cost through the use of perpetual inventory procedures and predeter-mined factory overhead rates.
   3) (　) Unit product cost is usually analyzed by two basic types of cost accounting systems.
   4) (　) Job order cost accounting and process cost accounting are quite different.
   5) (　) Product unit cost is made up of manufacturing cost, direct materials cost, direct labour cost and manufacturing overhead cost.

3. **Read & interpret the Following Passage**:

   ### Cost Accounting

   Cost accounting systems are widely used by all types of companies and factories. Managers and factory directors make use of them to determine unit costs of products and to control manufacturing cost overhead.

   In order to show the flow of product cost, there are six ledger accounts in the cost accounting system. These ledger accounts are made on the basis of computing unit cost.

4. **Put the Following Sentences into English and Pay Attention to the Expressive Ways of the Cardinal Numerals（基数词）**:

   1) **Hundreds of** new buildings have sprung in the city in recent years.
   2) The visitors came and paid a visit to our worksite **twos and threes** last few days.

3) It's said our manager is in her **early thirties** this year.

4) They joined the Building Industry in the **1980s**.

5) In fact, **five of** the young men are building engineering and technical personnel and **two of** them are economic managerial personnel.

5. Substitute the Following Words and Expressions:

Use the following **Ordinal Numeral** (序数词) to replace the black words in the the following sentence:

Zhaolin: Now don't laugh at me. I'm an unprofessional. If calculating unit cost, you should use cardinal numeral and not **ordinal numeral**, right?

赵林：我是外行，你可别见笑。计算单位成本，通常应使用基数词而不使用**序数词**，对吗？

Ordinal Numeral [ˈɔːdinl njuːmərəl] 序数词

first	1st	[fəːst]	第一
second	2nd	[ˈsekənd]	第二
third	3rd	[θəːd]	第三
fourth	4th	[fɔːθ]	第四
fifth	5th	[fifθ]	第五
sixth	6th	[siksθ]	第六
seventh	7th	[ˈsevnθ]	第七
eighth	8th	[eitθ]	第八
ninth	9th	[nainθ]	第九
tenth	10th	[tenθ]	第十
eleventh	11th	[iˈlevnθ]	第十一
twelfth	12th	[twelfθ]	第十二
thirteenth	13th	[ˈθəːˈtiːnθ]	第十三
twentieth	20th	[ˈtwentiiθ]	第二十
twenty-first	21st	[ˈtwenti fəːst]	第二十一
thirtieth	30th	[ˈθəːtiiθ]	第三十
thirty-second	32nd	[ˈθəːti ˈsekənd]	第三十二
fortieth	40th	[ˈfɔːtiiθ]	第四十
forty-third	43rd	[ˈfɔːti θəːd]	第四十三
fiftieth	50th	[ˈfiftiiθ]	第五十
fifty-fourth	54th	[ˈfifti fɔːθ]	第五十四

续表

sixtieth	60th	[ˈsikstiiθ]		第六十
seventieth	70th	[ˈsevntiiθ]		第七十
eightieth	80th	[ˈeitiiθ]		第八十
ninetieth	90th	[ˈnaintiiθ]		第九十
hundredth	100th	[ˈhʌndrədθ]		第一百
one hundred and first	101th	[wʌn hʌndrəd ənd fəːst]		第一百零一
thousand	1,000th	[ˈθauzəndθ]		第一千
two thousand nine hundred and seventy third	2,973th	[tuː ˈθauzənd nain ˈhʌndrəd ənd ˈsevnti θəːd]		第二千九百七十三

Explanatory Notes 注释：

1. 英语的序数词 1—19，除第一（first），第二（second），第三（third）有特殊形式以外，其余的均在基数词后加 -th，发 [θ] 音构成。

2. 英语序数词的缩写，除个位数 1，2，3 的序数词，在阿拉伯数词后加 st，nd，rd 构成外，其余的均在阿拉伯数词后加 -th 构成。例如：1st，2nd，3rd，4th，21st，43rd，90th，100th 等。

3. "第几十几"或第几百几十几的序数词，其百位数和十位数用基数词表示外，个位数用序数词表示；百位数和十位数之间还照样加"and"，十位数和个位数之间还用"-"连接，例如：第六百四十五应写成 six hundred and forty-fifth。

4. 对于十位整数的序数词可先将其词尾 -ty 中 y 变成 -ie，再加 -th，发 [θ] 音构成。如：twenty 变成 twentieth；seventy 变成 seventieth。

5. fifth，eighth，ninth，twelfth 等加 -th，属于不规则构词法，有必要逐个记。

Situational Dialogic Unit 33
第三十三情景对话单元

建筑经济管理人员英语情景会话

Learn to Speak English

Talking about Fixed Assets and Current Assets

Jielia: Sorry to bother you, Miss. What are you in charge of in the accounting department?

Alice: Fixed Asset, madam.

Jielia: I don't know anything about Fixed Assets. Could you tell me what Fixed Assets include?

Alice: Fixed Assets include contents like (usable period over a year) land and buildings, plants and machinery, vehicles and so on.

Jielia: I see. But what about Current Assets, I'd love to know?

Alice: Current Assets are cash and cash equivalents: raw materials, work in progress, stocks of finished goods, receivables.

Jielia: So many contents! Sundry debtors?

Alice: Various people who owe us money "debtors" is not only natural person, but also legal orgnization.

Jielia: I quite understand this. How do you distinguish between current liabilities and long term liabilities?

Alice: I think current liabilities are paid back within one year or one operating cycle, while long-term liabilities aren't due during the period.

Jielia: That's right. What does current liabilities involve?

Alice: It involves corporation short-term borrow or loan money, accounts payable, wages and salaries payable, bank loans payable, interst payable and taxes payable.

Jielia: You have many kinds of accounts, don't you?

Alice: Yes. We have controlling account, subsidiary account, cash account, banking account and so on.

Jielia: Thank you for your information, Miss.

Alice: Don't mention it.

学说英语

谈论固定资产和流动资产

吉莉娅：对不起打扰啦，小姐。您在会计部门主管什么业务？
艾丽斯：固定资产，女士。
吉莉娅：我对固定资产知之甚少。您能告诉我固定资产都包括哪些内容吗？
艾丽斯：固定资产包括的内容有（使用期在一年以上的）土地和构筑物、厂房和机械、运输设备诸如此类。
吉莉娅：我晓得了。流动资产又是怎么回事？
艾丽斯：流动资产是指现金和现金等价；像原材料、成品、半成品、有价证券、应收款项。
吉莉娅：这么多内容！什么叫债务人？
艾丽斯：拖欠我们钱的各种人。"人"可以是自然人，也可以是法人团体。
吉莉娅：我明白这点。流动负债和长期负债是怎么区别？
艾丽斯：我认为流动负债是指一年或一个经营周期内要偿还的债务；而不在这一时期内要偿还的债务则是长期负债。
吉莉娅：正是此意。流动负债这一项涉及哪些内容呢？
艾丽斯：流动负债涉及公司的债款、应付账款、应付工资、应付银行借款、应付利息和应交税款等项内容。
吉莉娅：你们有多种会计分类账，对吗？
艾丽斯：对呀！我们有总账、分类账、现金账、银行账等等。
吉莉娅：谢谢你提供的会计相关信息。
艾丽斯：没关系。

建筑经济管理人员英语情景会话

Spoken Practice 口语练习

1. **Pair Work:**

   Suppose A is an engineer, B is an accountant in a building company. They are talking how to differ Current Assets from Fixed Assets in accounting.

2. **Tell "true" or "false" in accordance with Learn to Speak English:**

   1) (　) An accountant is very sorry to disturb me.

   2) (　) Land and buildings, plants and machinery, vehicles and so on belong to Current Assets.

   3) (　) Fixed Assets are raw materials, work in progress, stocks of finished goods, and cash money at the bank.

   4) (　) Sundry debtor is a person who owes another person money.

   5) (　) Current liabilities involve corporation short-term borrow or loan money, accounts payable, wages and salaries payable, bank loans payable, interest payable and taxes payable.

3. **Read & interpret the Following Passage:**

   ### Fixed Assets

   Fixed Assets are often classified into tangible assets, intangible assets and natural resource.

   Tangible assets denote physical substance, as exemplified by land, building, machine and equipment. Land isn't subject to depreciation; Building, machine and equipment are subject to depreciation.

   Intangible assets have no physical substance and are non current. Examples included patents, copyrights, trademarks, franchises and goodwill.

   Natural resource is a site acquired for the purpose of extracting or removing some valuable resources such as oil, timber, minerals are classified as a natural resource.

4. **Substitute the Following Words and Expressions:**

   Use the following **Accounts and Others**（账目和其他）to replace the black words in the following sentence:

   Alice: Yes. We have **controlling account**, **subsidiary account**, **cash** account, banking account and so on.

艾丽斯：对呀！我们有总账、分类账、现金账、银行账等等。

Accounts and Others ［əˈkaunts ənd ˈʌθəz］账目和其他

account ［əˈkaunt］账目/会计科目

controlling account ［kənˈtrouliŋ əˈkaunt］总账

subsidiary account ［səbˈsidjəri əˈkaunt］分类账

real account ［riəl əˈkaunt］实账

capital account ［ˈkæpitl əˈkaunt］资本账

stock account ［stɔk əˈkaunt］股份账

asset account ［ˈæset əˈkaunt］资产账

cash account ［kæʃ əˈkaunt］现金账

income account ［ˈinkəm əˈkaunt］收入账

expense account ［iksˈpens əˈkaunt］支出账

mixed account ［mikst əˈkaunt］混合账

wage account ［weidʒ əˈkaunt］工资账

itemized account ［ˈaitəmaizd əˈkaunt］明细账

making an entry in the account ［ˈmeikiŋ ən ˈentri in ði əˈkaunt］记账

settling accounts ［ˈsetliŋ əˈkaunts］结账

keeping accounts ［ˈkiːpiŋ əˈkaunts］管账

auditing accounts ［ˈɔːditiŋ əˈkaunts］核账

examining accounts ［igˈzæminiŋ əˈkaunts］检查账

verifying accounts ［ˈverifaiiŋ əˈkaunts］核实账

transferring accounts ［trænsˈfəːriŋ əˈkaunts］过账

closing the books ［ˈklouziŋ ðə buks］暂停登账

account book ［əˈkaunt buk］账（簿）

slip ［slip］传票

invoice ［ˈinvɔis］发票

bill ［bil］汇票

wage/salary ［weidʒ ˈsæləri］工资/薪水

cheque，（Am.）check ［tʃek］支票

stock ［ˈstɔk］股票

Part Four
English Situational Conversations with Construction Testing and Surveying Personnel
(Situational Dialogic Unit 34 – 39)

第四部
建筑试验和测量人员英语情景会话
（第三十四至三十九情景对话单元）

Situational Dialogic Unit 34

第三十四情景对话单元

Learn to Speak English

Talking about Concrete Test

Helen: What time can you remove the anchors or fixtures of the prestressing steel bars, engineer Wang?

Tester: Oh, removing the anchors. It depends on whether the concrete strength reaches the designed value or not. At least the concrete test cube has shown the result is up to the standard.

Helen: Sound reasonable. What will happen if the anchors or fixtures are removed too early?

Tester: It'll cause big strength loss and even serious quality problem.

Helen: Yes, I guess so.

Tester: How can you ensure not to happen the above—mentioned quality problem.

Helen: The critical problem is time for removing the anchors, otherwise penment loss must be happened. But how do you avoid leakage from the heating in mass concrete?

Tester: Three points must follow. Firstly, we'll divide the mass concrete into several stages for concrete pouring by using construction joints properly.

Helen: Good method. This is first and what about second?

Tester: Secondly, we'll put the cold water in mixing concrete and embed chilling water pipe inside the concrete which can transfer the heating produced by the chemical reaction from the concrete.

Helen: What you said is right. Is there third?

Tester: Naturally. Thirdly, there's admixure (UFA) mixing in the concrete which can reduce the leakage from the shrinking.

Helen: Undoubtedly, concrete can avoid leakage, avert quality accident and ensure construction quality in this way.

Tester: You bet it is.

学说英语

谈论混凝土试验

海　伦：王工程师，你们何时才能松开预应力钢筋的锚具和固定件？

试验员：啊！松锚具。这要看混凝土的强度是否达到设计标准，至少混凝土试块的结果表明已达到设计标准才可以松。

海　伦：言之有理。如果锚具和固定件松开得过早会产生什么不良后果？

试验员：那将会造成较大应力的损失，甚至会造成严重的质量问题。

海　伦：是的，我也是这样认为的。

试验员：我还想知道怎样做才能不出上述质量问题？

海　伦：关键是锚具和固定件松开的时间，否则就会造成无法挽回的永久损失。那么你们怎样避免大体积混凝土中温度裂缝？

试验员：要做到三点。首先我们将通过正确设置施工缝来分段浇筑大体积混凝土。

海　伦：好法子。这是第一点，第二点是什么？

试验员：其次我们使用接近于0℃的冷水搅拌混凝土，并往混凝土中的预埋管道内加入冰水，带走混凝土硬化过程中产生的热量。

海　伦：说得好。那还有第三点吗？

试验员：自然有。最后就是把外加剂掺入混凝土中来减少因收缩产生的裂缝。

海　伦：毫无疑问，使用这种方法施工，才能避免混凝土裂缝，防止质量事故的发生以确保工程质量。

试验员：正是。

建筑试验和测量人员英语情景会话

Spoken Practice 口语练习

1. **Pair Work:**

   Suppose you're testing concrete in a laboratory. Ask your partner to tell you what you must pay great attention to if you do concrete test, and how to do concrete test well.

2. **Tell "true" or "false" in accordance with Learn to Speak English:**

   1) (   ) Removing the anchors or fixtures of the prestressing rebar depends whether the concrete strength reaches the design value or not.

   2) (   ) Big strength loss and even serious quality problem will be caused if the anchor or fixtures are removed too early.

   3) (   ) There're two points in avoiding leakage from the heating in mass concrete.

   4) (   ) Three points are dividing the mass concrete into several stages for concrete pouring; putting the cold water mixing in concrete and mixing admixture in the concrete.

   5) (   ) Admixture (UFA) mixing in the concrete can reduce the leakage from the shrinking.

3. **Read & Interpret the Following Passage:**

   ### Prestressed Concrete

   Prestressed concrete combines high-strength concrete with high-strength steel bar in an active manner. Tensioning the steel bar and holding it against the concrete, thus putting the concrete into compression. This active combination results in the much better behavior of the two materials. Steel bar is ductile and now is made to act in high tension by prestressing. Concrete is a brittle material with its tensile capacity now improved by being compressed while its compressive capacity is not really harmed. Thus prestressed concrete is an ideal combination of two modern high strength materials.

4. **Put the Following Sentences into Chinese and Pay Attention to the Use of "but"**:

1) Engineers and economists couldn't get the reference books anywhere **but** that bookstore. (prep.)

2) We have nothing to do **but** agree. (prep.)

3) Nick has been China **but** once during his all life. (adv.)

4) **But** for your investment, we shouldn't build the highway. (conj.)

5) It never rains **but** it pours. (conj.)

6) Maryann is tall and slim, **but** in good health. (conj.)

Explanatory Notes 注释：

but 用作并列连词时，可连接并列成分或分句，表示意思上的转折，可译为"但是"、"可是"、"然而"等；but 也可用作介词，意思为"除……以外"；but 还可用作副词，相当于 only, merely, 可译为"不过"、"只"、"仅"等。所以在翻译时，首先应搞清 but 用作什么词性，然后再根据其词性的具体词意来准确翻译才符合翻译法。

5. **Substitute the Following Words & Expressions**：

1) Use the following **Concrete Design and Test**（混凝土（级配）设计与检验）to replace the black words in the following sentence：

Tester: Oh, removing the anchors. It depends whether the concrete strength reaches the **designed value** or not. At least **the concrete test cube** has shown the result is up to the standard.

试验员：啊！松锚具。这要看混凝土的强度是否达到**设计标准**，至少**混凝土试块**的结果表明已达到设计标准才可以松。

Concrete Design and Test 混凝土设计与检验

['kɔnkriːt di'zain ənd test]

aggregate size ['ægrigit saiz] 骨料粒经

aggregates gradation ['ægrigits grə'deiʃən] 骨料级配

graded aggregate ['greidid 'ægrigit] 级配骨料

water requirement ['wɔːtə ri'kwaiəmənt] 需水量

water-cement ratio ['wɔːtə si'ment 'reiʃiou] 水灰比

cement-water ratio [si'ment 'wɔːtə 'reiʃiou] 灰水比

建筑试验和测量人员英语情景会话

cement-sand ratio ［siˈment sænd ˈreiʃiou］ 灰砂比
cement-aggregate ratio ［siˈment ˈægrigit ˈreiʃiou］ 灰集比
grading ［ˈgreidiŋ］ 级配
concrete mix proportion ［ˈkɔnkriːt miks prəˈpɔːʃən］ 混凝土配合比
mix proportion by weight ［miks prəˈpɔːʃən bai weit］ 重量配合比
crushed rock ［ˈkrʌʃid rɔk］ 碎石
cement paste ［siˈment peist］ 水泥浆
test cube ［test kjuːb］ 试块
slump test ［slʌmp test］ 坍落度试验
concrete stress ［ˈkɔnkriːt stres］ 混凝土应力
pressure testing record ［ˈpreʃə ˈtestiŋ ˈrekɔd］ 试压记录
concrete test cube ［ˈkɔnriːt test kjuːb］ 混凝土方块强度试验

2）Use the following **Defects of Concrete** （混凝土缺陷）to replace the black words in the following sentence：

Helen：Undoubtedly, concrete can avoid **leakage**, avert **quality accident** and ensure construction quality in this way.

海伦：毫无疑问，使用这种方法施工，才能避免混凝土**裂缝**，防止**质量事故**的发生以确保工程质量。

Defects of Concrete ［diˈfekts əv ˈkɔnkriːt］ 混凝土缺陷
crack ［kræk］ 裂纹，裂缝
cavity and pocket ［ˈkæviti ənd ˈpɔkit］ 空洞
void of paste ［vɔid əv peist］ 跑浆
stone pockets ［stəun ˈpɔkits］ 蜂窝状毛孔
shrinkage crack ［ˈʃriŋkidʒ kræk］ 收缩裂纹
rate of crack propagation ［reit əv kræk ˌprɔpəˈgeiʃən］ 裂缝扩张速度
reinforcement exposed ［ˌriːinˈfɔːsmənt iksˈpəuzid］ 露筋
vibratory test ［ˈvaibrətəri test］ 振动试验
shuttering mark ［ˈʃʌtəriŋ maːk］ 模板痕迹（混凝土面）
honey-comb and blasted surface 蜂窝麻面
［ˈhʌni koum ənd ˈblaːstid ˈsəːfis］

Situational Dialogic Unit 35
第三十五情景对话单元

Learn to Speak English

Talking about Steel Reinforcement Test

Booke: Are these the Steel Bars Quality Certificates and Test Reports from the manufacture, miss?

Oyang: That's right, sir. Can I help you in any way?

Booke: For sure. Are all physical character and chemical components complied with the specification, I'd like to know?

Oyang: It's hard to say. Now it's time for us to go to the laboratory and see the steel bar test in accordance with our schedule.

Booke: Yeah. Let's go.

Oyang: All right. I follow in your footsteps. I'd like to have a discussion with the laboratory technician for the steel bar testing. Can you introduce me about sequence of steel bar test?

Ridley: OK. Before doing test, we inspect the steel bar surface, and check if the size of the steel bar is complied with the specification, and if there're any leakages, scars or honnecombs on the surface.

Oyang: What do you test after the surface is accepted then?

Ridley: The steel bar will be tested by taking examples.

Oyang: What kind of tests do you do?

Ridley: We do most frequently physical tests.

Oyang: The physical test. How do you do such test?

Ridley: We take 6 segments of steel bar from each of 60 ton and cut one piece from each segment, and then divide six pieces into two groups (each group has three pieces) as testing samples.

Oyang: What do you do then?

Ridley: One of the group will be tensile test for its yieled point, tensile strength and the extension rate.

Oyang: Oh, I see this testing group. How about another?

Ridley: Another will be tested for its cold bending degree.

学说英语

谈论钢筋试验

布鲁克：这些是钢材生产厂家的钢筋产品合格证和检验报告吗，小姐？

欧　阳：对呀，先生。我能在某些方面帮你吗？

布鲁克：当然。我想了解这些材料的物理特性以及化学组成成分都符合规范要求吗？

欧　阳：这就难说。现在该是我们到试验室看一看日程表安排钢筋试验的时候了。

布鲁克：对呀！咱们走吧。

欧　阳：好的。我随你走，我想同试验技术员讨论一下钢筋试验相关事宜。给我介绍一下钢筋试验的程序好吗？

里德利：好的。在做钢筋试验之前，我们首先要检查钢筋的外观。核对是否标识的规格型号符合规范要求，检查是否钢筋表面有无坑凹，划痕或麻面缺陷。

欧　阳：如果表面合格的话，你们还要做哪些试验？

里德利：要对钢筋进行抽样试验。

欧　阳：你们都做些什么抽样试验呢？

里德利：通常所做的都是物理抽样试验。

欧　阳：物理试验。你们怎样做物理试验呢？

里德利：我们从每60吨钢筋中抽出6根，再从每根截取一小段，并把它们分成两组（每组三根）作为试验样品。

欧　阳：分成两组后怎么办？

里德利：其中一组做拉力试验，得出钢筋的屈服点、抗拉强度以及延伸率。

欧　阳：啊！我明白这组试验了。另一组做什么试验？

里德利：另一组做冷弯曲试验。

Oyang: If there're brittle leakages or bad welding performance occurred during test processing how to do, miss?

Ridley: It must have a chemical contentment analysis or other special tests to find out the problem.

Oyang: Yes. Your description is all right. Now I'd like to ask about the cold tensile processing.

Ridley: Cold tensile processing, please ask.

Oyang: OK. Under what situation do you test the cold tensile processing?

Ridley: If the extensile rate of the steel bar is already in excess of the defined maximum extension under the maximum strength during the cold tensile test, please tell me.

Oyang: What do you usually test, please tell me?

Ridley: No problem. In this case, we usually test the steel bar for its mechanical characters. The steel bar is adopted in works according to its actual grade found out in the test.

Oyang: I fully agree with you. I quite understand too, but can you give me an example?

Ridley: Oh, yeah. If it's a steel bar with lower grade found out by the test, it can't be used as the higher grade in the orignal.

Oyang: I know the relation betwen steel bar testing and its application.

Ridley: Right. So you'll avoid the bad result in your work for unknown.

Oyang: Yes, indeed. Thank you for your patient explanation.

Ridley: You're welcome.

欧　阳：如果加工中发生脆断或焊接性能不良怎么办，小姐？
里德利：那就一定要再做化学成分分析或做其他特殊试验来找出其原因。
欧　阳：对呀！你表述得很准确。我还想问一问冷拉加工的问题。
里德利：冷拉加工，请提问吧。
欧　阳：好吧。在什么情况下才做冷拉处理？
里德利：在力度最小而钢筋伸展率已经超过规定的最小伸展幅度的情况下才做钢筋冷拉处理。
欧　阳：你们通常做些什么试验，请讲给我听好吗？
里德利：没问题。在这种情况下，通常先做钢筋机械性能的试验，根据钢筋试验结果得出钢筋的实际等级再决定钢筋在工程中的使用。
欧　阳：我完全赞同你的做法，也基本上明白了相关试验，不过你能给我举一个例子吗？
里德利：喔，能。如果试验结果表明钢筋的等级和厂家表示不一致，较低，那就不能按照厂家所表示的高等级进行使用。
欧　阳：我对钢筋试验以及在工程中应用的关系有所了解。
里德利：对，这样就能避免因无知而造成的不良后果。
欧　阳：是的，的确实是这样。多谢你的耐心讲解。
里德利：不客气。

建筑试验和测量人员英语情景会话

Spoken Practice 口语练习

1. **Pair Work:**

   A acts as a rebar technician, B acts as a supervising engineer who wants to know something how to test steel bar. Use the following expressions:

   Can you expain me something about...?

   Yes, I'd like to...

   But what information...?

   It's...

2. **Tell "true" or "false" in accordance with Learn to Speak English:**

   1) (   ) Before processing, the Quality Certificates and Test Reports from the manufacture of all the reinforce steel bars must be checked.

   2) (   ) Most frequently steel bars tests are all the physical.

   3) (   ) The steel bar will be adopted in works according to its actual grade found out in the test.

   4) (   ) If the steel bar with lower grade found out by the test, it can be used as the higher grade in the orignal.

   5) (   ) One of the steel bar groups will be tensile test for its yielded point, ten sile strenght and the extension rate, the other group tested its cold bending degree.

3. **Read & Interpret the Following Passage:**

   Prestressing Steel Bar

   Prestressing steel bar is used in three forms: wire strands, single wires and high-strength bars. Wire strands are of the seven-wire type in which a central wire is enclosed tightly by six helically placed outer wires with a pith of 12 to 16 times the nominal diameter of the strand. Strand diameters range from 6.5 to 13 mm. Prestressing wire ranges in diameter from 4.9 to 7.0mm. It is made by cold drawing from high carbon steel, just as the individual wire strands. High strength alloy-steel bars for pre-stresssing are available in diameters from 19 to 35mm.

4. Substitute the Following Words & Expressions:

1) Use the following **Steel Bar Strength**（钢筋强度）to replace the black words in the following sentence:

Ridley: One of the group will be **tensile test** for its **yieled point**, **tensile strength** and the **extension rate**.

里德利：其中一组做拉力试验，得出钢筋的**屈服点**、**抗拉强度**以及**延伸率**。

Steel Bar Strength ［sti:l ba: streŋθ］钢筋强度

pretension ［'pri:'tenʃən］先张

post tensioning ［pəust 'tenʃəniŋ］后张

compression ［kəm'preʃən］压缩，压力

tension ［'tenʃən］张力，拉力，拉伸

tensile test ［'tensail test］拉力/拉伸的检验

principle bar ［'prinsəpl ba:］受力钢筋

tensile reinforcement ［'tensail ˌri:in 'fɔ:smənt］受拉钢筋

shear reinforcement ［ʃiə ˌri:in'fɔ:smənt］受剪钢筋

hooped reinforcement ［'hu:pt ˌri:in'fɔ:smənt］环向钢筋

radial bar ［'reidjəl ba:］径向钢筋（辐射伏）

compressive reinforcement ［kəm'presiv ˌri:in'fɔ:smənt］受压钢筋

transversal reinforcement ［trænz'və:səl ˌri:in'fɔ:smənt］横向钢筋

longitudinal reinforcement ［ˌlɔndʒi'tju:dinl ˌri:in'fɔ:smənt］纵向钢筋

2) Use the following **Types of Steel Bars**（钢筋式样）to replace the black words in the following sentence:

Ridley: **The steel bar** will be tested by taking examples.

里德利：要对**钢筋**进行抽样试验。

Types of Steel Bars ［taips əv ðə sti:l ba:z］钢筋式样

reinforcement bar ［ˌri:in'fɔ:smənt ba:z］钢筋

reinforcing steel ［ˌri:in'fɔ:siŋ sti:l］钢筋

steel bar / rod ［sti:l ba: rɔd］钢筋

steel reinforcement ［sti:l ˌri:in'fɔ:smənt］钢筋

main bar ［mein ba:］立筋

spacer bar ['speisə baː] 架立筋

splice bar [splais baː] 连接筋

anchor bar ['æŋkə baː] 锚固筋

starter bar ['staːtə baː] 插接钢筋

reinforcement skeleton [ˌriːin'fɔːsmənt 'skelitn] 钢筋骨架

mesh reinforcement steel fabric 钢筋网片
[meʃ ˌriːin'fɔːsmənt stiːl 'fæbrik]

Situational Dialogic Unit 36
第三十六情景对话单元

Learn to Speak English

Talking about Welding Test

Coke: I wonder whether you would weld the reinforcing steel after it has be cold tensioned, miss?

Liqin: Absolutely not. Because the cold tensioned reinforcing steels have improved the extension strength and yied point.

Coke: Only now do I know. What will happen if it's welded after cold tension?

Liqin: The mechanical property increased from the cold tension will be entirely lost.

Coke: Sound reasonable. So the low carbon steel wire can't be welded either after cold tensioned in the same principle, right?

Liqin: Right. It's not allowed to do in the specification.

Coke: What inspecting items must be usually done, I'd love to know?

Liqin: The pulling tension test, the bending plastic inspecting and the radiographic inspection radioscopy.

Coke: So many inspections and tests! What measures do you take to inspect the welding defects such as non-melted welding, air holes, leakage, slag in joints, welding seam size and such the like aren't conformed to the requirement?

Liqin: What you asked deals with many special questions There're many ways to inspect the quality of welding joints concerning different elements and design requirements.

Coke: What inspecting items should you pay attention to?

Liqin: Generally speaking, we should take care of the welding materials and electrodes, welding technological regulations, welders' technical skill and so forth.

Coke: How to inspect, miss?

学说英语

谈论焊接试验

科　克：小姐，我不知道冷拉后的钢筋能否进行焊接？

李　芹：绝对不能。因为冷拉后的钢筋已经改善了延伸力和屈服点。

科　克：我这才知道。如果冷拉后再进行焊接，会发生什么呢？

李　芹：冷拉后所增加的各种力学性能都会完全消失。

科　克：言之有理。所以同样的道理，冷拉过的低碳钢丝也不能进行焊接，对吗？

李　芹：对。规范是不允许这样做的。

科　克：我还想了解你们通常都进行哪些项目的焊接试验？

李　芹：进行拉伸应力试验、弯曲塑性检验和射线探伤。

科　克：要进行这么多的试验呀！你们还采用什么措施来检测像焊缝中未熔合、气孔、裂文、夹渣、焊缝尺寸诸如此类不符合要求的焊接缺陷？

李　芹：你所问的涉及到许多专业性问题。有许多检测焊接质量的方法来检测焊接构件和焊接设计的要求。

科　克：应留意哪些检查项目？

李　芹：一般来说，我们应检查焊接材料和电焊条，检查必要的工艺评定，制定焊接工艺规程，焊工的操作技能等诸多项目。

科　克：小姐，怎样进行检查呢？

Liqin: The surface areas of welding joints must be inspected by vision or magnifier (within 20 times magnification) in order to find out the surface defects.

Coke: You know what you are doing. What about the defects inside the joints?

Liqin: We adopt the extra-sound test, X-ray or R-ray test, magnetic powder test or colour test.

Coke: I think so many scientific instruments are to be tested and quality must be insured. Where can you carry out these tests without damaging the material and also the damage tests?

Liqin: Usually in our laboratory.

Coke: What mechanical character tests (the damage tests) can you do in your laboratory?

Liqin: We do the extension test, bending test and cold test for the welding joints.

Coke: Welded seams of the pipeline must have records, right?

Liqin: Yes, I suppose so according to welding code.

Coke: It's clear from the way we talked that you know the subject well.

Liqin: I'm pleased to hear your appreciation. Thank you!

Coke: Not at all.

李　芹：用肉眼或放大镜（放大20倍）来检查焊缝表面缺陷。
科　克：你很在行啰。那焊缝里面的缺陷该怎样进行检查呢？
李　芹：我们使用超声波检测法，X射线和R射线检测法，磁粉检测法或着色检测法进行检验。
科　克：我想用这么科学仪器来检测，质量一定能保证。那你们在哪儿能做这些无损检测，也做破坏性试验？
李　芹：通常都在试验室做。
科　克：你们在试验室还能做哪些机械性能（破坏性试验）的检测？
李　芹：我们能做焊接接头的拉伸试验，弯曲试验和冲击试验。
科　克：管线焊缝一定要有记录，是吗？
李　芹：是的。根据规范，我认为应该有。
科　克：从我们的对话中，可以看出你是一位有造诣的试验技术员。
李　芹：听到你的赞赏我深感欣慰。谢谢！
科　克：没什么。

Spoken Practice 口语练习

1. **Pair Work:**

    You're visiting a welding laboratory, and you're talking with a welding tester while you're watching how to carry out the welding test. Try to say what you personally see and hear here.

2. **Tell "true" or "false" in accordance with Learn to Speak English:**

    1) (   ) The strength increased from them will be lost if it is welded after cold tension reinforcing steel.

    2) (   ) The pulling tension test, the bending plastic inspecting and the radiographic inspection radioscopy must be usually done for the quality.

    3) (   ) The surface areas of welding joints must be only inspected by magnifier within 20 times magnification.

    4) (   ) The defects inside the welding joints are tested by the extra-sound test, X-ray or R-ray test, magnetic powder test or colour test.

    5) (   ) The extension test, bending test and colliding test for the welding joints can be done on the worksite.

3. **Read & Interpret the Following Passage:**

    ### Two Types of Welds

    The most two common types of welds are fillet welds and groove welds. Fillet welds are used to attach a plate to another plate or member in either a parallel (lapped) or protruding (tee) position. Groove welds retain the continuity of plate elements that are butt joined along their edges. Groove welds require special edge preparation and careful fit up, and when welded from both sides, or from one side with a backup strip on the far side, they may be said to achieve complete-penetration and may be stressed as much as the weakest piece that has been joined. Incomplete-penetration groove welds are used only when the plates are not required to be fully stressed and full continuity is not required. Complete-penetration groove welds are also used for corner or tee joints when full plate development is required.

4. Substitute the Following Words & Expressions:

1) Use the following **Welding Defects** (焊接缺陷) to replace the black words in the following sentence:

Coke: So many inspections and tests! What measures do you take to inspect **the welding defects** such as **non-melted welding**, **air holes**, **leakage**, **slag in joints**, **welding seam size** and such the like aren't conformed to the requirement?

科　克：要进行这么多的试验呀！你们还采用什么措施来检测象焊缝中未熔合、气孔、裂文、夹渣、焊缝尺寸诸如此类不符合要求的焊接缺陷？

Welding Defects [ˈweldiŋ diˈfekts] 焊接缺陷
melt/burn through [melt/bəːn θruː] 烧穿
fish eye [fiʃ ai] 白点
overlap [əvəˈlæp] 焊瘤
undercut [ˈʌndəkʌt] 咬边
slag inclusion [slæg inˈkluːʒən] 夹渣
excessive penetration [ikˈsesiv ˌpeniˈtreiʃən] 塌陷
weld crack [weld kræk] 焊缝裂纹
crater krack [ˈkrætə kræk] 弧坑裂纹
cold/hot crack [kould hɔt kræk] 冷/热裂纹
welding deformation [ˈweldiŋ ˌdiːfɔːˈmeiʃən] 焊接变形
erosion [iˈrouʒən] 溶蚀
complete penetration [kəmˈpliːt ˌpeniˈtreiʃən] 焊透
incomplete penetration [ˌinkəmˈpliːt ˌpeniˈtreiʃən] 未全焊透
pit [pit] 凹坑
lack of fusion [læk əv ˈfjuːʒən] 未熔合
incompletely filled groove [ˌinkəmˈpliːtli ˈfilid gruːv] 未焊满

2) Use the following **Terms about Welding Test** (焊接检验相关术语) to replace the black words in the following sentence:

Liqin: We do the **extension test**, **bending test** and **cold test** for the welding joints.

李芹：我们能做焊接接头的拉伸试验，弯曲试验和冲击试验。

Terms about Welding Test [tə:mz əˈbaut ˈweldiŋ ˈtestiŋ] 焊接检验相关术语

obtain a certificate [əbˈtein ə səˈtifikit] 获得证书

test piece [test pi:s] 试件

test specimen [test ˈspesimin] 试样

visual examination [ˈvizjuəl igˌzæmiˈneiʃən] 外观检查

destructive test [disˈtrʌktiv test] 破坏检验

penetrate inspection [ˈpenitreit inˈspekʃən] 渗透探伤

ultrasonic inspection [ˈʌltrəˈsɔnik inˈspekʃən] 超声波探伤

radioscopy [ˌreidiˈɔskəpi] 射线探伤

radiograph [ˈreidiəugra:f] (X) 射线照片

pulling tension test [ˈpuliŋ ˈtenʃən test] 拉伸试验

non-destructive testing [nʌn disˈtrʌktiv ˈtestiŋ] 无损检验

magnetic particle inspection [mægˈnetik ˈpa:tikl inˈspekʃən] 磁粉检验

bending plastic inspecting [ˈbendiŋ ˈplæstik inˈspektiŋ] 弯曲塑性检验

radiographic inspection radioscopy 射线探伤

[ˌreidiəuˈgræfik inˈspekʃən ˌreidiˈɔskəpi]

Situational Dialogic Unit 37
第三十七情景对话单元

Learn to Speak English

Talking about Piling Test

Alice: How many piling tests have you made on the building site, sir?

Dufu: At least ten pilling tests till now, miss.

Alice: Please tell me what the most important solution you obtain from your tests?

Dufu: The most important solution is that the maximum penetration to the last 3 groups with each 10 nos hammering and the bottom level of the piling can be fixed according to the designed loading capacity of the piles.

Alice: That's right. How many is the vertical tolerance for the piling?

Dufu: In accordance with the specification, the vertical error can not be more than 0.5% of the pile length after the driving operation.

Alice: For speeding up the construction progress, we want to drive piles by full height for each hammer, OK?

Dufu: No. The first several hammerings must be in low height to fix the piles in stable position, after that, hammer can be lifted to its full height.

Alice: Hammer of 8 tone is used to drive 350mm × 350mm square piles, isn't it?

Dufu: No, it isn't allowed to drive piles of this size by such a heavy hammer.

Alice: Why not, sir?

Dufu: Because 350mm × 350mm piles can't stand a stoke more than 2,000 kilogram Newtons (kN). But the hammer of 8 tone will produce more than 3,500 kN. stroke force.

Alice: OK. What test should you usually do after the pile has been already driven to the position?

Dufu: We should carry out the strength variation test to the piles to make sure that the piles are driven in good situation.

Alice: Right. Taking it all in all, you know what's what, I'm satisfied with your reply and sure that you can do your work better in the future.

Dufu: That's really good of you to say so.

Alice: There's no need to thank me.

学说英语

谈论打桩试验

艾莉斯：先生，你们在这家建筑工地已做过多少次打桩测试？
杜　傅：小姐，到目前为止最少十次。
艾莉斯：请谈谈从这些测试中你们获取的最重要的结论是什么？
杜　傅：最重要的结论是，根据桩的设计承载力，得出施打最后3阵，每阵10次的最大贯入度，以确定桩尖的打入标高。
艾莉斯：这就对啦！桩的垂直误差是多少？
杜　傅：根据规范，打入后桩的垂直误差不能超过桩长度的0.5%。
艾莉斯：为了加快施工进度，我们想把每一桩锤都调到最大的落差来打，行吗？
杜　傅：这不行。开始几次垂击落差必须低，这样才能使桩位更稳固，此后才可把桩锤提升到最大高度。
艾莉斯：用8吨桩锤打350毫米乘以350毫米的桩，可以不可以？
杜　傅：绝不可以，用这么重的桩锤打这种规格的桩是不允许的。
艾莉斯：那为什么不允许？
杜　傅：因为350毫米乘以350毫米桩不能承受2000千牛顿以上的冲击，而8吨锤的冲击力超过3,500千牛顿。
艾莉斯：是。桩已打到确定的位置后，你们通常还要做哪些必要的测试？
杜　傅：为了确保桩的质量，我们通常还要对桩进行应力变化测试。
艾莉斯：对！就整体而言，你做到胸中有数。我对你的回答感到满意，而且确信你们会在未来做得更好。
杜　傅：感谢你这样夸奖。
艾莉斯：没必要谢我。

Spoken Practice 口语练习

1. Pair Work:

Suppose your partner who is a supervising engineer, and comes to your new worksite where you've driven piles, he asks you to show him a piling test report. Try to say how to get the test result of driving piles during driving piles.

2. Tell "true" or "false" in accordance with Learn to Speak English:

1) ( ) The vertical error can not be above 5% of the pile length after the driving operation.

2) ( ) The first several hammerings must be in full height to fix the piles in stable position.

3) ( ) The hammer of 8 tone is allowed to drive 350mm × 350mm square piles.

4) ( ) Strength variation test to the piles have to be carried out after the pile has been already driven to the position.

5) ( ) I'm very unsatisfied with your piling test.

3. Read & Interpret the Following Passage:

Three Modern Piledriving Methods

1. **Driven piles**, where a prefabricated pile is driven into hard rock, providing a firm base.

2. **Driven and cast pile**, where the vibrator drives a steel tube into the ground, it is reinforced by steel grid and withdrawn after concrete is cast into it.

3. **Bored and cast piles**, where a hole is drilled and a concrete mixture is cast directly into the hole.

4. Put the Following Sentences into Chinese and Pay Attention to Translation Skill of Infinitive Phrases (动词不定式短语):

1) Victoria **came to see** he was wrong and I was right.

2) The old builder **appeared to be talking** with a foreign friend in English.

3) Manager **happened to have** once **been** to this beautiful and large city before.
4) We **got to know** all about the accident in fact.
5) Wilkinson **failed to understand** why I refused his invitation at that time.
6) I don't know why my memory sometimes **seems to play** tricks on me.
7) Xiao Wang **chanced to be** on the worksite where I was constructing.

Explanatory Notes 注释：

在英语中仅有 come, seem, appear, happen, chance, fail, get 等不及物动词后接动词不定式短语时，在意义上是从不同的角度对动词不定式所表示动作的进一步说明，和前面的动词不定式一同构成动词短语。这种短语带有某种情态意义，因此特提醒在翻译这种结构时，不能按动词不定式表示目的、结果以及原因等充当状语的常规进行翻译。

5. Substitute the Following Words & Expressions：

Use the following **Terms about Piling Test**（打桩试验相关术语）to replace the black words in the following sentence：

Alice：How many **piling tests** have you made on the building site, sir?

艾莉斯：先生，你们在这家建筑工地已做过多少次**打桩测试**？

Terms about Piling Test [təːmz əˈbaut ˈpailiŋ test] 打桩试验相关术语

pile load test [pail loud test] 桩荷载试验

pile pulling test [pail ˈpuliŋ test] 拔桩试验

penetration test [ˌpeniˈtreiʃən test] 贯入度试验

pile redriving test [pail ˈriːˈdraiviŋ test] 桩复打试验

field measurements [fiːld ˈmeʒəmənts] 现场测试

field identification [fiːld aiˌdentiˈfikeiʃən] 现场鉴定

field density test [fiːld ˈdensiti test] 现场密度测试

standard penetration test [ˈstændəd ˌpeniˈtreiʃən test] 标准贯入试验

field moisture equivalent [fiːld ˈmoistʃə iˈkwivələnt] 现场含水量等量

driving record ['draiviŋ 'rekɔːd] 打桩记录
over driving ['ouvə 'draiviŋ] 超打
pile capacity [pail kə'pæsiti] 单桩承载力
driving stress ['draiviŋ stres] 打桩应力
pile driving resistance [pail 'draiviŋ re'zistəns] 打桩阻力
depth of penetration [depθ əv ˌpeni'treiʃən] 贯入深度
specified penetration ['spesifaid ˌpeni'treiʃən] 指定贯入度
final penetration ['fainl ˌpeni'treiʃən] 最终贯入度
lateral pile load test ['lætərəl pail loud test] 桩的侧向荷载试验
standard penetration test blow count，N63.5 标准贯入试验锤击数
['stændəd ˌpeni'treiʃən test blou kaunt]

Situational Dialogic Unit 38
第三十八情景对话单元

Learn to Speak English

Talking about Surveying

Cathleen: Please tell me what surveying is defined as, sir?

Surveyor: OK. According to dictionary, it may be defined as the art of making measurements of the relative positions of natural and manmade features on the earth's surface.

Cathleen: And what about the term "surveying" in practice?

Surveyor: It is often used in the particular sense of meaning those operations which deal with the making of plans, that is to say, working in the two dimensions which form the horizontal place.

Cathleen: I see. What's surveying purpose?

Surveyor: It's the plotting of these measurements to some suitable scale to form a map, plan or section.

Cathleen: And what's the meaning of leveling?

Surveyor: The term "leveling" covers work in the third dimension, namely the dimension normal to the horizontal. Thus we have:

Cathleen: What, sir?

Surveyor: leveling and surveying.

Cathleen: What's surveying?

Surveyor: Operations connected with representation of ground features in plan.

Cathleen: What's leveling?

Surveyor: Operations connected with representation of relative difference in altitude between various points on the earth's surface.

Cathleen: What you said is right. And how many parts is a surveyor's work divided into?

Surveyor: Usually four parts, I think.

Cathleen: And what's the first part?

Surveyor: Field work: making and recording measurements in the field.

Cathleen: That's all right. And what's the second?

学说英语

谈论测量

凯思琳：先生，请给我讲一讲测量学的确切之意是什么？
测量员：好吧。根据字典对其的解释，测量学的定义应为对地面上的自然要素和人工地物的相对位置进行量测。
凯思琳：然而在实践中"测量"一词又是什么意思？
测量员：在实践中"测量"一词往往以特殊意义用来表示那些与测绘平面图有关的那些操作，也就是说，在构成水平面的二维平面上的工作。
凯思琳：我知道了。测量的目的是什么？
测量员：其目的是将这些测量成果按某种适当比例尺绘制成地图、平面图或断面图的技术。
凯思琳：那"水平测量"一词的含义又是什么？
测量员："水平测量"一词的含义则是指在第三维中的工作，即在垂直于水平方向的工作。这样有：
凯思琳：有什么，先生？
测量员：水平测量和平面测量。
凯思琳：什么是平面测量？
测量员：平面测量就是把地面上的要素表示在平面图上有关的操作。
凯思琳：水准测量是什么？
测量员：水准测量是与表示地面上各点高程之间相对差数有关的操作。
凯思琳：你说得对。那测量员的工作分几部分？
测量员：我想测量员的工作通常分四部分。
凯思琳：第一部分是什么？
测量员：外业：就是在野外进行测量并记录下测量结果。
凯思琳：对。第二部分呢？

Surveyor: Computing: mading the necessary calculations to determine locations, areas and volumes.

Cathleen: What you said is correct. What about next?

Surveyor: Mapping: that's plotted the measurements and drawing a map, I think.

Cathleen: OK. And what about last?

Surveyor: Stakeout: Setting stakes to delineate boundaries or to guide construction operations.

Cathleen: How nice! You're an experienced surveyor. I'm very pleased with your explaining.

Surveyor: I'm most grateful to your praise. But these're all essential knowledge to me.

Cathleen: Perhaps I'll come to learn some later on.

Surveyor: It's not trouble at all. Welcome to come anytime!

测量员：计算：就是进行必要的计算，以确定位置、面积和体积。
凯思琳：你说的没错。下一部分呢？
测量员：制图：我认为制图就是将测量成果绘制成地图。
凯思琳：对呀！那最后一部分呢？
测量员：放样：定立木桩用于表示边界或指导施工。
凯思琳：棒极了！你回答的令我满意。你真是一位富有经验的测量员。
测量员：多谢你的夸奖，其实这些都是我应具备的知识。
凯思琳：也许以后还会向你讨教的。
测量员：不必客气，欢迎随时光临！

建筑试验和测量人员英语情景会话

Spoken Practice 口语练习

1. **Pair Work:**

   You're a surveyor of a Construction Engineering Company, you're going to surveying with your surveying instruments. Try to say what surveying is and what surveying parts can be divided into.

2. **Tell "true" or "false" in accordance with Learn to Speak English:**

   1) (　) Surveying may be defined as the art of making measurements of the relative positions of natural and man-made features on the earth's surface.

   2) (　) The leveling covers work in the two dimension, namely the dimension normal to the horizontal.

   3) (　) Surveying is operations connected with representation of relative difference in altitude between various points on the earth's surface.

   4) (　) A surveyor's work is usually divided into five working parts.

   5) (　) A surveyor's first working part is computing, second is stake out.

3. **Read & Interpret the Following Passage:**

   ### The Level

   Strictly speaking the level is an instrument designed primarily to furnish a horizontal line of sight. The line is determined by a telescope with the usual components consisting of object glass, focusing arrangement, diaphragm with cross—lines, and eyepiece. In practice, the telescope must be capable of rotation about a vertical axis so that it can be pointed in any direction.

   The levels in use nowadays can be grouped into three main classes: dumpy levels, automatic levels and tilting levels often called quickset or engineer's levels.

4. **Substitute the Following Words & Expressions:**

   1) Use the following **Types of Surveying** （测量的种类） to replace the black words in the following sentence:

Cathleen: And what about the term "**surveying**" in practice?
凯思琳：然而在实践中"**测量**"一词又是什么意思？

Types of Surveying [taips əv səːˈveiiŋ] 测量的种类

plane surveying [plein səːˈveiiŋ] 平面测量

geodetic surveying [ˌdʒiːouˈdetik səːˈveiiŋ] 大地测量

topographic surveying [ˈtɔpəˈgræfik səːˈveiiŋ] 地形测量

route survey [ruːt səːˈvei] 路线测量

hydrographic survey [ˌhaidrouˈgræfik səːˈvei] 水文/河道测量

construction survey [kənˈstrʌkʃən səːˈvei] 施工测量

photogrammetric survey [ˌfoutəˈgræmitrik səːˈvei] 摄影测量

2) Use the following **Geometry** (**几何图形**) to replace the black words in the following sentence：

Surveyor: Computing: mading the necessary calculations to determine **locations**, **areas** and **volumes**.

测量员：计算：就是进行必要的计算，以确定**位置**、**面积**和**体积**。

Geometry [dʒiˈɔmitri] 几何图形

horizontal [ˌhɔriˈzɔntl] 水平线，水平面

vertical [ˈvəːtikəl] 垂直线，竖向

incline [inˈklain] 斜面，斜坡

circle [ˈsəːkl] 圆形，圆周

square [skwɛə] 正方形

trapezium [trəˈpiːzjəm] 梯形

triangle [ˈtraiæŋgl] 三角（形）

pyramid [ˈpirəmid] 棱锥形，棱锥体

tangent [ˈtændʒənt] 切线，正切

plane [plein] 平面

area [ˈɛəriə] 面积

cubature [ˈkjuːbətʃə] 体积

content volume [ˈkɔntent ˈvɔljum] 容积

locality [louˈkæliti] 位置

radius [ˈreidjəs] 半径

diameter [dai'æmitə] 直径

shape [ʃeip] 形状

circumference [sə'kʌmfərəns] 圆周，周线

polygon ['pɔligən] 多边形，多角形

Situational Dialogic Unit 39
第三十九情景对话单元

Learn to Speak English

Talking about Construction Surveys

Edison: It's said that survey has many types, I'd like to know how many exactly, Engineer Don?

Donna: Usually there're seven, young chap.

Edison: Seven. Why so many? Please tell me what they are?

Donna: OK. Plane surveying, geodetic surveying, topographic surveys, route surveys, hydrographic surveys, construction surveys and photogrammetric surveys.

Edison: Oh. really seven. Are they all concerning construction?

Donna: Not all. Main route surveys, hydrographic surveys and construction surveys are concerned in it.

Edison: I'm a student of architecture. Would you mind telling me about them in short way?

Donna: Certainly not, young chap.

Edison: Thank you. I'd like to know what route surveys are?

Donna: Route surveys are for high-ways, rail-roads, canals, pipelines and other projects which do not close upon the starting points.

Edison: I quite understand it. What about hydrographic surveys?

Donna: Yes. Since they survey of lakes, streams, reservoirs and other bodies of water, reservoirs, dams etc. belong to construction works.

Edison: I'm special interested in construction surveys, what does it mean?

Donna: This is the key to your question, I suppose. Construction surveys are important to you, they provide locations and elevations of buildings.

Edison: A topographic surveys on constraction area is the first problem solved in locating or positing a structure, right?

Donna: For sure. Because reference points to control the construction stakes and check the progress of work are needed.

Edison: But how to do construction surveying work well, Please explain it to me, Engineer Don?

学说英语

谈论施工测量

爱迪生：听说测量有许多种，我想知道究竟有几种，唐工？

唐　娜：通常说七种，小伙子。

爱迪生：就有七种！怎么这么多？请说说都是哪七种？

唐　娜：好吧。有平面测量、大地测量、地形测量、路线测量、水文/河道测量、施工测量和摄影测量。

爱迪生：啊，果然有七种。那这些测量和建筑都有关系吗？

唐　娜：并非所有都有关系。与建筑有关的主要是路线测量、水文测量和施工测量。

爱迪生：我是学建筑学的学生。你不介意的话扼要地给我讲讲相关测量可以吗？

唐　娜：当然不介意。小伙子。

爱迪生：谢谢！我想知道什么是路线测量？

唐　娜：路线测量是为兴修公路、铁路、开挖河道、铺设管道和其他工程而进行的不闭合于起始点上的测量工作。

爱迪生：我清楚了。但水文测量和建筑有什么关系吗？

唐　娜：有。因为水文测量是有关湖泊、溪流、水库以及水域方面的测量工作。水库、水坝等不都属于建筑工程。

爱迪生：我对施工测量特感兴趣，什么是施工测量？

唐　娜：我想这应是你的关键问题，施工测量对于你来说尤为重要。施工测量是用于提供建筑物的位置和高程的测量工作。

爱迪生：施工区的地形测量是在建筑物定位工作中首先要解决的问题，是吗？

唐　娜：那当然是。因为我们需要一些用于控制施工标桩并依据其检查施工进度的参考点。

爱迪生：那怎样才能搞好建筑测量工作呢，唐工，请给我讲讲？

Donna: The work is best learned on the job by adapting basic principles to practice. Because each work has its own characteristic.

Edison: That's reasonable. Is accuracy absolutely essential in setting out large buildings which are mainly adopted the prefabricated parts?

Donna: Yes, of course. Precision is absolutely necessary, not err by hair's breadth at all.

Edison: What procedure should surveyors carry out for highly accurate measurements, I'm longing for them?

Donna: Several procedures must be followed, for instance, using a good quality tape which has never been broken; whenever possible, don't allow the tape to sag.

Edison: That's right. This is about measuring tool. Have you anything to stress?

Donna: Yes. Using a spring balance or constant-tension handle in order to adjust the instrument accurately.

Edison: Good. That's about adjusting instrument.

Donna: Right. Last procedure is computing the various corrections and applying the corrections to the distance set out.

Edison: The last one is about surveying and measuring results. So many procedures should be followed, is it?

Donna: Certainly. For the absolute accuracy, every surveyor must do so. Only following such procedures can you guarantee surveying accuracy.

Edison: I bear in mind. Thank you for your patient explanation.

Donna: Not at all. Such a trifling thing is hardly worth mention.

唐　娜：最好是在工作中把测量的基本原理同实践相结合的过程中学习。因为每项工作都有其本身的特点。

爱迪生：有道理。在放样过程中，主要在使用预制构件的大型建筑物时，精度是绝对必要的吗？

唐　娜：当然精度是绝对必要，决不能有丝毫偏差。

爱迪生：我渴望知道为了确保高精度的测量，测量员必须履行哪些步骤？

唐　娜：有许多步骤都必须履行，比方说，使用未曾受损的优质卷尺；无论什么时候，要尽可能不使卷尺弯曲。

爱迪生：对呀。这一步骤是有关量具的，还有其他要强调吗？

唐　娜：有。使用弹簧秤或拉力稳定的拉力架以便校准仪器。

爱迪生：很好，这一步骤是校准仪器用的。

唐　娜：对。最后的步骤是计算各种改正数并将它们施加到所放样的距离上去。

爱迪生：最后的步骤是有关测量结果。如此多的步骤都得遵循吗？

唐　娜：那当然是。为了测量的绝对准确，每一位测量人员都应这样做。只有这样，才能保证其准确性。

爱迪生：我记住啦，多谢你不厌其烦地讲解。

唐　娜：不客气，区区小事何足挂齿。

Spoken Practice 口语练习

1. **Pair Work:**

   One acts as a surveyor, the other acts as an inspector who wants to know what surveying procedures should be carried out by any surveyor for highly accurate measurements. Use the following expressions:

   ——Can I help...?

   ——Yes...

   ——What surveying procedures should...?

   ——First... then... finally

2. **Tell "true" or "false" in accordance with Learn to Speak English:**

   1) ( ) Plane surveying and geodetic surveying are concerned construction works.

   2) ( ) A topographic survey on the construction area is the first problem solved in locating or positing a structure.

   3) ( ) Reference points to control the construction stakes and to check the progress of work are needful.

   4) ( ) Every surveyor must use a spring balance or constant-tension handle to adjust the instrument accurately.

   5) ( ) The surveyors should carry out four procedures for highly accurate measurements.

3. **Read & Interpret the Following Passage:**

   ### The Theodolite

   The theodolite is an instrument designed for the measurement of horizontal and vertical angles. It is a precision surveying instrument for measuring angles, and is of wide applicability in surveying. There are repeating theodolites and direction theodolites nowadays.

   A theodolite may be regarded as a mechanical realization of the geometry of three concurrent straight lines—the telescope axis, the so-called transit axis to which the telescope axis should be perpendicular, and the main rotation axis to which the transit axis should be perpendicular.

If the geometry of the instrument is perfect, then when the main rotation axis is vertical, the transit axis will be horizontal; and the line of sight will sweep out a vertical plane when the telescope is elevated or depressed.

4. **Match the Following Antonyms A with B:**

(A) antonym	(B) antonym	(A) antonym	(B) antonym
correct 正确的	hot 热	elder 较长的	outside 外面
cold 冷	worst 最坏的	night 夜间	thin 瘦
east 东	opened 打开的	strong 强壮的	right 右
empty 空的	dark 黑暗	fat 肥	slow 慢
best 最好的	wrong 错误	inside 里面	most 最多的
absent 缺席	west 西	fast 快	low 低
bright 光明	wet 潮湿的	least 最少的	younger 较幼的
big 大的	present 出席	left 左	near 近
closed 关闭的	small 小的	far 远	bad 坏的
dry 干燥	angry 愤怒	high 高	day 白天
pleased 喜悦	full 满的	good 好的	weak 虚弱的

5. **Substitute the Following Words & Expressions:**

1) Use the following **Surveying Lines**（测量线）to replace the black words in the following sentence:

Donna: Yes. Because **reference points** to control **the construction stakes** and to check the progress of work are needed.

唐娜：是的。因为我们需要一些用于控制**施工标桩**并依据其检查施工进度的**参考点**。

Surveying Lines [səːˈveiiŋ lainz] 测量线

straight line [streit lain] 直线

broken line [ˈbroukən lain] 折线

solid/full line [ˈsɔlid ful lain] 实线

base-line [beis lain] 基线

building line [ˈbildiŋ lain] 建筑红线，房基线

datum line [ˈdeitəm lain] 基准线，水准线

datum point ['deitəm pɔint] 基准点
central point ['sentrəl pɔint] 中心点
axis ['æksis] 轴线
site location [sait lou'keiʃən] 定位线，定位
center line ['sentə lain] 中心线
outline ['aut-lain] 轮廓线
string line [striŋ lain] 标线
perpendicular line [ˌpə:pən'dikjulə lain] 垂直线，定线
line of level [lain əv 'levl] 水平线
dimension line [di'menʃən lain] 尺寸线

2) Use the following **Surveying Instruments and Others**（测量仪器与其他）to replace the black words in the following sentence：

Donna：Yes. Using a **spring balance** or **constant-tension handle** in order to adjust **the instrument** accurately.

唐娜：有。使用弹簧秤或拉力稳定的拉力架以便校准仪器。

Surveying Instruments and Others 测量仪器与其他
[sə:'veiiŋ 'instrumənts ənd 'ʌðəz]

theodolite [θi'ɔdəlait] 精密经纬仪
high-precision theodolite [hai pri'siʒən θi'ɔdəlait] 高精度经纬仪
repeat theodolite [ri'pi:t θi'ɔdəlait] 复测经纬仪
direction theodolite [di'rekʃən θi'ɔdəlait] 方向经纬仪
transit ['trænsit] 经纬仪
leveling instrument ['levəliŋ 'instrumənt] 水平仪
spirit level ['spirit 'levl] 水平器
dumpy level ['dʌmpi 'levl] 定镜水平仪
quickset level ['kwikset 'levl] 速调水平仪
engineer's level [ˌendʒi'nəz 'levl] 工程水平仪
automatic level [ˌɔ:tə'mætik 'levl] 自动安平水平仪
telluric meter [te'ljuərik 'mi:tə] 微波测距仪
cross-hair ring [krɔs hɛə riŋ] 十字丝环
support [sə'pɔ:t] 支架，支座

leveling rod ['levəliŋ rɔd] 水准标尺
ranging pole ['reindʒiŋ poul] 标杆，测杆
readjust focusing [ˌriːə'dʒʌst 'foukəsiŋ] 调整聚焦
leveler ['levlə] 水准测量员
surveyor [sə:'veiə] 测量员
transitman ['trænsitmən] 经纬测量员
rodman ['rɔdmən] 标杆员，司尺员

Part Five
English Situational Conversations with Administrative Personnel in Construction Company
(Situational Dialogic Unit 40-45)

第五部
建筑公司后勤人员英语情景会话
（第四十至四十五情景对话单元）

Situational Dialogic Unit 40
第四十情景对话单元

Learn to Speak English

Talking about Booking Airline Tickets

Janet: I'd like to book some flights to Washington on Sunday, sir.

Hexi: OK. I'll find out for you. Which flight, miss?

Janet: Any flight, but I'd like to book non-stop flight, economy class and open return.

Hexi: I see. BA has got a DC-9 leaving at 07:30, and I have to remind you open return tickets must be firmed up 3 days in advance.

Janet: I rememder it already. Anything to declare, sir?

Hexi: Yeah. We reserve the right to retain the whole or part of the fare in the case of booking cancelled within two hours of scheduled departure.

Janet: (Say half joking) I'm not the first time to book a ticket. I know this regulation.

Hexi: Although you know this, our duty is to explain this to you clearly.

Janet: Thank you for your kindness. What's the fare to Washington?

Hexi: US $500, miss.

Janet: How long does it take and when does it arrive at Washington?

Hexi: Let me look in the time-table for you. Oh, taking about 15 hours. It's going to arrive at 08:00 a.m. next day.

Janet: What time should check in, sir?

Hexi: Do be there before 06:30 if you're checking in at the airport, OK. Here's your ticket, miss. It's all in order.

Janet: Here's your money. Thanks.

Hexi: Not at all.

建筑技术与管理英语情景会话

学说英语

谈论订购机票

珍妮特：先生，我想订几张星期日飞往华盛顿的机票。

贺　喜：好吧，我先给您查一查。订哪个航班，小姐？

珍妮特：任何航班都可以，但我要订直达航班，普通舱，不限回来时间的往返票。

贺　喜：我明白了。正好英航有个 DC-9 班机，07：30 起飞。不过我还得提醒你"不定日期机票要在开航 3 天前落实"。

珍妮特：我记住了。先生，还有什么规定要说明的吗？

贺　喜：有。旅客在开机前两小时以内要求退票，我们有权将已付票款的全部或部分扣下，不予退还。

珍妮特：（半开玩笑地说）我并非是第一次订票。我知道这条规定。

贺　喜：尽管你知道，但我们有义务向你们讲解清楚我们的相关规定。

珍妮特：谢谢您的好意。到华盛顿的机票价钱是多少？

贺　喜：500 美元，小姐。

珍妮特：要飞行多长时间？何时才能抵达华盛顿？

贺　喜：我给您查一下时刻表。啊，大约飞行 15 小时。次日上午八点到达。

珍妮特：先生，什么时候办登机手续？

贺　喜：你来机场办登机手续的话，务必在 06：30 之前到达。好了，小姐，这是您的机票，手续全办妥了。

珍妮特：给钱，谢谢！

贺　喜：不客气。

Explanatory Notes 注释：

　　open return 是不定时间的来回机票，即往返机票。购买这种机票要比单程票便宜，有效期长达一年，旅客确定归期后，可凭此票向航空公司办理返回事宜。

Spoken Practice 口语练习

1. **Pair Work:**

    A acts as a rear service manager of a Building Company, B acts as a ticket seller who wants to know what air-tickets A likes to book. Use the following expressions:

    ——Can I help you?

    ——Yes, I'd like to...

    ——What tickets...?

    ——We have...

2. **Tell "true" or "false" in accordance with Learn to Speak English:**

    1) (　) I'd like to book some flights to Beijing on Sunday.

    2) (　) The fare of confirmed date ticket to Warsaw is ＄500.

    3) (　) I'd like to book economy class, open return.

    4) (　) If you're checking in at the airport, you must be there after 06:30.

    5) (　) Here's your money, sir. It's all in order.

3. **Read & interpret the Following Passage:**

    Booking Airline Tickets

    You can go to a travel agency or talk directly to the airlines to book your airline ticket. Remind you that some large cities have more than one airport. Be sure to know which airport and terminal your flight leaves from.

4. **Put the Following into English:**

    道　歉

    因东西搁置找不到（暂时丢失）而道歉时，经常使用"似乎是"这一说法。这是因为这里有模棱两可之意，说话人想把事情轻描淡写地告诉物主而不使其过于惊慌。有时候在东西丢失了甚至于打碎了的时候也用这种说法。

5. **Substitute & Reference Words and Expressions:**

    1) Use the following **Air Routes and Others**（航线和其他用语）to

replace the black words in the following sentence:

Janet: Any flight, but I'd like to book **non-stop flight**, **economy class** **and open return**.

珍妮特：任何航班都可以，但我要订**直达航班**，**普通舱**，**不限回来时间的往返票**。

Air Routes and Others [εə ruːts ənd ˈʌðəz] 航线和其他用语

Internal Air Route [inˈtəːnl εə ruːt] 国内航线
flight schedule [flait ˈʃedjuːl] 航班时刻表
non-stop flight [nʌn stɔp flait] 直达航班
first class [fəːst klaːs] 头等舱
economy class [iˈkɔnəmi klaːs] 经济舱
single/ one way (Am.) [ˈsiŋgl wʌn wei] 单程票
return/ round trip (Am.) [riˈtəːn raund trip] 往返票
open date ticket [ˈoupən deit ˈtikit] 不定日期客票
confirmed date ticket [kənˈfəːmid deit ˈtikit] 定日期客票

International Air Routes [ˌintəˈnæʃənl εə ruːts] 国际航线

JAL Beijing-Tokyo（日航）北京—东京
RO Beijing-Karachi-Bucharest（罗航）北京—卡拉奇—布加勒斯特
JAL Beijing-Shanghai-Osaka-Tokyo（日航）北京—上海—大阪—东京
AA San Francisco-Shanghai-Beijing（美航）旧金山—上海—北京
IR Tokyo-Beijing-Teheran（伊航）东京—北京—德黑兰
PR Manilla-Guangzhou-Beijing（菲航）马尼拉—广州—北京
PK Tokyo-Beijing-Karachi（巴航）东京—北京—卡拉奇
ET Beijing-Bombay-Addis Ababa
（埃航）北京—孟买—亚的斯亚贝巴
SR Beijing-Bombay-Athens-Geneva-Zurich
（瑞航）北京—孟买—雅典—日内瓦—苏黎世
JU Beijing-Karachi-Belgrade-Zurich
（南航）北京—卡拉奇—贝尔格莱德—苏黎世
AF Tokyo-Beijing-Karachi-Athens-Paris
（法航）东京—北京—卡拉奇—雅典—巴黎

AA New York-San Francisco-Shanghai-Beijing

(美航）纽约—旧金山—上海—北京

2）Use the following **Main Air Corporations throughout the World**（世界主要航空公司）to replace the black words in the following sentence：

Hexi：I see. **BA** has got a DC-9 leaving at 07:30, and I have to remind you open return tickets must be firmed up 3 days in advance.

贺　喜：我明白了。正好**英航**有 DC-9 班机，07:30 起飞。不过我还得提醒你"不定日期机票要在开航 3 天前落实。"

Main Air Corporations throughout the World 世界主要航空公司

AC Air China （中航）中国国际航空公司

BA British Airways （英航）英国航空公司

AA American Airlines （美航）美国航空公司

AC Air Canada （加航）加拿大航空公司

AF Air France （法航）法国航空公司

AY Finnair （芬航）芬兰航空公司

CX Cathay Pacific Airways （香航）国泰航空公司

ET Ethiopian Airlines （埃航）埃塞俄比亚航空公司

IB Iberia （西航）西班牙航空公司

JAL Japan Airlines （日航）日本航空公司

LH Luft hansa （德航）汉莎航空公司

MX Mexicana （墨航）墨西哥航空公司

OA Olympic Airways （希航）奥林匹克航空公司

PR Philippine Airlines （菲航）菲律宾航空公司

QF Qantas Airways （澳航）澳大利亚航空公司

RG Varig （巴航）巴西航空公司

RO Tarom （罗航）罗马尼亚航空公司

SN Sabena （比航）比利时航空公司

SQ Singapore Airlines （新航）新加坡航空公司

SR Swissair （瑞航）瑞士航空公司

TE Air New Zealand （新航）新西兰航空公司

Situational Dialogic Unit 41
第四十一情景对话单元

Learn to Speak English

Talking about Telephoning an International Call or Sending a Telegram

Linda: Do you want to book a trunk-call, sir?

Jiaxin: No, I don't want to book a trunk-call. I'd like to book a telegram. Can you help me, miss?

Linda: Sorry, sir. It's a telephone counter here and telegram counter is over there.

Jiaxin: There, I see. Thanks. By the way, which do you think is worthwhile and better, sending a telegram to Shanghai, China or making a phone call there?

Linda: It depends on the concrete condition.

Jiaxin: What's your meaning?

Linda: Paying a telegram is according to the words, however, paying a phone call is time.

Jiaxin: Comparatively speaking, sending a telegram reckon up, I've a few words to say.

Linda: That's probably true.

Jiaxin: (a few minutes later) I want to book an ordinary telegram to Shanghai, China. It needs to be sent out as soon as possible, miss.

Maria: OK, sir. More people want to send their telegrams, so we're very busy today. But I'll try my best to do so for you.

Jiaxin: Thank you. But how should I go through formalities?

Maria: Please fill in the telegraph form first. Do write down the addressee's name, address and others correctly and write them legibly.

Jiaxin: OK, miss. Should I fill in the information strictly according to the fact?

Maria: Certainly. Please hand it to me after filling it in, sir.

Jiaxin: Thank you for your warm reception.

Maria: Not at all.

学说英语

谈论打国际电话还是拍电报

琳　达：先生，你想挂个长途电话吗？
贾　欣：不，我不想挂长途电话。我想拍一个电报。小姐，你能帮我办理相关手续吗？
琳　达：很抱歉，先生。这儿办理打电话手续，拍电报在那边柜台。
贾　欣：那边，我知道了，谢谢。顺便问一句，你说给中国上海打电话、拍电报哪种合算些？
琳　达：这要根据具体情况而定。
贾　欣：此话怎讲？
琳　达：拍电报是按字的多少记费，而打电话则按时间长短收费。
贾　欣：我要说的话并不多，相对而言拍电报还是合算些。
琳　达：也许是这样。
贾　欣：（几分钟过后）小姐，我想给中国上海拍个普通电报。希望尽快办理。
玛丽亚：好的，先生。今天拍电报的人较多，所以业务也就很繁忙，但我会尽快给您办理的。
贾　欣：谢谢！怎样办理相关手续呢？
玛丽亚：请先填写这张电报文稿。务必填准收报人姓名、地址和其他相关信息，而且字迹得写清楚。
贾　欣：好的，小姐。要如实填写吗？
玛丽亚：当然是。先生，填完后交给我就可以了。
贾　欣：感谢您的热情服务！
玛丽亚：不用谢。

Explanatory Notes 注释：

1. 英美人士打电话的习惯和中国人相比有所不同，下列几点应予以注意：
    1) 在接对方电话时，应主动先告诉对方你是谁或你在何处。例如：This is Mary.（我是玛丽。）或 David is speaking.（大卫在讲话。）等，而不要用汉语习惯先问对方，诸如"喂，你是谁？你在哪儿？"这类话。
    2) 在打电话的过程中，习惯用 this 指代自己；用 that 指代对方。如：This is Tom.（我是汤姆。）Who is that?（你是谁？）
    3) 你给对方打电话时，当你听到对方话音后，问对方是谁时，一般习惯应说"Is that…?"而不说"Who are you"或"Are you…?"
    4) 如你接到一个打错的电话，一般应说"I'm afraid you have the wrong number"（对不起，你拨错了号码）。应有礼貌地告诉对方打错了电话，并把你的电话号码或所处的位置主动的告诉对方，以免对方再打这个号码，而不应该很不耐烦或粗暴地回答对方。

2. 电报的计费办法：
    英文电报是按"词"计费的，这里的词不等于汉语的字。但这种"词"也不同于英文的自然"词"。它是电报的计费单位，其基本规则如下：
    1) 英文的自然词、复合词、普通文字、暗语和字码符号混合书写的词组，凡不超过十个字母均按一个"词"收费，例如：AT ONCE 是两个单词，有六个字母算一个词；英文电报十个字母为一个词，超过此数而不足二十个字母则算两个"词"。例如：TELECOMMUNICATION 为十七个字母，算两个词。
    2) 密码、商业标志、数字和缩写，每五个字码算一个词。

Spoken Practice 口语练习

1. **Pair Work:**

   Work in groups or pairs. Suppose you are a cadre of a Building Company. Try to say how to make an international phone call and how to send a telegram in a post office.

2. **Tell "true" or "false" in accordance with Learn to Speak English:**

   1) (   ) The fee of telegram and phone call are paid the same standard.
   2) (   ) The telegram needs to be put through as soon as impossible.
   3) (   ) I'd like to book an ordinary call to Xi'an, China.
   4) (   ) "I'm afraid you have the wrong number" means your phone number is incorrect.
   5) (   ) "I am Jiaxin, and who are you?" is conformed to the saying way of British & American custom.

3. **Read & interpret the Following Passage:**

   ### Telephoning

   The telephone system in the foreign countires also has an area code. If you know it and the phone number, it's usually easy and cheap to dial the number yourself. You can dial direct to many countries overseas or you can ask for the overseas operator.

4. **Substitute the Following Words & Expressions:**

   1) Use the following **Terms about Telegram**（电报相关术语）to replace the black words in the following sentence:

   Linda: Sorry, sir. It's a telephone counter here and **telegram** counter is over there.

   琳达：很抱歉，先生。这儿办理打电话手续，**拍电报**在那边柜台。

   Terms about Telegram ［təːmz əˈbaut ˈteligræm］电报相关术语

   telegraph fee ［ˈteligraːf fiː］电报费

   original copy ［əˈridʒənəl ˈkɔpi］原报底稿

   telegraph building ［ˈteligraːf ˈbildiŋ］电报大楼

   destination ［ˌdestiˈneiʃən］收报地址

sender's signature ['sendəz 'signitʃə] 发报人署名
ordinary telegram ['ɔːdinəri 'teligræm] 普通电报
urgent telegram ['əːdʒənt 'teligræm] 加急电报
Please fill in the telegraph form 请填写电报纸
[pliːz fil in ðə 'teligrɑːf fɔːm]
addressee's name and address 收报人姓名和地址
[ˌædreˈsiːz neim ənd əˈdres]

Telegram Form ['teligræm fɔːm] 电报格式

Free：报费　　　　　Serial：流动号码
Account No：记账号码　Transmitting Date and Time：发出日期
Original No：原来号码　Operator：值班人
Clerk：营业员
Please Write Legibly：请把字迹写清楚
Robert Wood 567 Chinatown New York city U. S. A.
美国　纽约市　唐人街　第567号，罗伯特·伍德
AWAITING YOUR INSTRUCTION SOONEST.
请速指示。
Zhao Yuan 赵元
P/bag 04988 CSCEC London U. K.
英国伦敦　中建总公司 04988 信箱

Class 报类	Name of Transmitting Office 发报局名	Number of Word 字数	Date 日期	Time 时间

2) Use the following **Telephone and Its Idioms**（电话以及相关习语）
to replace the black words in the following sentence：
Linda：Do you want to book **a trunk-call**, sir?
琳　达：先生，你想挂个**长途电话**吗？
Telephone and Its Idioms 电话以及相关习语
['telifoun ənd its 'idiəmz]
public telephone ['pʌblik 'telifoun] 公用电话
urban telephone ['əːbən 'telifoun] 市内电话
business telephone ['biznis 'telifoun] 业务电话
megnetic telephone card [mæg'netik 'telifoun kɑːd] 磁卡电话

mobile phone ['moubail foun] 移动电话
SPC telephone [spk 'telifoun] 程控电话
radio telephone ['reidiou 'telifoun] 无线电话
telephone number ['telifoun 'nʌmbə] 电话号码
telephone directory ['telifoun di'rektəri] 电话号码簿
area code ['ɛəriə koud] 区号
book a trunk-call to... [buk ə trʌŋ kɔ:l] 挂个到……电话
make a phone call [meik ə foun kɔ:l] 打电话
call/ring sb. up [kɔ:l riŋ 'sʌmbədi ʌp] 给某人打电话
phone sb. [foun 'sʌmbədi] 给某人打电话
You're wanted on the phone. [juə 'wɔntid ɔn ðə foun] 有你的电话。
A phone calls for you. [ə foun kɔ:lz fə ju:] 你的电话。
The line is busy/engaged. [ðə lain iz 'bizi in'geidʒid] （电话）占线。
The line is dead. [ðə lain iz ded] 电话断了。
The telephone is ringing. [ðə 'telifoun iz 'riŋiŋ] 电话铃响了。
Please answer it. [pli:z 'ɑ:nsə it] 请接电话。
The line is clear. [ðə lain iz kliə] 电话接通了。
There's no answer. [ðɛəz nou 'ɑ:nsə] 没人接电话。
Hello, I'm listening. ['he'lou aim 'lisniŋ] 喂，说/讲吧！
I have to hang up. [ai hæv tu hæŋ ʌp] 我该挂断了。
Someone wants you on the phone. 有人来电找你。
['sʌmwʌn wɔnts ju: ɔn ðə foun]

Situational Dialogic Unit 42
第四十二情景对话单元

Learn to Speak English

Talking about Posting Letters and Parcels

Mike: I want to post a letter to Xi'an, China.

Clerk: OK. By airmail, sir?

Mike: Oh, yes. What's the postage?

Clerk: I'll check it for you. 90 P is enough.

Mike: OK. I'm a philatelist and I like to collect stamps.

Clerk: I sell all kinds of stamps here. Which do you prefer, commemorative stamp or common one?

Mike: I pay same postage, and naturally I prefer to buy a commemorative stamp rather than a common one.

Clerk: I think so. Do you want an envelope, sir?

Mike: Yes. And how much is it?

Clerk: Two P. Here you are. Please write address, post code and name begibly, I have to remind you.

Mike: Thank you for your goodwill reminding. Sure. By the way, how long does it take to get there?

Clerk: Usually, it takes about two days. Do you have other business to do, sir?

Mike: Yes. I've got some parcels to mail, too.

Clerk: What parcels, bulky parcel or small one?

Mike: They're private parcels, and belong to small, I think.

Clerk: All right. Please fill in one dispatch and two declaration forms.

Mike: (after a while) OK. Here you are. How much is the charge?

Clerk: I've to examine if there's any dangerous articles in them. OK. It comes ten dollars.

Mike: Ten dollars. Here's the money.

Clerk: Here's your receipt, sir.

Mike: Thanks very much.

Clerk: Small thanks to me.

学说英语

谈论邮寄信件和包裹

迈　克：我想邮寄一封到中国西安的信。
营业员：好的。航空邮寄吗，先生？
迈　克：哦，是的。邮资是多少？
营业员：我给你查一下。90便士就够了。
迈　克：好吧。我是一名集邮爱好者，我喜欢集邮。
营业员：我这儿售各种邮票。您喜欢哪种邮票，纪念邮票还是普通邮票？
迈　克：花同样的钱，我自然喜欢纪念邮票而不喜欢普通邮票。
营业员：我也这样认为。先生，还买信封吧？
迈　克：对呀！多少钱一个？
营业员：2便士。这是你的邮票和信封。我得提醒你一句，请把地址、邮编、姓名写清楚。
迈　克：多谢你温馨地提醒，我会的。顺便问一声，这封信寄到西安需要多长时间？
营业员：通常需要两天。先生，你还有其他业务要办理吗？
迈　克：是的。我还有几件包裹也要邮寄。
营业员：什么包裹，大宗包裹还是小件包裹？
迈　克：是个人包裹，我想都属于小件包裹吧。
营业员：好吧。请填写一张发递单，两张税单。
迈　克：（过了一会儿）行。填写好了。该交多少邮资费？
营业员：我先检查一下有无危禁物品。检查通过了，总共要支付10美元。
迈　克：10美元。给钱。
营业员：给你的收据，先生。
迈　克：非常感谢！
营业员：一点也不用感谢。

Spoken Practice 口语练习

1. **Pair Work:**

   A is a rear service cadre in a Building Company, B is one of clerks in a big Post Office. B tries to tell A how to post letters and parcels.

2. **Tell "true" or "false" in accordance with Learn to Speak English:**

   1) (   ) I want to post a letter by airmail to Guangdong, China.

   2) (   ) Usually the postage to China is 90 P.

   3) (   ) I'm a stamp fan and I like to collect rare stamps.

   4) (   ) I prefer to buy a commemorative stamp rather than a common stamp.

   5) (   ) I've got some parcels to post too.

3. **Read & interpret the Following Passage:**

   ### What Is A Return Receipt?

   When the addressee receives the letter or parcel, he signs a receipt which the Post Office returns to you by mail. It is your proof, in case you ever need it, that the letter or parcel was delivered. There is some charge for it in some countries.

4. **Put the Following Sentences into Chinese and Point out the Function of "as":**

   1) Is there a difference between the English language **as** it is spoken by the Englishmen and by the Americans?

   2) **As** chief engineer is away at present, the technical meeting has to be put off till next Wednesday.

   3) Please construct **as** the drawing says.

   4) Busy **as** he is, he often goes to the building site and inspect engineering quality.

   5) I'll solve the technical problem **as long as** it takes place on the worksite.

   6) His English spoken is as good as I, and his translation is not so good as I.

Explanatory Notes 注释：

As 也是英语中非常活跃而又十分有用的单词之一，看似简单，但使用复杂，很难掌握，因为它不仅能用作介词、连词、关系词和许多短语，而且作为连词时还具有不同的词意，因此也能构成不同状语从句。例如：

1）as 连词，当……的时候之意，引导时间状语从句。
2）as 连词，鉴于、由于之意，引导原因状语从句。
3）as 连词，按照、象之意，引导方式状语从句。
4）as 连词，尽管、虽然之意，语序倒装，引导让步状语从句。
5）as/so long as 连词，只要之意，引导条件状语从句。
6）as… as 和……一样、not so…as 不如……那样之意，连词，引导比较状语从句。

5. Substitute the Following Words & Expressions：

1）Use the following **Terms about Letter**（信件术语）to replace the black words in the following sentences：

Mike：I want to **post a letter** to Xi'an, China, miss.
迈　克：小姐，我想**邮寄一封**到中国西安的信。
Clerk：OK. By **airmail**, sir?
营业员：好的。航空邮寄吗，先生？

Terms about letter ［təːmz əˈbaut ˈletə］ 信件术语
registered letter ［ˈredʒistəd ˈletə］ 挂号信
express letter ［iksˈpres ˈletə］ 快信
double-registered letter ［ˈdʌbl ˈredʒistəd ˈletə］ 双挂号信
postcard ［ˈpoustkaːd］ 明信片
letter paper ［ˈletə ˈpeipə］ 信纸
envelope ［ˈenviloup］ 信封
address ［əˈdres］ 地址
sender/addressor ［ˈsendə ˈədresə］ 寄件/信人
recipient/addressee ［riˈsipiənt ˌædreˈsiː］ 收件/信人
post code ［ˈpoust koud］ 邮政编码
postmark ［ˈpoustmaːk］ 邮戳

post office [poust 'ɔfis] 邮局

post office box (POB) [poust 'ɔfis bɔks] 邮政信箱

postman ['poustmən] 邮递员

2) Use the following **Stamps** (邮票) to replace the black words in the following sentence：

Clerk：I sell all kinds of **stamps** here. Which do you prefer, **commemorative stamp** or **common one**?

营业员：我这儿售各种邮票。您喜欢哪种邮票，**纪念邮票**还是**普通邮票**？

Stamp [stæmp] 邮票

stamp collecting [stæmp kə'lektiŋ] 集邮

philatelic stamp [ˌfilə'telik stæmp] 集邮邮票

rare stamp [rɛə stæmp] 珍贵邮票

(un)used stamp [(ˈʌn)ˈjuːzd stæmp]（未用过的）旧邮票

commemorative stamp [kə'memərətiv stæmp] 纪念邮票

special stamp ['speʃəl stæmp] 特种邮票

airmail stamp ['ɛəmeil stæmp] 航空邮票

pair [pɛə] 双联

block of four [blɔk əv fɔː] 四联

souvenir card ['suːvəniə kaːd] 小型张

complete set [kəm'pliːt set] 整套

face value [feis 'væljuː] 面值

perforation [ˌpəːfə'reiʃən] 齿孔

stamp-album [stæmp 'ælbəm] 集邮册

philatelist/stamp collector [fi'lætəlist stæmp kə'lektə] 集邮者

3) Use the following **Kinds of Parcel** (包裹的种类) to replace the black words in the following sentences：

Clerk：What **parcels**, **bulky parcel** or small one?

营业员：什么包裹，**大宗包裹**还是小件包裹？

Mike：They're **private parcels**, and belong to small, I think.

迈克：是**个人包裹**，我想都属于小件包裹吧。

Kinds of Parcel [kaindz əv ˈpɑːsl] 包裹种类

insured parcel [inˈʃuəd ˈpɑːsl] 保价包裹

small parcel [smɔːl ˈpɑːsl] 小件包裹

bulky parcel [ˈbʌlki ˈpɑːsl] 大宗包裹

parcel postage [ˈpɑːsl ˈpoustidʒ] 包裹邮资

parcel form [ˈpɑːsl fɔːm] 包裹详情单

notice of arrival [ˈnoutis əv əˈraivəl] 领取包裹通知

return receipt [riˈtəːn riˈsiːt] 回执

Situational Dialogic Unit 43
第四十三情景对话单元

Learn to Speak English

Talking about Shopping

Forster: Are you being served, sir?

Gaogui: No. I want to buy some office articles. Can you show me those red note books and blue ball pens?

Forster: OK. Here you are. Have a look and try!

Gaogui: Oh. Very nice. I like them very much. How much is it?

Forster: One mark for per book and per piece.

Gaogui: It's too expansive, it seems to me. Can you make a reduction?

Forster: Yeah. The best I can offer is 10% discount.

Gaogui: But the price is reasonable. OK. I'll take ten each. How much should I pay you?

Forster: And the next article, sir?

Gaogui: Oh, yes. Some cigarettes and lights. . . .

Forster: I'm afraid I can't help you. But it sells them just over that counter.

Gaogui: I saw it. Your money, please.

Sophie: OK. Thanks. (After a while) Anything I can do for you?

Gaogui: Yeah, Thirty lights and twenty cartons of Hilton cigarettes made in England. Can you show a sample?

Sophie: Yes. Here you are. Please look at the words "Made in England".

Gaogui: Yes, quite good and the quality is excellent. It's up to the sample. How much do I owe you?

Sophie: Three hundred and sixty-five marks in all.

Gaogui: That's too dear. Any cheaper?

Sophie: To tell the truth, that's almost cost price. As you want more. I advocate small profits but quick turnover. So you just pay me a wholesale price, not retail price. Three hundred and fifty is OK, my former customer.

Gaogui: Many thanks. Here's your money.

Sophie: Thank you. Hope to have more chance to serve you.

学说英语

谈论购物

福斯特：先生，有人招呼您吗？

高　贵：没有。我想买一些办公用品。您能给我看看那些红色笔记本和蓝色圆珠笔吗？

福斯特：好吧。这就是。看看怎样？

高　贵：啊！很不错，我很喜欢。这要多少钱？

福斯特：每本1马克，每支也是1马克。

高　贵：似乎太贵了。能打折吗？

福斯特：能。最多打九折。

高　贵：不过价格还算合理。好吧，各买10个。该付多少钱？

福斯特：先生，不知你是否还想买些其他的东西？

高　贵：啊，是的。再买些香烟和打火机……。

福斯特：我这就恐怕无能为力。不过就在那边的柜台出售（香烟）。

高　贵：我看见啦。请把钱收好。

索菲娅：好的。谢谢！（过了一会儿）我能为你效劳吗？

高　贵：是呀。买30个打火机，20条英国制造的希尔顿香烟，能给我先看看样品吗？

索菲娅：好的。请看吧。瞧"英国制造"这字样。

高　贵：是的，不错，质量上成，符合样品规格。我该付多少钱？

索菲娅：总共365马克。

高　贵：太贵啦！还能便宜点儿吗？

索菲娅：老实说这几乎是成本价。因为你买的量大，薄利多销嘛，我还是按批发价卖给你的，不是零售价。老顾客，付350马克就可以了。

高　贵：请收好钱。多谢！

索菲娅：谢谢！希望今后再度光顾。

Spoken Practice 口语练习

1. **Pair Work:**

   Supposing A is a salesgirl of a supermarket, B is a purchaser (采购员) of a building company. They're talking about the price of some daily articles that B needs to buy.

2. **Tell "true" or "false" in accordance with Learn to Speak English:**

   1) (   ) I want to sell some note books and ball pens.
   2) (   ) The note books are too expansive for me to buy, I think.
   3) (   ) The best price I can offer is 5% discount.
   4) (   ) The quality of Hilton cigarettes made in England is excellent.
   5) (   ) To tell the truth, that's almost retail price.

3. **Read & interpret the Following Passage:**

   ### Asking Favours

   If you ask for things, it's important to be polite. Especially English people use rather elaborate and roundabout ways of asking for things. The most important thing about asking favours of people is how you ask, rather than the actual words you use. The intonation you use in making your request is as important as what you actually say. If you think someone will refuse yours, you can ask the question in such a way that the refusal doesn't cause embarrassment.

4. **Put the Following Sentences into Chinese and Point out the Function of "as":**

   1) These foreigners regard Chinese builders **as** their real friends and loyal partners.
   2) The matter isn't considered **as** settled.
   3) There're different types of work in construction, **such as** civil construction workers, building installers, building mechanics and building decorators, etc.
   4) I want to find **such** English-Chinese Dictionary **as** you are using right

now.

5）**As** is known to us, China has a huge building industry now.

6）What our manager wants to mention is **as above.**

7）The contract copy reads **as follows.**

8）The construction problem of safety and quality should be considered **as whole.**

Explanatory Notes 注释：

　　1）as 介词，引入宾语补足语，2）as 介词，引入主语补足语。除了上述 as 用作介词外，as 还可用作代词，如3）such as 诸如之意，引导同位语，4）as 关系代词作宾语，引导定语从句，5）as 关系代词作主语，引导定语从句。as 短语的使用频率也相当高，如6）as above 如上之意，用作表语，7）as follows 如下之意，用作状语，8）as whole 整体来说之意，用作状语。由于 as 短语在英语口语中很有用，因此再列举几条在日常生活中出现频率较高的供参考使用，如：as a rule（通常，照常）、as a result（结果）、as well（也）、as usual（照常）、as a matter of fact（事实上）、so as to（do）（以便，为了）、as matters stand（照目前的情况看）、as likely as not（说不定）、as if（好像）、as concerns（关于）、as ever（仍旧，照常）等。

5. Substitute the Following Words & Expressions：

1）Use the following **Stores and Others**（商店及其他）to replace the black words in the following sentence：

Forster：I'm afraid I can't help you. But it sells just over that **counter.**
福斯特：我这就恐怕无能为力。不过就在那边的**柜台**出售（香烟）。

Stores and Others ［stɔːz ənd ˈʌðəz］ 商店及其他

supermarket ［ˈsjuːpəˌmaːkit］ 超级市场

department store ［diˈpaːtmənt stɔː］ 百货商店

shopping centre ［ˈʃɔpiŋ ˈsentə］ 商业中心

shop ［ʃɔp］ 店铺

antique shop ［ænˈtiːk ʃɔp］ 古玩店

clothes market ['klouðz 'maːkit] 衣服市场
electrical department [i'lektrikəl di'paːtmənt] 电器部
jewellery/jewelry counter ['dʒuːəlri 'kauntə] 首饰部
cash desk [kæʃ desk] 交款处，收银台
salesman/boy ['seilzmən bɔi] 男售货员
saleswoman/girl ['seilzˌwumən gəːl] 女售货员
customer ['kʌstəmə] 顾客
cashier [kæ'ʃiə] 收银员
bargain sale ['baːgin seil] 大廉价
Not for sale [nɔt fə seil] 非卖品
We never close [wi 'nevə klouz] 通宵营业

2) Use the following **Some Terms of Articles**（部分商品术语）to replace the black words in the following sentence：

Sophie: OK. Thanks. (After a while) Anything I can do for you?

索菲娅：啊，谢谢！（过了一会儿）我能为你效劳吗？

Gaogui: Yeah, Thirty **lights** and twenty cartons of Hilton **cigarettes** made in England. Can you show some samples?

高贵：是呀。买30个**打火机**，20条英国制造的希尔顿**香烟**，能给我先看看样品吗？

Terms of Some Articles [təːmz əv sʌm 'aːtiklz] 部分商品术语

evening/dinner suit ['iːvniŋ 'dinə sjuːt] 男礼服
evening dress ['iːvniŋ dres] 女礼服
jacket ['dʒækit] 上衣
trousers ['trauzəz] 裤子
shirt [ʃəːt] 衬衣
fur coat [fəː kout] 皮大衣
skirt [skəːt] 裙子
tie/necktie [tai 'nektai] 领带
bow tie [bou tai] 领结
shoes [ʃuːz] 鞋
electric razor [i'lektrik 'reizə] 电须刀

camera ['kæmərə] 照相机
colour film ['kʌlə film] 彩色胶卷
sun-glasses [sʌn 'glaːsiz] 太阳镜
toilet articles ['tɔilit 'aːtiklz] 盥洗用品
umbrella [ʌm'brelə] 雨伞
diamond (finger) ring ['daiəmənd 'fiŋgə riŋ] 钻戒
pearl necklace [pəːl 'neklis] 珍珠项链
gold brooch [gould broutʃ] 金胸针
fake pendant [feik 'pendənt] 假坠子
silver bracelet ['silvə 'breislit] 银镯子
genuine ear ring ['dʒenjuin iə riŋ] 真耳环

Situational Dialogic Unit 44
第四十四情景对话单元

Learn to Speak English

Talking about Seeing a Doctor

(A) Seeing a Surgeon

Doctor: What's wrong with your leg, young man?

Brown: I didn't take a care and sprained it when I was working on the work-site, doctor.

Doctor: Well, Let me have a look. Please show me your tender spot, OK?

Brown: OK. Here it is. Don't touch it. It pains if touch my sore spot.

Doctor: Does it hurt when I press here?

Brown: Yes, it hurts terribly.

Doctor: For it's swollen, and hard to diagnose. You'll go and have to be taken an X-ray first, I think.

Brown: Is it serious, doctor? Why to take an X-ray?

Doctor: I want to judge if it's fracture or dislocation.

Brown: I understand what you mean. Thank you for your kindness.

Doctor: Don't mention it. (after half an hour) Let me have a look at the X-ray, well. It says nothing serious.

Brown: What should I do, doctor?

Doctor: Take it easy. Have a plaster applied and a wound dressed first.

Brown: And what will I do then?

Doctor: Take the antiphlogistic and stop pain as indicated in the prescription after you go home.

Brown: Where is your pharmacy, doctor?

Doctor: Oh. It's over there.

Brown: OK. Anything else, doctor?

Doctor: Yes. After you got home, you won't walk up and down and must stay in bed for at least three or four days.

Brown: I see. Thank you very much, doctor.

Doctor: Not at all. May you get well sooner!

学说英语

谈论看病

（A）看外科医生

大　夫：小伙子，你的腿怎么啦？
布　朗：大夫，我在工地上干活，一不小心就把腿扭伤了。
大　夫：啊，让我检查一下吧。请给我看看疼痛的位置好吗？
布　朗：好。就在这儿。不能碰，一碰就痛。
大　夫：我按这儿时，你觉得痛吗？
布　朗：是的，痛得厉害。
大　夫：由于这儿肿了，所以很难诊断清楚。我想你得先去拍一张片子。
布　朗：严重吗，大夫？为什么还得拍片子？
大　夫：拍片子就能看清到底是骨折还是脱臼。
布　朗：我理解你的用意。多谢你的好意。
大　夫：不必谢。（半小时以后）我看看片子，啊！没什么大问题。
布　朗：大夫，那我该咋办？
大　夫：别紧张！先涂抹点药，包扎起来。
布　朗：然后怎么办？
大　夫：我再给你开点消炎止痛药，回家后，请按处方说明服用就是了。
布　朗：大夫，药房在那儿？
大　夫：嗬，就在那边。
布　朗：对，我看见啦。大夫，还有什么要嘱咐的吗？
大　夫：是的。到家后，你不要来回走动，至少卧床休息三四天。
布　朗：我明白了。非常感谢，大夫。
大　夫：没什么。祝你早日康复！

(B) Seeing a Physician

Patient: I feel unwell, doctor.

Doctor: What's the matter with you, young man?

Patient: Maybe I've a fever.

Doctor: Anything else?

Patient: I've also a headache. I'm aching all over. You don't know how unwell I feel!

Doctor: Please tell me how long you've been like this?

Patient: Since last night.

Doctor: Oh. By looking, you only have a cold, I suppose.

Patient: Perhaps a bad cold.

Doctor: Let me examine you carefully again.

Patient: OK. But how to examine?

Doctor: Don't breathe while I'm listening to your heart and lunge. (After a while) Now take a deep breath, please.

Patient: Is it OK?

Doctor: Not yet, Let me feel your pulse... a little fast. Open your mouth and say "Ah". Have your temperature taken.

Patient: What about my illness, doctor?

Doctor: Your temperature is higher and your heart and lunge beating a little fast, but it's not serious. To be frank, you just have a cold.

Patient: What ought I to do, doctor?

Doctor: It's nothing serious. Have an injection taken first, and it's ally a fever and relieve pain, and then you'll be better soon. Here's your prescription, and have more hot water when you're taking your medicine at your home.

Patient: Thanks. I'm sure it'll give me relief after I take my medicine.

Doctor: Not at all. I think so.

（B）看内科医生

病　人：大夫，我觉得身上很不舒服。
大　夫：年轻人，你怎么不舒服？
病　人：也许我是发烧吧。
大　夫：还有哪儿不得劲吗？
病　人：还有点头痛，浑身都不舒服，你可不知道，多么难受呀！
大　夫：请告诉我像这样症状有多久啦？
病　人：自昨晚以来一直是这样。
大　夫：啊！从表面上诊断，我觉得你只是患了感冒。
病　人：也许是感冒吧。
大　夫：让我再给你仔细检查一下。
病　人：那好。不过怎么检查？
大　夫：我听你的心脏时，屏住气。（过了一会儿）请现在做深呼吸。
病　人：好了吗？
大　夫：还没呢。你的脉搏……也有点快。把嘴张开，说"啊"。让我再量一下你的体温。
病　人：怎么样，大夫？
大　夫：你的体温比较高，心跳有点快。但没什么大问题，坦率地说，你只是着凉了。
病　人：那我就放心了。大夫，我该怎么办？
大　夫：不要紧，先打一针，解热止痛，很快就会缓解点儿。这是给你开的处方，回到家后服药时要多喝点儿热水。
病　人：谢谢。服药后肯定会解除我的疾苦的。
大　夫：不必谢。我也是这样想的。

Spoken Practice 口语练习

1. **Pair Work:**

   Suppose your partner who is ill, and comes to a Hospital / Clinic. A doctor looks at the patient's clinical symptom, makes a diagnosis and gives him/her the result. But the patient is deeply concerned to ask how to treat it and what to be payed attention to.

2. **Tell "true" or "false" in accordance with Learn to Speak English:**

   1) (   ) I've sprained my arm in my office building.

   2) (   ) Because the leg hurts terribly, you'll have to stay in bed for one or two days.

   3) (   ) I've a fever and a headache.

   4) (   ) You only have a cold by looking.

   5) (   ) After being taken an injection and medicine, you must get well sooner.

3. **Read & interpret the Following Passage:**

   ### Foreign Hospital

   Foreigners take ill or involved in accidents while in the U. K. are entitled to free medical treatment under the British National Health Service. Maybe things are defferent in other countries. It's usually best to go to see a doctor that someone has recommended. In an emergency, you may go to the emergency entrance of the nearest hospital. Medical services abroad are generally very expensive.

4. **Substitute the Following Words & Expressions:**

   1) Use the following **Medical Staff and Departments of Hospital**（医务人员和医院的科室）to replace the black words in the following sentence:

   Patient: Where is your **pharmacy**, **doctor**?

   病人：大夫，药房在哪儿？

   Medical Staff and Departments of Hospital 医务人员和医院的科室

['medikəl sta:f ənd di'pa:tmənts əv 'hɔspitl]

doctor ['dɔktə] 大夫，医生

nurse [nə:s] 护士

pharmacist/ pharmaceutist ['fa:məsist ˌfa:mə'sju:tist] 药剂师

clinic ['klinik] 医务所，诊所

out-patients department [aut 'peiʃənts di'pa:tmənt] 门诊部

registration office [ˌredʒis'treiʃən 'ɔfis] 挂号室

consult room [kən'sʌlt ru:m] 诊断室

emergency room [i'mə:dʒənsi ru:m] 急诊室

medical department ['medikəl di'pa:tmənt] 内科

surgical department ['sə:dʒikəl di'pa:tmənt] 外科

ear-nose-throat department [iə nouz θrout di'pa:tmənt] 耳鼻喉科

orthop(a)edics department [ˌɔ:θou'p i:diks di'pa:tmənt] 骨科

laboratory [lə'bɔrətəri] 化验室

operation room [ˌɔpə'reiʃən ru:m] 手术室

dressing/injection room ['dresiŋ in'dʒekʃən ru:m] 包扎/注射室

ward [wɔ:d] 病房

in-patients department [in 'peiʃənts di'pa:tmənt] 住院部

2）Use the following **Surgical Disease, Treatment and Medicine/Drug**（外科疾病，治疗和药物）to replace the black words in the following sentence：

Doctor：Have a **plaster applied** and a **wound dressed** first, and then take the **antiphlogistic and stop pain** as indicated in the prescription after you go home.

大夫：先涂抹点药，包扎起来，然后我再给你开点消炎止痛药，回家后，请按处方说明服用就是了。

Surgical Disease, Treatment and Medicine/Drug 外科疾病，治疗和药物

['sə:dʒikəl di'zi:z, 'tri:tmənt ənd 'med(i)sin/drʌg]

burns [bə:nz] 烧伤

bruise [bru:z] 挫伤，伤痕

trauma ['trɔ:mə] 创伤，外伤

frostbite ['frɔstbait] 冻伤
suture ['sju:tʃə] 缝合
excision [ek'siʒən] 切除/开
extraction of pus [iks'trækʃən əv pʌs] 抽脓
change dressings [tʃeindʒ 'dresiŋz] 换药
apply a plaster [ə'plai ə 'pla:stə] 上药膏
perform an operation [pə'fɔ:m ən ˌɔpə'reiʃən] 实施手术
relieve/stop pain [ri'li:v stɔp pein] 止痛
replace dislocated joints [ri'pleis 'dislə̄keitid dʒɔints] 脱臼复位
disinfectant [ˌdisin'fektənt] 消毒剂
hemostatic [ˌhi:mə'stætik] 止血药剂
pain-killer [pein 'kilə] 止痛药
antiphlogistic ['æntiflou'dʒistik] 消炎药
avoid reinfection [ə'vɔid ˌri:in'fekʃən] 防止再感染

3) Use the following **Diagnosis, Symptoms and Medicine/Drug**（诊断/检查，症状和药物）to replace the black words in the following sentence：

Doctor：Don't breathe while I'm **listening to your heart and lunge**. (After a while) Now **take a deep breath**, please. Let me feel your **pulse... a little fast**. Open your mouth and say "Ah". Have your **temperature taken.**

大夫：我听你的**心脏**时，屏住气。(过了一会儿)请现在**做深呼吸**，你的**脉搏**……**也有点快**。把嘴张开，说"啊"。让我再量一下你的**体温**。

Diagnosis, Symptoms and Medicine/Drug 诊断/检查，症状和药物
[ˌdaiəg'nousis, 'simptəmz ənd 'med(i)sin/drʌg]
consult a doctor [kən'sʌlt ə 'dɔktə] 看病
check one's blood pressure [tʃek wʌnz blʌd 'preʃə] 量血压
make a cardiogram [meik ə 'ka:diəgræm] 做心电图
make out a prescription [meik aut ə pris'kripʃən] 开处方
acupuncture and moxibustion ['ækjupʌŋktʃə ənd ˌmɔksi'bʌstʃən] 针灸

chill [tʃil] 发冷
nausea ['nɔːsjə] 恶心
cough [kɔf] 咳嗽
diarrh(o)ea [ˌdaiə'riə] 腹泻
stomachache ['stʌməkeik] 胃痛，肚子痛
constipation [ˌkɔnsti'peiʃən] 便秘
vomiting ['vɔmitiŋ] 呕吐
dizziness ['dizinis] 头昏
insomnia [in'sɔmniə] 失眠（症）
dysentery ['disəntri] 痢疾
tonsillitis [ˌtɔnsi'laitis] 扁桃腺炎
pharyngitis [ˌfærin'dʒaitis] 咽炎
heat stroke [hiːt strouk] 中暑
indigestion [ˌind(ə)i'dʒesʃən] 消化不良
food poisoning [fuːd 'pɔizniŋ] 食物中毒
pill/tablet [pil 'tæblit] 丸/片药
glucose ['gluːkous] 葡萄糖
sleeping pill ['sliːpiŋ pil] 安眠药
antipyretics ['æntipai'retiks] 退烧药
antidote ['æntidout] 解毒药

Situational Dialogic Unit 45
第四十五情景对话单元

Learn to Speak English

Talking about Purchasing Some Food for Site Canteen
A. Buying Some Grain and Oil

Hanbin: There's no more grain and oil in our canteen. I've to buy some. (After a while)

Service: You're welcome, sir. Our Grain & Oil Shop is the biggest one in the city. Quality fine, price cheap and repulation high. you can count it.

Hanbin: Thank you. I'm a Chinese builder. I've come here to buy some grains and edible oil for our site canteen. Can you show me some, please?

Service: OK, sir. But what kind of grain do you like?

Hanbin: Oh, some flour and rice.

Service: Please come and see the sample.

Hanbin: Hm. It's nice. It's just what I hope so. How much per bag?

Service: Ninety lire. The price of flour and rice are the same. How many do you want?

Hanbin: I'll take one hundred bags each.

Service: So many, which oil do you like, vegetable oil or animal oil, sir?

Hanbin: Vegitable oil is good for people's health, so I buy it, I think.

Service: Do you prefer soybean oil or rapeseed oil?

Hanbin: Soybean oil is much better, boss. How much is it?

Service: Two lire per kilogram.

Hanbin: But it's nice and cheap. We'll need five hundred kilogram. How much should I pay you in all?

Service: Let me calculate them. That's 2,000 lire in all

Hanbin: OK. Here's money for you.

学说英语

谈论给工地食堂采购食物

A. 买粮油

韩　斌：食堂粮油所剩无几。我得去买些（粮和食油）。
　　　　（过了一会儿）
塞维斯：先生，欢迎光顾。我们店是本市最大的粮油店。质量优、价格兼、信誉高，这一点你可放心。
韩　斌：谢谢。我是中国建筑工人。我前来贵店是给我们工地食堂买些粮油。请给我看一下贵店里的货物好吗？
塞维斯：好吧，先生。但不知您要看哪种粮？
韩　斌：哦，面粉和大米。
塞维斯：请过来看一看样品吧。
韩　斌：啊，不错，正合我意。多少钱一袋？
塞维斯：90里拉，面粉和大米一个价。您要买多少？
韩　斌：每种100袋。
塞维斯：买得还不少呢。先生，想要哪种油，植物油还是动物油？
韩　斌：植物油对人体益处多多，因此我想买些植物油。
塞维斯：你喜欢豆油还是菜子油？
韩　斌：豆油更好。老板，这要多少钱呢？
塞维斯：每公斤2里拉。
韩　斌：不过还挺便宜。要500公斤。算算总共该付多少钱？
塞维斯：让我算算。总共2,000里拉。
韩　斌：好吧。给你钱。

B. Buying Vegetables, Fruits and Condiments

Caimai: Oh, it's a large market. There're various kinds of vegetables and fruits here.

Sophia: Yes, sir. Can I help you in any way?

Caimai: For sure. I wonder if you have any good tomatoes, celeries...?

Sophia: Of course, we have. But how many do you need?

Caimai: I need more. How much does each box cost?

Sophia: The charge for the tomatoes is 2.9 pounds per box, and celeries 2.5.

Caimai: That's rather expensive, isn't it?

Sophia: Yes, a bit, but they're very fine.

Caimai: Can you come down a bit?

Sophia: That's our standard price, but how much would you like to buy, sir?

Caimai: I know that's a fair price but nothing is immutable. I'll take twenty boxes each. If apples and oranges are quite nice, I'll buy some, too.

Sophia: OK. That's settled then. They're all 2 pounds for each box. How many kilogram apples and oranges?

Caimai: That's right. Two hundred kilogram, too.

Sophia: Is there anything else you'd love to buy?

Caimai: Yes. Dried day-lily, fungus and some condiments.

Sophia: It sells three pounds a bag. Does it suit you?

Caimai: Yes, I'll take ten bags each. How much is it altogether?

Sophia: Let me see. It's 649 pounds. Pay 600 pounds sharp is OK.

Caimai: Here's the money for you. Please count it.

Sophia: Thank you. Hope you come again if you need something.

Caimai: Sure to come next time.

B. 购买蔬菜、水果和调味品

采　买：嗨，这真是个大市场。这儿有各种各样的蔬菜和水果。

索菲娅：是的，先生。我能帮你点儿忙吗？

采　买：肯定能。但不知你这儿是否有优质西红柿，芹菜……？

索菲娅：当然有。你要买多少？

采　买：我需要量较大。一箱多少钱？

索菲娅：一箱西红柿是 2.9 英镑，芹菜是 2.5 英镑。

采　买：太贵啦，不是吗？

索菲娅：是的，有点贵，不过质量可上乘。

采　买：能便宜点吗？

索菲娅：这是标准价。那你想出什么价，先生？

采　买：我知道这个价差不多，但一成不变的事是没有的。那每样菜买 20 箱。苹果，橘子以及其他水果不错的话，也买些。

索菲娅：那好，一言为定，每箱都按 2 英镑付款。苹果，橘子要买多少？

采　买：这就对啦。也要 200 公斤。

索菲娅：还要买什么菜吗？

采　买：是的。买些黄花菜，木耳和调味品。

索菲娅：一袋 3 英镑，价钱合适吧？

采　买：合适。每种要 10 袋。总共该付多少钱？

索菲娅：我算一算。总共 649 英镑。付 600 英镑整就可以啦。

采　买：这是付给你的钱。请收好。

索菲娅：谢谢。如果再需要什么的话，敬请再度光顾。

采　买：下次肯定会来。

C. Buying Some Meat and Sea Food

Roger: May I be of any service for you, sir?

Buyer: Thank you. I'd like to buy some meat, eggs and fowl, miss.

Roger: OK. We've beef, mutton, pork, and fowl in my shop. What would you like to buy, please?

Buyer: Let me look at your pork. It's nice and lean, really good. How much for each kilogram, please?

Roger: The price for pork is eight dinars per kilogram.

Buyer: That's kind of steep.

Roger: But how many do you need?

Buyer: More than two hundred lean pork.

Roger: Six Dinars. You can't be wrong on that, I think.

Buyer: Just so-so.

Roger: New Year is coming. I suppose you must buy something else.

Buyer: Yes. But next time I'll buy some lobsters, hairtail...

Roger: The sea food we've just got are quite fine, sir. If you don't mind, you have a look. It won't take you too much time, does it?

Buyer: Obviously not. Oh, nice!

Roger: There're too much sea food to store. I'll sell some prime price to you if you buy some today. It's also for you to help me.

Buyer: Yours are worth the price and top quality. Is that right?

Roger: Certainly. Business is striking a bargain that both sides agree.

Buyer: OK. fifty kilogram each type.

Roger: Thank you for your help.

Buyer: Not at all.

C. 购买肉和海味

罗　杰：先生，我可以为您效劳吗？
购买者：多谢，小姐。我想买些肉、蛋和禽类。
罗　杰：好的。我店有牛肉、羊肉、大肉和禽类。请问您想买些什么？
购买者：瞧一瞧大肉吧，挺瘦，确实不错。请问1公斤多少钱？
罗　杰：每公斤大肉价格是8个第纳尔。
购买者：这价有点高吧。
罗　杰：不知您想买多少？
购买者：200多公斤瘦肉。
罗　杰：6个第纳尔。我认为这价钱您不会吃亏的。
购买者：还可以吧。
罗　杰：新年即将来临，我想你们一定还得买些海味品吧。
购买者：是的。不过下次来买些龙虾，带鱼……
罗　杰：先生，我们刚进的海味品相当不错。你不介意的话，可以先看看，不会占用你过多时间，对吗？
购买者：显然不会。啊，真不错！
罗　杰：我们进的货太多，库存不下。如果你今天能购买的话，也算帮我个忙，我按进价卖给你。
购买者：你们的海味品货真价实、质量上乘。是这样吗？
罗　杰：当然。生意就是双方同意就成交。
购买者：好吧。每种各买50公斤。
罗　杰：多谢你的帮助。
购买者：没什么。

Explanatory Notes 注释：

　　nice + and + a. 短语在英语口语中是一种很有用的表达方式，一般译为"挺...", 例如：nice and lean 挺瘦、nice and cheap 挺便宜、nice and high/tall 挺高等。

Spoken Practice 口语练习

1. Pair Work:

One acts as a saleslady in a supper market, the other acts as a purchasing agent (采购员) who wants to buy some vegetables, fruits, grains, meat and others for his site canteen. Use the following expressions:

——Can I ... ?

——Yes, ...

——How ...

——It's...

2. Tell "true" or "false" in accordance with Learn to Speak English:

1) (   ) I've to buy some grain and vegetables in the supermarket.

2) (   ) I've come here to buy some flour and rice for our site canteen.

3) (   ) There are various kinds of vegetables and fruits in the large grain market.

4) (   ) Let me look at your mutton. It's really excellent.

5) (   ) You must buy something for the coming New Year, I suppose.

3. Read & interpret the Following Passage:

Asking People to Repeat

As long as you ask politely, most people don't mind repeating what you didn't hear or understand. Don't say the word "please" in U. K. when you want somebody to repeat what he/she says. This point should be reminded you so as to talk with others abroad.

4. Substitute the Following Words & Expressions:

1) Use the following **Kinds of Grain** (粮食种类) to replace the black words in the following sentence:

Service: OK, sir. But what kind of **grain** do you like?

塞维斯: 好吧, 先生。但不知您要看哪种**粮食**?

Kinds of Grain [kaindz əv grein] 粮食种类

grain shop [grein ʃɔp] 粮店

super flour ['sjuːpə 'flauə] 精(面)粉

corn flour [kɔːn ˈflauə] 玉米粉
wheat flour [hwiːt ˈflauə] 麦面粉
rice [rais] 大米
rice flour [rais ˈflauə] 米粉
soybean [ˈsɔiˈbiːn] 黄豆
broad bean [brɔːd biːn] 蚕豆
pea [piː] 豌豆
sesame [ˈsesəmi] 芝麻
green pease [griːn piːz] 青豆

2) Use the following **Sorts of Edible oil**（食油种类）to replace the black words in the following sentence：

Service：OK, which oil do you like, **vegitable oil** or **animal oil**, sir?

塞维斯：好的。先生，想要哪种油，**植物油**还是**动物油**？

Sorts of Edible oil [sɔːts əv ˈedibl ɔil] 食油种类
vegetable oil [ˈvedʒitəbl ɔil] 植物油
pork fat [pɔːk fæt] 猪/大油
animal fat [ˈæniməl fat] 动物油
sesame oil [ˈsesəmi ɔil] 芝麻油，香油
soybean oil [ˈsɔiˈbiːn ɔil] 黄豆油
peanut oil [ˈpiːnʌt ɔil] 花生油

3) Use the following **Kinds of Vegetable**（蔬菜种类）to replace the black words in the following sentence：

Caimai：Sure. I wonder if you have any good **tomatoes, celeries**...?

采买：肯定能。但不知你这儿是否有**优质西红柿，芹菜**……？

Kinds of Vegetable [kaindz əv ˈvedʒitəbl] 蔬菜种类
greengrocer's [ˈgriːnˈgrousəz] 蔬菜店
Chinese cabbage [ˈtʃaiˈniːz ˈkæbidʒ] 白菜
greens [griːnz] 青/油菜
cabbage [ˈkæbidʒ] 甘蓝，卷心菜
carrot [ˈkærət] 胡萝卜
spring onion [spriŋ ˈʌnjən] 大葱

green pepper [gri:n 'pepə] 青椒
lotus root ['loutəs ru:t] 莲藕
mushroom ['mʌʃrum] 蘑菇
bamboo shoots [bæm'bu: ʃu:ts] 竹笋

4) Use the following **Dried Vegetables and Condiments**（干菜和调味品）to replace the black words in the following sentence：

Caimai：Yes. **Dried day-lily**, **fungus** and some **condiments.**

采 买：是的。买些**黄花菜**，**木耳**和**调味品**。

Dried Vegetables and Condiments 干菜和调味品
[draid 'vedʒitəblz ənd 'kɔndimənts]

ginger ['dʒindʒə] 生姜
garlic ['ga:lik] 大蒜
peanut ['pi:nʌt] 花生米
picklex ['pikl] 泡菜，腌制菜
salted vegetable ['sɔ:ltid 'vedʒitəbl] 咸菜
pickled tuber mustard ['pikld 'tju:bə 'mʌstəd] 榨菜
seasoning ['si:zniŋ] 作料，调味品
gourmet powder ['guəmei 'paudə] 味精
table salt ['teibl sɔ:lt] 精盐
soy sauce [sɔi sɔ:s] 酱油
aromatic vinegar [ˌærou'mætik 'vinigə] 香醋
baking powder ['beikiŋ 'paudə] 发酵粉
pepper ['pepə] 胡椒
spice powder [spais 'paudə] 香料粉/五香粉

5) Use the following **Fresh Fruits**（鲜果）to replace the black words in the following sentence：

Sophia：OK. They're all 2 pounds for each box. How many kilogram **apples and oranges**?

索菲娅：那好，每箱都按2英镑付款。**苹果，橘子**要多少?

Fresh Fruits [freʃ fru:ts] 鲜果

lemon ['lemən] 柠檬

olive ['ɔliv] 橄榄
coconut ['koukounʌt] 椰子
haw [hɔː] 山楂
litchi /lichee ['liːtʃiː] 荔枝
mango ['mæŋgou] 芒果
musk melon [mʌsk 'melən] 香瓜，甜瓜
cherry ['tʃeri] 樱桃

6）Use the following **Meats**, **Eggs** and **Fowl**.（肉类，蛋和禽类）to replace the black words in the following sentence：

Buyer：Thank you. I'd like to buy some **meat**, **eggs** and **fowl**, miss.
购买者：多谢，小姐，我想买些**肉**、**蛋**和**禽类**。

Meats [miːts] 肉类
the butcher's [ðə 'butʃəz] 肉店
pork [pɔːk] 猪肉
spareribs ['spɛəribz] 排骨
mutton ['mʌtn] 羊肉
beef [biːf] 牛肉
cured meat [kjuəd miːt] 腊肉
bacon ['beikən] 烟/熏猪肉
sausage ['sɔsidʒ] 香肠
game [geim] 野味
fowl [faul] 禽类
salt egg [sɔːlt eg] 咸蛋
duck [dʌk] 鸭
preserved egg [pri'zəːvd eg] 皮蛋
pigeon ['pidʒin] 鸽
goose [guːs] 鹅
chicken ['tʃikin] 鸡
game bird [geim bəːd] 猎禽

7）Use the following **Fish and Sea Food**（鱼类和海味）to replace the black words in the following sentence：

Buyer: Yes. But next time I'll buy some **lobsters**, **hairtail**...
购买者：是的。不过下次来再买些龙虾，带鱼……。

Sea Food [siːfuːd] 海味

Sea Food Store [siːfuːd stɔː] 海味店

prawn [prɔːn] 对/明虾

shelled shrimp [ʃeld ʃrimp] 虾仁

lobster ['lɔbstə] 龙虾

sea cucumber [siː'kjuːkəmbə] 海参

crab [kræb] 蟹

seaweed ['siːwiːd] 海带

conch [kɔŋk] 海螺

red laver [red 'leivə] 紫菜

fishmonger's ['fiʃˌmʌŋgəz] 鱼店

carp [kaːp] 鲤鱼

grass carp [graːs kaːp] 草鱼

squid [skwid] 鱿鱼

silver carp ['silvə kaːp] 鲢鱼

turtle ['təːtl] 甲鱼，鳖

mud eel [mʌd iːl] 黄鳝

cuttlefish ['kʌtlfiʃ] 墨鱼

octopus ['ɔktəpəs] 章鱼

meat frog [miːt frɔg] 田鸡

pomfret ['pɔmfrit] 鲳鱼

Key to Spoken Practice 口语练习答案——Chinese Reference Translation 汉语参考译文

第一部　建筑企业管理人员英语情景会话

第一情景对话单元

公　司

公司是一个法律实体，与其业主分离而独立存在。公司的资产属于公司，而不属于股东个人。公司的业主称之为股东，他们的所有权是通过可转让的股份得到确认的。公司为其债务服务的同时，还必须为其盈利支付所得税。作为一个"独立的法律实体"，公司可以签订合同，在法庭上同自然人一样起诉和应诉。

第二情景对话单元

欢迎辞

女士们，先生们：

随着我国对外交往日益增多，我们每天要接待大量的来自不同国家的专家和学者。今天，我们很荣幸能和亨利·史密斯先生欢聚一堂。史密斯教授在建筑领域卓有成就，在世界上享有一定的威望。

首先，让我代表在座的各位向我们的贵宾表示热烈的欢迎和真挚的问候。

现在请亨利·史密斯先生做关于建筑企业管理的报告。

> **Invitation Card**
> Mr. and Mrs. Smith
> Request the pleasure of your company At dinner
> In Wild Cloud Guest House
> On Friday the 16th Oct. 2005
> From 7:00 to 8:00 p. m

第三情景对话单元

董事会的职能

董事会最基本的职能就是制订公司政策，并保护股东的利益。董事会的具体职责包括雇用公司高级职员，确定其工资待遇，宣布发放股利，以及审核内外审计人员的审计结果。

Business Card

> CSCEC
>
> **Wei Hua Manager**
> Overseas Company
> **China State Construction Engineering Corporation**
> Address: Baiwanzhuang Beijing China
> Post code: 100037　　　　　Fax: 010 – 8548986
> Tel: 010 – 87654321（Home）　010 – 81234567（office）
> E – mail: Weihua@yahoo.com　www.China.com

第四情景对话单元

公司的职业化管理

股东拥有公司，但他们不参与公司的日常管理工作，只是通过选举董事会管理公司事务。而董事雇用职业经理人管理公司经营，股东个人则无权参与管理，除非他/她被董事聘为公司经理。

建筑技术与管理英语情景会话

Notice

All the section managers are requested to have a meeting in the conference room at 8:00 on Thursday, Mar. 20th 2003.

President Office

Mar. 19th. 2003

第五情景对话单元

公司高级职员与其职责

公司最高管理层应包括总经理或首席执行官、秘书、主计长、财务主任。此外,每个职能部门都有一位副总经理主管,如人事、生产和经销等。

秘书在许多契约和法律方面代表公司,还负责保管董事会和股东大会的会议记录。主计长负责内部控制,编制会计账簿和财务报表。财务主任对公司资金有保管责任,并主要负责对公司现金的计划和控制。

Reply to accept the invitation

Mr. John Smith

accepts with pleasure the kind invitation

of General manager Mr. Wang Hai of

China State Construction Engineering Corporation

to the New Year's Eve Party

on Thursday, the thirty-first of December 1992

at seven p. m.

in the Hall of Hilton Hotel

第六情景对话单元

发函投标

敬启者：

我们研究了贵方筹建处提供的法定方式和条件，现随函附上在塞百路兴建泰莱宾馆的标书，并有信心能中标。

谨上

附件：如文

第七情景对话单元

承建友谊宾馆合同

华夏旅行社（以下简称甲方），和天山建筑总公司（以下简称乙方）就承建友谊宾馆一事，订立合同。双方同意下列事项：

1. 甲方委托乙方承建一座宾馆，其设计图纸由甲方提供。
2. 双方同意承建费定为600万美元整。甲方在合同签订后十天内支付给乙方30%的承建费，其余部分应在宾馆建成后两周之内全部付清。
3. 承建宾馆的所有建筑材料由甲方提供，并且必须符合一致同意的标准和规格。

（待续）

第八情景对话单元

（续上单元）

4. 该宾馆限定在本合同签订后十二个月内建成。1995年10月1日交工。
5. 所承建的宾馆保证五十年不倒不漏，如果出现倒漏现象，应由乙方负责免费修理。
6. 本合同书于1994年10月1日在伦敦签订，共两份，每份均用中文和英文写成，两种文本具有同等的法律效力。

杨明　　　　　　　　　　　　　　大卫·史密斯

（签名）　　　　　　　　　　　　（签名）

华夏旅行社代表　　　　　　　　　天山建筑总公司代表

　　附件略

Cocktail Party

There're several parties, such as banquet, dinner-party, cocktail party, reception party and tea party. But cocktail parties are popular for both business and social functions. They may be formal or informal and are often held between 6:00 and 8:00 in the evening. Guests are usually served with drinks and hors d'oeuvres or snacks.

第九情景对话单元

修改合同条款

敬启者：

贵公司 2001 年 5 月 1 日函及所附合同草本已收悉，谢谢。

关于合同第八款，我们建议作一些修改，修改后的文字如下：

"任何一方均不得将对方收到的任何资料，图纸，信件以及其他文件转让给第三者。任何一方只可把收到的任何资料，图纸以及其他文件用于本合同项目下工程的建筑，安装，维修，培训和操作。而任何一方在取得对方的书面同意之前，不得擅自将其用于任何其他目的或任何其他工程"。

上述修改后的条款更切合实际，需要并将证明是可行和互利的。盼能来信确认。

谨上

第十情景对话单元

验收、验交与保修期

工程每一阶段完工后，由甲、乙双方人员组成验收小组，按照工程设计要求和规范进行验收。

在验收过程中，如发现施工有不符合设计要求，应由乙方采取必要补救措施，使之达到图纸设计的质量标准，但所产生的费用，应由乙方承担。

工程保修期应为每阶段的竣工移交书签字之日起一年。在此期间，如发现因施工原因造成的质量问题，应由乙方无偿修复，达到施工图标准为止。

第十一情景对话单元

恭贺庆祝福斯特大桥竣工

王先生阁下：

我和我的夫人获悉中国建设者们已建成了福斯特大桥。

在你们收到的许多贺信中，我和我的夫人也想再加上一份。因为在您领导下，中国建设者们克服了种种困难，自始至终都在努力的工作，所以我们对于你们所取得的成绩根本不感到惊奇。

我和我的夫人真诚地希望您和您的职工们在将来工作中取得更大成就。

您热诚的（签全名）敬贺
1996 年 12 月 26 日
于英国伦敦

第二部　建筑工程技术人员英语情景会话

第十二情景对话单元

一幢旋转大楼

这幢旋转大楼如此与众不同，以至于许多人首次看到它时简直都无法相信自己的眼睛。这幢旋转大楼有 54 层，包括 10 层的办公室、147 套公寓以及顶部两层楼的许多会议室。从底部到顶端可旋转 90°，所以每层楼上的公寓都拥有充足的光线。这幢 190 米高的大楼是瑞典最高的建筑，也是欧洲最高的住宅楼之一。许多人都认为这幢旋转大楼是人们建造的奇观。难道你就不想亲眼目睹一次吗？

第十三情景对话单元

世界七大奇观之一
——中国的长城

长城，人类的杰作，中华之魂，是世界上最长的城墙，像一条巨龙一样跨越群山、横穿峡谷、横跨中国，始发于西边沙漠向东边大海弯曲向前。长城具有两千多年的历史。长城汉语叫做"万里长城",实际上超过9000米长、6~7米高、4~5米宽。中国的长城不仅是世界七大奇观之一,也是一个世界人造奇观,1978年即被联合国列为首批世界文化遗产。

1)我认为你不对。
2)约翰并非是因为生病而迟到。
3)汽油价格今年可能不会下跌啦。
4)看来小明的钱是要不回来了。
5)我看王海是满不在乎,是吗?

第十四情景对话单元

建筑图

建筑图有许多种。例如:平面图、立面图、剖面图、平面布置图、鸟瞰图、仰视图、标准图、施工图……。图纸在建筑施工中起着至关重要的作用,因此图纸被视为施工的准则和指南。施工就是把设计转化为现实。

1)油漆干了才能触摸。(直译)油漆未干,不许触摸。
2)有运动,就有做功。(直译)没有运动,就没有做功。
3)有空气,生物才能生存。(直译)没有空气,生物都不能生存。
4)人皆有弱点。(直译)没有无弱点的人。
5)他们在一起工作就互相帮助。(直译)没有互相帮助,他们就不在一起工作。
6)有了你的帮助,我才能在学习建筑英语中取得这样大的进步。(直译)如果没有你的帮助,我就不可能在学习建筑英语中取得这样大的进步。

第十五情景对话单元

建筑材料询价

敬启者：

我们得知贵公司从事建筑材料经销业务有多年。

目前我们有意询问一些建筑材料价格，并随附上所需的材料名称，供你方参考。

如果你方有意经营这些所需材料，我方将在近期内与你方进行相关事宜洽商。

谨上

附件：如文

Wall Papers

Nowadays, PVC. (Polyvinyl Choride) wall paper is widely used in architectural decorative field and overcomes the disadvantage of common plastic wall paper such as lower wet strength, easy to become midewed. Besides it, there are other varieties of wall papers, such as vermiculite wall paper, which has a surface coat of inorganic grain.

第十六情景对话单元

安装材料的报价

敬启者：

从报纸上看到贵公司的广告，我方想请贵公司尽快地邮寄来安装材料的最新价目表和附有图片的商品目录，以及最优惠的报价。

如蒙贵方函告最优惠的交易条件及有关贵公司资信情况，我们不胜感激。

盼早日回复为荷。

谨上

A New Material——Plastics

Plastics find wide application not only in our daily life but also in modern engineering. For example, there are plastics floors and window frames, plastic water pipes and fittings in the new buildings. In mechanical engineering, machine parts are made of plastics. And in electrical engineering, plastics serve as good insulator.

Plastics are very useful because they have many good properties. They are light and strong. They do not rust at all. Besides, they can be easily made into any forms for different purposes.

第十七情景对话单元

什么是合金？

如果你把两种或更多的金属熔化在一起，就会获得一种新金属，这种金属就叫合金。合金与原来的金属是截然不同的。

假如你给一种金属里掺杂甚至于很小比例的另一种金属，它的性能都会改变。例如镍能增加钢的强度和硬度，如果你把镍掺入钢里，就成为镍钢，镍钢用于制作切割工具。同样，铝合金有结构钢的强度却仅有钢的三分之一的重量。不锈钢已消除了锈的威胁。不同的合金有着不同的性能特点，因此在建筑工业中要根据不同目的选用不同的合金材料。

第十八情景对话单元

梁的类型

梁是用于在横向空间隙上支撑垂直荷载的水平构件。从广义而言，梁是外力趋于弯曲的结构构件。根据支撑方式，梁通常分为简支梁、悬臂梁、探头梁、连续梁等类。

在建筑施工中，梁是由木材、钢材以及钢筋混凝土建造而成的。对于重型梁，特别是铁路桥梁以及大跨度横梁均广泛使用钢筋混凝土。

1) 看看这张施工图，你就明白怎样施工。

2）因为我是一位土木工程师，而他是一位经济师。

3）咱们去检查你们刚完成的给水工程吧。

4）我们的老师举出许多例子来解释'and'的用法，所以我们都完全理解了。

5）尽管李明是一位小男孩，却制服了飞跑的马。

6）祝兄弟的中国人民兴旺并幸福。

第十九情景对话单元

住　宅

世界上有许多不同类型的住宅。它们可能是大的或小的，古代的或是现代的，中式的或是西式的，或是中西式相结合的住宅。绝大多数住宅都是方形的，极少数住宅是圆形的。有些住宅仅有一层，而另外的一些住宅却有两层或几层，甚至还有不少多层的建筑。

许多住宅的设计都是相似的，楼上设有两三个卧室和浴室，而楼下设有餐厅、厨房和客厅，在房前屋后还拥有一个小花园。

绝大多数住宅都是由混凝土、钢材、木材、石块或砖建造而成的。

House Structures and Equipments

structure	reinforced concrete framework, pressure and quake resistance, fireproof features, etc.
roof	waterproof fittings and covering slabs of heat insulation
external wall	stone foundation and high-class bricks
internal wall	building block, coat with Eco-paint
elevator	brand name elevator
stair	public staircase with hard wooden rails and antiskid tiled landings and steps
flooring	marble tiles and solid wooden compound floor used
door & window	colour aluminum alloy energy-saving windows with double paned glass by two kinds of opening type. Unit main door with fire prevention & security function

续表

master bath	marble wall & floor, sanitary ware with faucets
kitchen	unit cupboard and water heater
air – condition	central air-conditioning system
power supply	an independent electric meter, 20kw. / standard unit, 30kw. / house
gas	pipe natural gas (2.5m^3 meter)
telephone	3 ADSL lines per household
CATV	equipped with satellite and public antenna receiver
security system	Each household can carry intellectual door management, visiting confirmation by video intercom and monitoring cameras.

第二十情景对话单元

柱子的作用

垂直结构构架的构件称之为柱子。柱子把楼层和屋面的荷载传到基础上。柱子，特别是用木材制作而成的，常称之为支柱；承载压应力的桁架结构叫做支杆，支杆的作用与柱子的作用相同。

4. 1) 据我所知他的口语通常错误很少。
   2) 我想这个工具太重我单手拿不起。
   3) 他以前没有遵守诺言。
   4) 约翰的操作技能现在并不比我好多少。
   5) 恐怕王林太累了，简直走不动了。
   6) 说实话，我们宁愿学建筑英语而不愿学文学英语。
   7) 你们今天不喝咖啡，喝茶好吗？
   8) 马克把这些单词写了多少遍，都没记住。
   9) 近来我很少见到总经理黄先生。
   10) 在学建筑英语之前，许多建筑工人对于这一专业英语几乎是一无所知。

口语练习答案——汉语参考译文

第二十一情景会话单元

对产品质量问题的回函

敬启者：

参阅贵方 2005 年 3 月 4 日函，承告第 286 号合同下的钢屋架，经我方初步检验后，发现表面粗糙，有裂纹、起皱等缺陷。

愿提醒你方，该钢屋架是在参观过你方产品陈列间所展示的样品后达成交易。因此，检验标准应以该样品质量为依据。我公司现已电告陈列间技术人员与我方检验人员会同检验，待收到他们的报告后，再进一步与贵方磋商。

谨上

---

4. 1）日夜   2）先后
  3）一再   4）到处
  5）进出（来龙去脉） 6）方式方法
  7）日复一日   8）亲密
  9）来回   10）时常

第二十二情景会话单元

伸缩缝

材料随着温度的变化会膨胀与收缩，所以建筑材料在不同的温度下就有着不同大小尺寸。某些建筑材料随着温度变化，在某种程度上，膨胀力是很大的，可能会引起结构构件破裂，这就是在所有大型结构构件之间（构件的总长度超过 60 米）必须留有伸缩缝的原因所在。

4. 1）我们并不能把我们所学的英语单词都记住。
   我们不能把我们所学的英语单词记住。
  2）这里的建筑机械并非都是中国制造的。
   这里的建筑机械都不是中国制造的。
  3）这两种教科书并非都适合我们学习。
   这两种教科书都不适合我们学习。

4）王先生对这一技术问题解答得很准确，但不够清楚。
王先生对这一技术问题解答的既不准确，也不清楚。

5）多数学生只会笔译，但不会口译。
多数学生既不会口译，也不会笔译。

第二十三情景对话单元

一个繁忙的建筑工地

这是华山建筑工程公司的一个建筑工地，工地上十分整洁而且材料堆放地井然有序。

一些高大的塔吊耸立在工地上。许多幢单元公寓大楼已竣工，一幢高层大楼还正在施工之中。

吊车司机们正在开起吊车吊运各种建筑材料，砂浆搅拌机正在搅拌砂浆，好多组瓦工正在高高的脚手架上砌筑砖墙，水暖工们正在铺设水管道，工地上所有的建设者们都在忙着各自的工作。

Two Critical Men on Worksite

The two most important men on a worksite are the contractor's agent and laborer, but their duty is not same at all. The agent is important because he has the authority of the contractor and acts for contractor on the site. The laborer is important because of him, with perhaps hundreds of other laborers, undertaking and accomplishing all the work on the construction site.

第二十四情景对话单元

失火索赔

敬启者：

本人抱歉地报告我们工地库房昨晚发生火灾，起火原因尚未查明。

估计库存损失约值 85989 美元。很侥幸，并无任何记录受损，故此计算损失不会有太大困难。

敬请贵处尽快安排代表来访，并请指示处理水渍货物。

谨上

第三部 建筑经济管理人员英语情景会话

第二十五情景对话单元

什么是会计？

会计是识别、计算和传递经济信息的过程。目的是让信息的使用者（决策者与经营者）能够在获得充分信息基础上，做出客观的判断和正确的决策。当然，这种信息主要是财务性的，并以货币的形式表述。

每一个拥有货币、机械以及建筑物等经济资源的盈利团体，都使用会计信息。所以，会计被称之为商业语言。在21世纪，世界经济的全球化鼓舞着会计行业向前发展。

Form of I. O. U

Jun. 8, 2002

To the Finance Section of the Company
　I. O. U one thousand dollars ($1,000) only.

Hao Zheng

第二十六情景对话单元

开立账户

如果你要到银行开立账户，你也许要通过下列大部分程序：首先，你得到新账户部门填写好一份签字卡。然后，你得提供你的身份证明以便开立账户。你在都市应有个永久住址，同样要求你提供愿意你推荐永久住户的名字。最后并非至少，你随身携带一些现金以便开立账户用。很多银行要求最少存100美元现金。

建筑技术与管理英语情景会话

Form of Receipt

Jun. 18, 2002

Received from Mr. Hao Zheng one thousand dollars
($1,000) only.

John Smith
For the Finance Section of the Company

第二十七情景对话单元

美国和英国的货币体制

不同的国家政府颁布不同的纸币和硬币。每个政府决定其货币单位和价值标准。通常其标准都是以金银为价值基础。

美国国会1785年选择美元作为货币单位，而且把十进位制用作计算方法的基础。1美元等于100美分或便士。在美国英语中，使用'bill'钞票这一单词是指纸币。

英镑是英国基本的货币单位。英国于1971年将其货币转换成十进位制，1英镑由100便士构制而成（1英镑=100便士）。在英国英语中，使用'note'钞票这一单词是指纸币。

第二十八情景对话单元

银行业务

中国绝大多数银行都是国有的，由国家对其监管。银行经营着各种人民币业务，也从事着国际金融货币交易。银行的功能就是提高、利用、积累和管理国内资金或兑换外汇。

银行履行许多功能——开立储蓄账户、支取现金和现金核对、授予抵押贷款。现在，计算机联网系统有助于银行为客户或用户提供更加快捷、更加精确的服务，信用卡就是一个典型实例。

总而言之，有了银行的服务，人们的生活是可想而知的方便。

1) A is more than B.   2) A is less than B

3) A approximately equals to B   4) A is not equal to B

第二十九情景对话单元

通知已付汇款函

敬启者：
  为支付贵公司 369 号发票，现随函附上本公司银行支票一张，面值为 13,120 美元。值得一提的是，我们对贵方处理订单的方式相当满意。货物已准时由中国航空空运到，正好能投入到建筑用料之中。感谢贵方对此事给予即时处理。

谨上

附件：如文

Informing the Receipt of Remittance

Dear Sirs,
  We were pleased to receive your bank cheque for US $13,120. It has been credited to your account, which is now completely clear. Please give us the opportunity of serving you again in any way we can.

Yours faithfully

第三十情景对话单元

会计师与簿记员

  会计师能分析解释财务信息、编制财务报表、进行审计、设计会计体系、进行预算和编制预算、并能提供税务服务。专门从事这些工作的人就是会计师。
  簿记员的工作就是正确登记日常财务记录，不设计或不建立记账制度。财务记录通常就是指记账。

1) 10 +/− 5 = ?
2) 100 + 55 = 155
3) 16 − 8 = 8
4) 12 ×/÷ 2 = ?
5) 90 × 4 = 360
6) 300 ÷ 5 = 6
7) 100 ÷ 20 + 5 × 2 − 6 = 9

第三十一情景对话单元

成本－数量－利润分析

咱们选择等式法讨论下面例子：

混凝土构件厂销售混凝土楼板。每块混凝土楼板的销售价是48英镑。每块混凝土楼板变动成本销售价是8英镑，而每月的固定支出是24,800英镑。该厂必须销售多少块混凝土楼板才能不盈不亏或略有利润？

销售＝变动成本＋固定支出＋利润

假设 X ＝ 销售数量的保本点是不盈不亏，利润就是零，这个等式是：

48 英镑 X = 70 英镑 + 24,800 英镑 + 0

40 英镑 X = 29,760 英镑

X = 620 块楼板

（或总销售29,760英镑，每块楼板销售价是48英镑）

这个事例告诉我们：这个厂每月必须销售620块楼板才能达到保本点；这个厂每月必须销售620块楼板才能略有利润。

第三十二情景对话单元

成本会计

成本会计系统广泛应用于各类公司和工厂。经理们和厂长们利用成本会计系统决定产品的单价，并控制其制造加工费用。

为了显示产品造价的流动，成本会计系统有六种分类账目。这些分类账目是在计算单价的基础上而建立的。

1) 近年来这个城市已建起了数以百计栋楼房。
2) 在过去几天里，参观者三三两两前来参观我们的工地。

口语练习答案——汉语参考译文

3）据说我们的经理今年有30来岁。
4）他们在20世纪80年代就加入到建筑行业。
5）实际上,这些青年人中的五位是建筑工程技术人员,而两位则是经济管理人员。

第三十三情景对话单元
固定资产

固定资产包括有形资产、无形资产和自然资源。

有形资产是指拥有的物质形态,如土地、房屋或机械设备。土地不折旧,房屋或机械设备则要折旧。

无形资产是指没有物质形态的、非流动的固定资产,如专利权、商标权、版权、专卖权以及商誉。

自然资源是指为了从中开采或获取某些有价值的资源,如石油、木材、矿藏而取得的,并非作为地基使用的场所。

第四部　建筑实验与测量人员英语情景会话

第三十四情景对话单元
预应力混凝土

预应力混凝土把高强混凝土与高强钢筋'积极'地结合起来。张拉钢筋并依靠混凝土使之保持着受拉状态,从而使混凝土受压。这种积极结合的结果使两种材料的性能都能更好地发挥其作用。钢是韧性材料,现在由于预加应力而使它在高拉下进行工作;混凝土则是脆性材料,现在它的抗拉能力由于受压而得到提高,而它的抗压能力却丝毫也没有受到影响。因此预应力混凝土是现代两种高强度材料的理想结合。

4.1）除了那家书店,工程师们和经济师们在别处再也买不到这类参考书。
　2）除了同意,我们毫无办法。
　3）尼克一生仅到过中国一次。

4) 要不是你的投资，我们就不可能建起这条公路。

5) 不雨则已，一雨倾盆。

6) 玛丽安长得又高又瘦，可是很健康。

第三十五情景对话单元

预应力钢筋

预应力钢筋由三种形式：钢铰线、单根钢丝和高强钢丝组成，其中一根位于中间，剩余六根以螺旋形式紧紧包住这根钢丝，其螺距是钢铰线标定直径的 12~16 倍。钢铰线的直径在 6.6~13 毫米范围之内。预应力钢丝的直径在 4.9~7.0 毫米范围之内。正像钢铰线中的钢丝一样，它也是由冷拔高碳钢筋制成的。高强合（金）钢筋适合于做预应力钢筋，它的直径在 19~35 毫米之间。

第三十六情景对话单元

两种焊接

最常用的两种焊接形式是角焊和坡口焊。角焊用于将互相平行（搭接）或互相垂直（成 T 型）的两块板或构件焊接在一起。坡口焊则是沿着板件的边缘对接，从而保持了板件的连续。坡口焊要求对被焊接件的边缘进行专门的处理和仔细的拼装。当从两面焊接或从一面焊接而在另一面设有背垫板时，这种坡口焊称之为完全焊透，焊缝能承受的应力与被焊接的最弱的那块板所能承受的应力相同。不完全焊透的坡口焊仅用于不要求板全部受力的情况和不要求全部连续的情况。当要求整块板受力时，完全焊透的坡口焊也用于角连接或丁字形接头焊接。

第三十七情景对话单元

三种现代打桩方法

1. 打入桩：将预制桩打入基岩中，就可以提供坚固的基座。
2. 沉管灌注桩：用震动锤将钢管打入地下后，在钢管里放入钢筋，浇完混凝土后再把钢管拔出。
3. 钻孔灌注桩：先进行钻孔再把混凝土直接灌入桩孔中。

1）维多利亚终于明白了他是错的而我是对的。
2）这位年长的建筑工人似乎能用英语和外国朋友进行交谈。
3）经理正巧以前曾到过那个美丽的大城市。
4）我们终于获悉事故的全部真相。
5）威尔金森弄不明白在那时我为什么竟然拒绝了他的邀请。
6）我弄不懂有时我的记忆似乎在捉弄我。
7）小王正好也在我施工的工地。

第三十八情景对话单元

水准仪

严格地说，水准仪主要是为提供一条水平视线而设计的一种仪器。这条视线是由具备物镜、调焦装置、十字丝环和目镜这些常规部件组成的望远镜所决定的。在实用中，望远镜应能绕竖轴旋转，使它能瞄准任何方向。

目前使用的水准仪可归纳为定镜水准仪、自动安平水准仪和微倾水准仪（通常称作为速调水准仪或工程水准议）等三种。

第三十九情景对话单元

经纬仪

经纬仪是为量测水平角和竖直角而设计的一种仪器。它是一种量测角度的精密测量仪器，并在施工测量中得到广泛的应用。经纬仪有复测经纬仪和方向经纬仪两大类。

经纬仪可以认为是三条共点直线的几何条件在机械上的实现，这三条共点直线就是视准轴，视准轴应与之垂直的所谓横轴，以及横轴应与之垂直的竖轴。

假如仪器的几何条件都能得到完全满足，那么当竖轴垂直时，横轴就会是水平的；而当俯仰望远镜时，视线就描画出一个垂直平面。

第五部 建筑公司后勤人员英语情景会话

第四十情景对话单元

预订飞机票

如果你准备乘飞机出行,那么你可以到旅行社订购机票,也可以直接同航空公司通话预订。提醒你,有些大城市不止一个机场,务必弄清楚,你应从哪个机场,哪个候机楼登机起飞。

Apology

The phrase "seem to have" is often heard in apologies when things are mislaid (temporarily lost). This is because it gives the idea of doubt, and the speaker wishes to break the news gently to the owner and not to alarm him too much. Sometimes it's also used when things have been lost, or even broken.

第四十一情景对话单元

打电话

外国电话系统同样有区号。如果你知道区号和电话号码的话,你可以自己直接打电话,这样打电话通常很容易,也比较经济。你也可以直接拨号与海外很多国家通话,也可以找国际长途台的接线员转接。

第四十二情景对话单元

回执是什么?

当收信人收到信件时,在回执上签字,然后邮局再把这个回执给你寄回来。一旦你需要时,它就是个证据,证明你的信件已寄到了。在一些国家索要回执还收些费。

4. 1)英美人讲英语时,他们讲的英语有区别吗?
  2)鉴于此时总工程师不在,技术工作会议不得不推迟到下周三召开。
3）请照图施工。
4）虽然他很忙，但却常到建筑工地检查工程质量。
5）只要在工地出现技术问题，我都能迎刃而解。
6）他的英语口语和我一样好，但笔译却不如我。

第四十三情景对话单元

求　助

如果你向别人求助的话，尽量以礼相求尤为重要。特别是英国人用相当含蓄和婉转的方式提出要求。要求别人帮忙，最重要的是怎么问，而不是你实际使用的字眼。你提出请求时所用的语调与你实际要说的内容同样重要。如果你觉得对方有可能会拒绝你的请求的话，你可以用一种即使遭到回绝也不会引起尴尬的方式询问对方。

第四十四情景对话单元

国外医院

外国人在联合王国得病或出了意外事故可以享受英国国家健康服务部门的公费医疗。也许在其他国家，情况就不同了。平时最好到别人推荐的医院去就医。紧急情况应直接去最近医院的急诊室。国外的医疗费普遍都很贵。

第四十五情景对话单元

请人重复

只要你以礼相求，绝大多数人并不介意重说你没有听清或听懂的话。在英国，当你想叫人复述一句话时别说"请"这个字。这一点应该提醒你以便与国外人更好的交谈。